ORCHESTRATION

Books by Walter Piston

HARMONY

COUNTERPOINT

ORCHESTRATION

ORCHESTRATION

BY *Walter Piston*

W · W · NORTON & COMPANY

New York · London

Music autographed by MAXWELL WEANER

Drawing of the violin by KATHRYN NASON

All other illustrations by the author

W. W. Norton & Company, Inc., 500 Fifth Avenue, New York, N.Y. 10110

PRINTED IN THE UNITED STATES OF AMERICA
FOR THE PUBLISHERS BY THE VAIL-BALLOU PRESS
0

ISBN 0-393-09740-4

CONTENTS

TWO · ANALYSIS OF ORCHESTRATION

THREE · PROBLEMS IN ORCHESTRATION

⇛ ⇚

FOREWORD

THE true art of orchestration is inseparable from the creative act of composing music. The sounds made by the orchestra are the ultimate external manifestation of musical ideas germinated in the mind of the composer. One skilled in the technique of orchestration may practice a somewhat lesser art of transcribing for orchestra music originally written for another medium. This can be a fine though difficult art, provided the orchestrator is able to put himself momentarily in the composer's place, and, so to speak, to think the composer's thoughts. Failing this, the result is unlikely to amount to more than a display of skill and craft, often of a superficial and artificial nature.

Orchestration, in the sense here employed, refers to the process of writing music for the orchestra, using principles of instrumental combination essentially those observed operating in the scores of Haydn, Mozart, and Beethoven. It is a common technique, employed in present-day symphonic music as well as in that of the classical and romantic periods. For the present purposes it will not be considered to embrace earlier processes based on improvisation, fortuitous instrumental balance, and the stabilizing influence of a keyboard instrument, with *basso continuo*.

The technical equipment of both composer and orchestrator must include a thorough knowledge of the individual instruments, their capabilities and characteristics, and a mental conception of the sound of each. Then the effects and resources of instrumental combination must be learned, involving such matters as balance of tone, mixed tone colors, clarity in texture, and the like. Finally, the orchestra is to be sensed as itself an individual instrument, flexibly employed to present the music, in form and content, with fidelity and effectiveness.

A multitude of obstacles and unsolved problems has prevented the establishment of a science of orchestration. The imperfection and vagueness of our musical notation makes it impossible to indicate with accuracy dynamic and rhythmic quantities as well as pitch, to say nothing of shades of tone color, warmth and intensity. One consequence of this is the preponderance of the role played by the performers and the conductor in the translation of written notes into sound. It is a well-known fact that no two performances of a work sound alike, and we find pleasure and satisfaction in this versatility of music as written. But for the student anxious to know the effect in sound of what he has put on paper, the unknown quantity of the performer's understanding has to be acknowledged in his calculations.

There are also mechanical and physical influences that cause variants in the sound of an orchestral score. No two orchestras sound alike. They may differ in the number of strings, in the quality and make of the instruments, and quite naturally in the capabilities of the players. A wide difference exists in the acoustic properties of the various auditoriums in which the individual orchestras habitually play, and the same orchestra will sound different in a different place.

Because of this variety in the sounds produced from the same given notes, and also because the student of orchestration seldom has an opportunity to hear those notes played at all, the student works under severe handicaps in striving to cultivate a capacity for the mental hearing of orchestral scores.

In the event that his opportunities are limited to hearing phonograph records and radio broadcasts, he must be cautioned that these resources often have serious and misleading deficiencies. It is possible to doubt that the usual commercial recording of a symphonic work can stand the test of comparison with the printed score. At least in this writer's experience, almost every recording produces some sounds that do not exist in the score, and fails to produce some of the notes printed therein, besides showing numerous other discrepancies. The phonograph record is valuable as a means of conveying the over-all effect of a composition, but it is an insecure medium through which to store up instrumental sounds in the memory, or to ascertain the sound effect of a printed page of orchestration.

The shortcomings of radio broadcasting of music are too well known to need description here. The complex vicissitudes suffered by a musical tone from the time it leaves the orchestra until it is perceived by the ear of the listener all have their effect upon the quality of the tone. When recordings are broadcast, the efficiency of the initial "pick up" is improved, but often the records are worn, and frequently the pitch is clearly not the same as the pitch of the performance from which the recording was made. This means that a variation in speed has been introduced at some stage of the recording or reproducing process. This, in turn, means a loss of fidelity not only in pitch, but also in tempo and in the tone color of each instrument.

Through a realization of these existing conditions, a philosophy of musical experience can be formed, so that conclusions are drawn not from one or two examples of actual sound, but from the cumulative evidence of many experiences, and even then held subject to subsequent revision.

The three essential aspects of the study of orchestration are treated in the three divisions of this book. In Part One, the instruments and their playing techniques are studied in detail. In Part Two, an approach to the analysis of orchestration is suggested, and in Part Three, typical problems in orchestration are given with some examples of their solution.

Throughout the book emphasis is placed on the method of study, the orientation of the student's program of action, to help him in continuing further studies along the paths suggested. The material covered is designed for a year's course in orchestration at the college level, but it is the author's conviction that the subject matter is too flexible to be presented as a course of graduated steps and exercises. A presentation is called for that will be adaptable to varied musical backgrounds, although it will always be difficult for persons lacking a knowledge of harmony and counterpoint to work out problems in orchestration. The student should be stimulated to make acquaintance with scores, and to develop self-reliance and initiative in seeking a deep knowledge of the instruments and how they are combined. Such a presentation will be found, it is hoped, in this introduction to the art of orchestration.

ONE
THE INSTRUMENTS OF THE ORCHESTRA

CHAPTER ONE

STRINGED INSTRUMENTS

Throughout the comparatively brief history of orchestration the string group—violins, violas, 'cellos, and double-basses—has maintained its position as dominant element of the symphony orchestra. Countless scores from all periods bear evidence that their composers regarded woodwind and brass rather as accessories and were hesitant to entrust much of their essential musical material to any but stringed instruments.

Such an attitude is partly justifiable because of the superiority of the strings in so many important respects. Strings are tireless and can play virtually any kind of music. They have a greater dynamic range than wind instruments and far more expressive capacity. The tone color of the string group is fairly homogeneous from top to bottom, variations in the different registers being much more subtle than in the winds. At the same time, stringed instruments are the most versatile in producing different kinds of sound. As string tone is rich in overtones all manner of close and open spacing is practical. One does not tire of hearing string tone as soon as one tires of wind tone; in fact, there exists a sizable literature of compositions written for string orchestra without wind instruments.

The string section of a typical symphony orchestra usually consists of sixteen first violins, fourteen second violins, twelve violas, ten violoncellos, and eight double-basses. Variations in these proportions may be found, reflecting the predilections of individual conductors, or perhaps determined by some such circumstance as the size of the concert stage.

The four strings of each of these instruments are tuned as follows.

Fig. 1

In the case of the double-bass the actual sound is an octave lower than the written notes.

The pitch of a vibrating string can be expressed in terms of the frequency, or rapidity, of its vibrations. For instance, the upper string of the viola sounds the A which in present-day tuning has a frequency of 440 vibrations per second.

A stretched string can be varied in pitch by varying the tension. Stringed instruments are tuned by turning the tuning pegs to which the strings are attached. Tightening a string increases the frequency of its vibration; hence raises its pitch.

The weight of the string has an important influence on the frequency of its vibration. Thus the four strings on the same instrument may be identical in length, but may differ widely in pitch because they are made to differ in weight. Furthermore, by making use of this principle, the strings can be tuned to their various pitches without the necessity of too great a difference in their tensions. The lower-pitched strings are not only thicker, but they are made still heavier by winding the gut or steel with fine wire of copper, silver, aluminum, or other metals.

Variation in the length of the string produces proportional variation in pitch. A longer string vibrates more slowly than a shorter one, other conditions being equal. It is found, for example, that halving the string length doubles the frequency and raises the pitch an octave.

FINGERING

The action of the left-hand fingers stopping the string firmly against the fingerboard shortens the sounding length of the string, thereby raising the pitch.

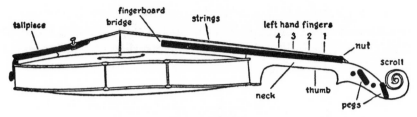

Fig. 2. Violin

In the diagram, note that the sounding length of the string, to be set in motion by the bow, is that between the stopping finger and the bridge. The remainder of the string will of course be silent.

Since halving the string length raises the pitch an octave, the point at which a string is stopped to sound the octave above its open, or un-stopped, pitch will be exactly one-half the distance from nut to bridge. If we wish to raise the pitch another octave we will find the point of stopping one-half the distance from this middle point to the bridge, or three-fourths the total string length from the nut.

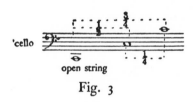

Fig. 3

The principle demonstrated is that fingering a given interval does not imply covering a fixed length of string, but a length that diminishes as the hand moves toward the bridge. When playing a succession of equal intervals on one string, the fingers measure off not equal divisions of string length but proportional divisions. For example, on the viola a major second above an open string means a distance of about 1½ inches, whereas the same interval in a very high position measures less than ½ inch. A major second above an open string on the violin meas-ures about 1¼ inches, on the 'cello about 2⅝ inches, and on the bass about 4¼ inches.

Another characteristic of string fingering is that when the hand is in a given position on one string the fingers can readily stop tones on any of the four strings, without the necessity of moving the hand. Each position is identified by a number derived from the number of diatonic steps between the first finger and the open string. In string technique, and also in the fingering of wind instruments, the index finger, not the thumb, is called first finger.

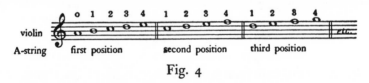

Fig. 4

Detailed description of the fingering systems of the several stringed instruments will be given in succeeding chapters.

DOUBLE-STOPS

It is possible to stop notes on two adjacent strings in such a way that the bow can sound both notes at once. This is called double-stopping. Triple- and quadruple-stops (chords) are also feasible, although it will presently be seen that the simultaneous sound of three or four notes cannot be prolonged by the bow.

Fig. 5

DIVIDED STRINGS

In the orchestra, double notes are customarily divided between the two players reading from the same desk. The part should be marked *divisi*, Italian for divided (Fr., *divisés;* Ger., *geteilt*), most often abbreviated to *div*. The right-hand player at each desk takes the upper note. When the part returns to single notes it should be marked *unisoni* (Fr., *unis;* Ger., *nicht geteilt*), usually abbreviated *unis*. If double notes are written, and the composer wishes each player to play all the notes, using double-stops, he writes a precautionary *non div.* (in German scores usually *Doppelgriff*). This indication is used only when there is more than one note, to prevent dividing.

A division of a section into more than two parts would be marked
div. in 3 (Fr., *div. à 3;* Ger., *dreifach geteilt*), necessitating indications
in the individual players' music to show which part each is to play.
Sometimes the divided parts are given separate lines in the score, for
legibility. If the parts are complex, better results may be obtained by
dividing by desks (It., *da leggìi;* Fr., *par pupitres;* Ger., *pultweise*), the
odd-numbered desks taking the upper part.

If only half the members of a section are to play, the part is marked
half (It., *la metà;* Fr., *la moitié;* Ger., *die Hälfte*). The players on the
left at each desk will then remain silent until given the indication *all*
(It., *tutti;* Fr., *tous;* Ger., *alle*).

VIBRATO

In the playing of stringed instruments the tone is given life and
warmth through the use of vibrato of the left hand. This is a combination of impulses involving the muscles of the hand, wrist, and arm, and
its effect at the fingertip is an almost imperceptible oscillation in pitch
of the note. The vibrato is employed on all stopped tones except those
of short duration and needs no indication for its use. However, there
are times when one prefers the peculiar tone quality obtainable only
by suppressing the vibrato, in which case the direction *senza vibrato*
should be given.

BOWING

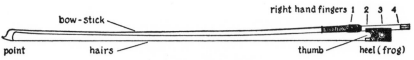

right hand fingers 1　2　3　4
bow-stick
point　　　hairs　　　　　　　thumb　　heel (frog)

Fig. 6. Violin Bow

The bow-stick is of fine, light wood, generally Pernambuco, which
is remarkable for its elastic quality. The stick is curved inward toward
the hair, and, when the hair is tightened by means of the screw at the
heel of the bow, the resulting tension brings into play the resilience of
the stick, an important factor in the various bow strokes. The hair is
horsehair, although in recent times other materials, such as nylon, have

been tried. There are over a hundred hairs in a violin bow. It is the habit of string players to rub a specially prepared rosin on the bow hairs to help in securing the right amount of friction on the strings.

The bow is held firmly, yet lightly, between the fingers and thumb of the right hand, as shown in Fig. 6. The first finger is in a position to exert varying pressure on the bow-stick, while the little finger is used mainly to balance the bow, according to its position on the string. (The so-called German style of bowing for the double-bass will be described later.)

The bow is drawn at right angles to the string, ordinarily at a place about halfway between the bridge and the end of the fingerboard. For a louder and more brilliant tone, and for the normal production of high notes, the bow is played nearer the bridge. For softer tones it is moved nearer to the fingerboard. The hair may be placed flat, so that all the hairs are in contact with the string; but usually the bow is turned on edge, so that only part of the hair is engaged. This enables the player to control the amount of hair being used. For the violin and viola the tilt is away from the player; for the 'cello and bass the opposite is more convenient.

The part of the bow near the point is called the upper part of the bow; that nearer the heel, the lower part. When the bow is drawn starting at the lower part and proceeding toward the point, straightening the elbow joint, the stroke is called down-bow. The opposite is up-bow. Both are more clearly expressed by the French *tiré* (drawn) for down-bow, and *poussé* (pushed) for up-bow. The signs ⊓ (down-bow) and ∨ (up-bow) are in universal use.

LEGATO

If no slurs are marked, each note calls for a change in the direction of the bow.

EX. 1. Franck—*Symphony*   p. 17, ed. Eulenburg

These changes in the direction of the bow are made by a good player with practically no break in the continuity of the tone, by virtue of a supple wrist and a skillful coördination of all muscular movements.

When slurs are marked, all notes under one slur are to be played "in one bow"; that is, with no change in direction of the bow.

EX. 2. Schubert—*Symphony no. 5*   p. 24, ed. Eulenburg

A violinist would instinctively begin the phrase shown above with an up-bow. The up-bow, in string style, is associated with the up-beat, or anacrusis, whereas the down-beat, as in Ex. 1, suggests a down-bow to the player. It is impossible, and often inadvisable, to apply this principle to every up-beat or down-beat, but the principle is continually in evidence in good bowing.

For a vigorous attack on a long note, to be followed by a down-bow chord or accent, it is well to begin down-bow, changing immediately to up-bow. This change of bow will not be perceived by the ear if properly performed, and will permit the use of the more energetic down-bow for both attacks.

EX. 3. Beethoven—*Coriolanus Overture*   p. 1, ed. Philharmonia

There is a natural tendency towards *crescendo* in the up-bow, due to the increasing leverage of the length of bow to the left of the string, and likewise a tendency towards *diminuendo* in the down-bow. While these tendencies are guarded against by the player, it is advisable to recognize them when planning the bowing of a passage.

It is evident that the bow must move up as much as it moves down. But if the up and down motions are of unequal time value it means that the bow must move at an uneven speed, thus making it difficult to maintain an even dynamic level. The bowing indicated in Fig. 7 will inevitably cause the third and sixth beats to sound louder than the others, since the same length of bow must be used to play two sixteenth notes in up-bow as was used to play four sixteenths in down-bow.

Fig. 7

A more even tone will be achieved by a bowing which restores the balance of up and down, both in quantity and rate of motion.

Fig. 8

In a legato phrase the changes in direction of the bow are determined by combined factors of intensity, dynamic level, tempo, the length of the bow, fingering, etc. Any melody can be bowed effectively in many different ways, and it is no wonder that concertmasters often disagree

as to the best way to bow a given phrase, and are seen even now marking changes in the bowing of such well-established classics as the
Beethoven symphonies.

EX. 4. Beethoven—*Symphony no. 4*   p. 41, ed. Kalmus

NONLEGATO

Perhaps the commonest bow stroke is that which changes direction
for each note. As mentioned above, the change can be made without
break in the tone. But this stroke, known by the French term *détaché*,
is usually performed so that one hears the articulation of the bow
changes. The notes are not so detached from one another that the effect
could be called staccato. The *détaché* can be described as nonlegato.
Ordinarily it is played in the middle or upper third of the bow.

EX. 5. Schubert—*Symphony no. 8*   p. 57, ed. Philharmonia

This nonlegato bow stroke is sometimes used at the point of the bow
to take advantage of its extreme lightness there, and at the heel for the
added weight occasionally wanted.

At the point (Fr., *à la pointe;* It., *a punta d'arco;* Ger., *an der Spitze*):

EX. 6. Bartók—*Concerto for Orchestra*   p. 79, ed. Boosey & Hawkes

At the heel (Fr., *au talon;* It., *al tallone;* Ger., *am Frosch*):

EX. 7. Strauss—*Don Quixote*   p. 56, ed. Philharmonia

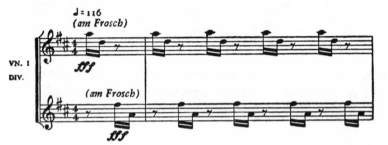

For vigorous emphasis and equality of stress, a series of down-bows can be used, near the heel of the bow, the bow being lifted with a swift up-bow motion between the notes.

EX. 8. Stravinsky—*Le Sacre du Printemps*   p. 11, ed. Russe

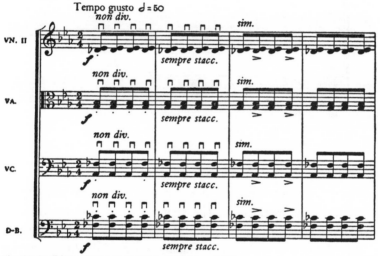

A combination of legato and nonlegato is found in the bowing known as *louré*. This is indicated by a dash over each note, with slurs to show the bow changes. The first finger regulates the rather gentle break in the continuity of the tone by controlling the pressure on the stick, aided by a subtle slowing of the bow with the wrist.

EX. 9. Sibelius—*Symphony no. 2*   p. 3, ed. Breitkopf

STACCATO

Staccato bowing is of two types—"off the string" and "on the string." In moderate tempo and at a dynamic level from *piano* to *mezzo forte*, the bow is dropped on the string with a sort of semicircular motion at the middle of the bow. The bow rebounds, although it is partly lifted by the wrist. The Italian word *spiccato* (detached) is applied by string players to bowing that makes use of a springing or bouncing of the bow-stick. It is also called *saltando* (jumping). There is much disagreement over the exact application of these terms. But fortunately the composer or orchestrator is not called upon to indicate more precisely than by dots over the notes, together with dynamic signs and tempo marks, the quality of music that means to a string player *spiccato*, *saltando*, or off-the-string staccato.

EX. 10. Beethoven—*Symphony no. 1*   p. 38, ed. Kalmus

Staccato playing in fast tempo does not call for a lifting of the bow, but the short, quick down- and up-bows made by the wrist alone, in the middle of the bow, cause the stick to bounce, and this in turn causes the hair to spring off the string with each stroke.

EX. 11. Rossini—*Overture to William Tell*   p. 45, ed. Kalmus

Another type of bouncing bow is usually called by the French *jeté* (thrown). It is played near the point, and the bow is not thrown but dropped upon the string with a slight down-bow motion, and allowed to bounce of its own accord. Groups of two to six notes can be played in this way, the indication being dots under a slur, sometimes with the word *saltando,* or *saltato,* to make sure of the bouncing effect.

EX. 12. Rimsky-Korsakoff—*Capriccio Espagnol*   p. 73, ed. Kalmus

The bowing called *martellato* (hammered) is an on-the-string staccato (Fr., *martelé*). The bow is not permitted to leave the string and
the stroke is very swift, with abrupt start and stop. The sound of the
note, whether in *piano* or *forte*, might be imagined in the shape of an
oblong block with square ends. Although it is usually played with the
upper part of the bow, the martellato stroke may be used at the heel,
where the added weight of the bow contributes to the vigor of the
staccato.

EX. 13. Bruckner—*Symphony no. 9* p. 142, ed. Philharmonia

When several notes under a slur are marked with dots, the intended staccato may be accomplished with a bouncing bow, usually up-bow, as in Ex. 14, or with the bow held firmly on the string, sharp stops being made by the wrist, as in Ex. 15. The latter bowing is known as slurred staccato.

EX. 14. Mahler—*Symphony no. 4* p. 3, ed. Philharmonia

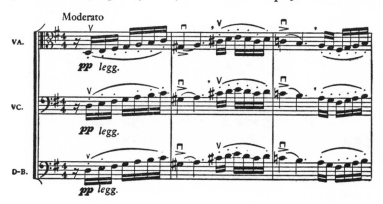

EX. 15. Stravinsky—*Orpheus*   p. 40, ed. Boosey & Hawkes

The rhythm of dotted eighth and sixteenth, in fast tempo, is most often played as slurred staccato, even when not so marked. This bowing is indicated by a slur, with a dot on the sixteenth note. It is the first note that is shortened, however. The same bowing is used for the quarter note followed by an eighth in six-eight time.

EX. 16. Berlioz—*Fantastic Symphony*   p. 153, ed. Eulenburg

For a light, crisp effect, this may be done at the point of the bow, with up-bow on the beats.

EX. 17. Weber—*Euryanthe Overture*   p. 22, ed. Philharmonia

The various bow strokes described are to be found in countless combinations. True knowledge of their appropriate use comes from long study and experience in playing a stringed instrument, to which must be added real understanding of the music. The student of orchestration should begin early the practice of marking the bowing of string parts. Whenever he thinks of a phrase for strings he must always imagine how it would best be bowed, within the limits of his knowledge. Through trial and observation much can be learned about this most important aspect of string writing.

It should be realized that bowings marked in printed scores are not always literally followed in performance. Composers are seldom careful to indicate all bowings, and some markings are the result of editing. What the composer actually wrote is evidence of his wishes, and this forms the basis for study by conductor and concertmaster as to the best way to realize the composer's intentions. Here, as in all matters of art, there is plenty of room for differences of opinion and interpretation.

ACCENTS

Accents are made principally with the bow, but an accent may also be imparted by the left hand, by means of a sudden quickening of the vibrato, by a more forceful finger stroke, or by both. It depends on whether the accented note is made by lifting the finger (Fig. 9*a*), or by dropping it on the string (Fig. 9*b*). This left-hand accent is nearly always combined with the bow accent in vigorous and rhythmic passages.

Fig. 9

Accents are of course relative to the general nuance of a particular tone, whether soft or loud. There are different kinds of accents, created by different modes of attack. The following figure attempts to show graphically the shape of the tone in the most important of these forms.

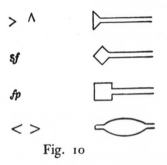

Fig. 10

Composers in general seem to have been indifferent to these distinctions, one reason being perhaps that they are impossible to produce on the pianoforte. Therefore it becomes a responsibility of the conductor to decide which type of accent is meant by the composer's sign, and to see that it is properly executed.

EFFECTS OF COLOR

To obtain a tone of very soft floating quality the strings may be directed to play on the fingerboard (Fr., *sur la touche;* It., *sulla tastiera* or *sul tasto;* Ger., *am Griffbrett*). The bow is placed so far from the bridge that it is actually over the upper part of the fingerboard, where there is greater amplitude in the vibration of the string.

EX. 18. Debussy—*Rondes de Printemps*   p. 36, ed. Durand

Permission granted by Durand et Cie., Paris, copyright owners; Elkan-Vogel, Philadelphia, Pa., agents

In this bowing, care must be taken that too much pressure is not put upon the bow, lest it strike more than one string. Playing over the fingerboard is impractical on the E-string of the violin, since the curve of the body of the instrument interferes with the proper placing of the bow. It is often indicated, nevertheless, for passages running up to high positions on the E-string; although the directive cannot be followed literally, it serves to suggest the tone quality desired.

Playing with the bow very close to the bridge, or even upon it (Fr., *au chevalet;* It., *sul ponticello;* Ger., *am Steg*), produces a special kind of sound, due to the bringing out of upper partials not usually heard. The sound has been called glassy and metallic. This effect is generally combined with the bowed tremolo.

EX. 19. Strauss—*Symphonia Domestica*

p. 67, ed. Associated Music Publishers

With authorization of the original publishers Ed. Bote & G. Bock, Berlin, Wiesbaden.

When *sulla tastiera* or *sul ponticello* is no longer wanted, the part is marked *modo ordinario,* or *naturale.*

The bow may be turned over, so that the strings are struck with the wood instead of the hair (It., *col legno*). This is a bowing used for dry staccato effects, the bow-stick tapping with a kind of off-the-string staccato.

EX. 20. Britten—*Passacaglia from Peter Grimes*

p. 16, ed. Boosey & Hawkes

Obviously, one can expect little sound to come from drawing the wood across the string, since the amount of friction is very small. There are, nevertheless, some instances in scores of tremolo and legato bowing *col legno*. It is interesting that Gustav Mahler felt it necessary to add a footnote in the score of his First Symphony to explain that the indication *col legno* and the bowing marked were no error.

EX. 21. Mahler—*Symphony no. 1*   p. 91, ed. Universal

These effects, although not common, are much better known today. Some composers write *col legno battuto* (Ger., *geschlagen*) for the tapping, and *col legno tratto* (Ger., *gestrichen*) to indicate that the wood

is to be drawn across the string. The return to normal bowing after *col legno* is indicated by *arco*.

PIZZICATO

The strings are frequently plucked, instead of bowed. The direction *pizzicato* (abbreviated *pizz.*) indicates that this manner of playing is to be continued until the word *arco* signifies that playing with the bow is to be resumed.

The right first finger plucks the string, over the fingerboard, and the other three fingers hold the bow against the palm of the hand. The thumb may rest on the edge of the fingerboard to steady the hand, although this position is not always necessary or practical. The playing position of 'cello and bass permits pizzicato also with the thumb, especially for chords arpeggiated from the bottom note upward.

Changing from arco to pizzicato requires an appreciable amount of time, varying according to the position of the bow at the instant. A larger interval must be allowed if the pizzicato follows a down-bow at the point, whereas after an up-bow at the heel the change can be practically instantaneous.

EX. 22. Debussy—*Pelléas et Mélisande*   p. 231, ed. Durand

The return to arco after pizzicato is slightly more inconvenient, as it involves the quick adjustment of the bow into playing position. Activity like that in the following example is not uncommon, however.

EX. 23. Berlioz—*Harold in Italy*   p. 145, ed. Eulenburg

Reprinted with the permission of the sole agents for Eulenburg Miniature Scores: C. F. Peters Corporation, New York.

The pizzicato is by its nature a form of staccato. The sound dies away quite promptly. Differences are to be noted in this respect between small and large instruments, violin and double-bass, for instance. The longer and heavier strings sustain the tone much better than the shorter ones. Open strings are more resonant than those stopped by the fingers. The sound of the fingered notes can be prolonged a little by vibrato.

The quality of tone in pizzicato can be varied by plucking at different points on the string, and by the manner of plucking, from a gentle stroking with the fleshy part of the fingertip to a twanging of such violence that the string strikes against the fingerboard. There is also a difference according to the position of the left hand. In higher positions the string is so short that the pizzicato is of a hard, dry quality, which at times may be used to advantage.

EX. 24. Ravel—*Daphnis et Chloé* p. 132, ed. Durand

The rapidity of passages in pizzicato is necessarily limited by the difficulty of continued plucking by one finger. The trick of alternating first and second fingers in fast pizzicato, acquired by some players, is by no means universal. Factors affecting the practicability of fast pizzicato playing include the size of the instrument, the dynamic level of the music, the amount of continuous pizzicato demanded, and the complications in the passage from the standpoint of changes from one string to another. The following is an example of successful pizzicato writing at a rapid tempo.

EX. 25. Dukas—*L'Apprenti-Sorcier*   p. 51, ed. Kalmus

Pizzicato may also be performed with the fingers of the left hand when the notes are so arranged that a finger is free to pluck the string, or when a finger is so placed that it can pluck as it is raised after stopping a note. Left-hand pizzicato is indicated by a cross over or under the notes.

EX. 26. Stravinsky—*Symphony in C*   p. 21, ed. Schott

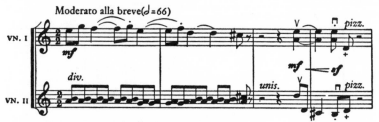

Chords of three and four notes in pizzicato are arpeggiated from the bottom up, unless otherwise marked. A series of quickly repeated chords may be more effectively played by alternating back-and-forth movements, using one or several fingers. The direction of the strokes may be shown by perpendicular arrows, or by the usual signs for up- and down-bow. Sometimes *quasi guitara* is added.

EX. 27. Ravel—*L'Enfant et les Sortilèges*   p. 38, ed. Durand

The arpeggiated effect can be held to a minimum by a sharp, sudden finger stroke. Two notes can be plucked simultaneously with two fingers. A straight bracket is the accepted indication for this.

EX. 28. Stravinsky—*Ragtime* p. 4, ed. Chester

Although possibilities of new sounds to be obtained by pizzicato have not been explored by composers in general, some new effects have been used, such as pizzicato *sul ponticello* and *sul tasto;* pizzicato harmonics; picking with the fingernail near the nut; and snapping the string against the fingerboard. The last is indicated by the sign ⊙.

EX. 29. Bartók—*Violin Concerto* p. 51, ed. Boosey & Hawkes

HARMONICS

The vibration of a string is a composite of a number of separate, simultaneous vibrations, whose frequencies vary in the ratio 1, 2, 3, 4, 5, etc. These vibrations are represented in the following diagrams. Points marked *n* are called nodes.

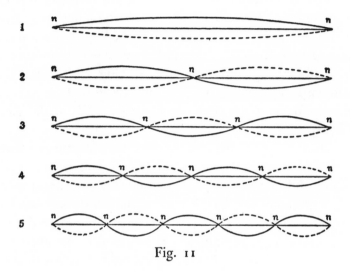

Fig. 11

Let us assume the string to be the G-string of a violin. Fig. 11 could then be translated into musical sounds, thus:

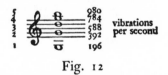

Fig. 12

It will be noticed that the ratio of the divisions of the string shown in Fig. 11 is the same as that of the frequencies shown in Fig. 12.

These sounds present in a single tone are called harmonics. Number one is the first harmonic, or fundamental tone. The others are called second, third, fourth, and fifth harmonics, overtones, or partials. Higher harmonics than these are present also, in diminishing strength. The number and comparative strength of the harmonics making up a tone give it its individual tone color, or *timbre*, enabling us to distinguish the sound of a clarinet from that of a 'cello playing the same note. We do not hear this combination of harmonics as a chord. The fundamental tone is so much stronger than its upper partials that we are regularly deceived into assuming that it alone is what we hear.

If a vibrating string is touched very lightly at one of the dividing nodes shown in Fig. 11, it will be prevented from sounding its fundamental, but it will continue to vibrate as in the diagram, according to the node chosen, and it will sound the corresponding note shown by Fig. 12. For example, the G-string is touched lightly at a point one-third of its length from the nut, while maintained in vibration by the bow. The entire string vibrates as in no. 3 of Fig. 11. The note sounded is that shown as no. 3 of Fig. 12. The same result is obtained by touching the other node of the same number, two-thirds of the way from nut to bridge.

Tones produced in this manner are called by string players *harmonics* (Fr., *sons harmoniques;* It., *armonici;* Ger., *Flageolettöne*). Their timbre is quite different from normal stopped tones, since only those partials are sounding that have a node at the point touched. They are indicated in notation by (*a*) placing a small circle over the note intended to sound as a harmonic, or (*b*) writing a diamond-shaped note at the pitch where the node producing the desired note is found on the string.

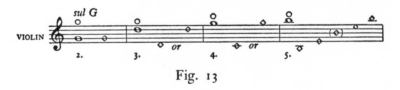

Fig. 13

The indication *sul G* means that all is to be played on the G-string (Ger., *G-Saite*). Another means of designating the string to be used, preferred by the French, is that of Roman numerals, the highest string being always I (*e.g.,* IVe corde).

ARTIFICIAL HARMONICS

On the violin and viola it is possible to stop a tone with the first finger and at the same time touch a node with the fourth finger. This can also be done on the 'cello, using the thumb and third finger. The node which has been found the most dependable is that of the fourth harmonic, one-fourth the new string length, at a point represented in notation by the interval of a perfect fourth above the note stopped by the first finger. The resulting tone is therefore two octaves above the stopped tone. These harmonics are called artificial harmonics, as differentiated from natural harmonics, which have open strings as fundamental tones. Artificial harmonics are indicated in notation by (*a*) placing a small circle above the note to be heard as a harmonic, or (*b*) writing the fundamental to be stopped by the first finger as a normal note and the node a fourth above as a diamond-shaped note (Fig. 14). The actual pitch of the tone intended is often added above, as (*c*).

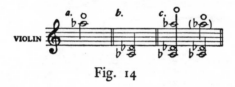

Fig. 14

Composers frequently use the notation (*a*) for all harmonics, leaving the method of production to the player, whether as artificial or as natural harmonics. The notation (*b*) is sometimes used when the lower tone is an open string. This is incorrect but easily understood.

TRILLS

Trills are performed by the motion of one finger, since the finger stopping the lower of the two tones is held down throughout. Both major and minor trills are good in all ranges, the only exception being those on the lowest note of the instrument, where the alternation of open string and stopped note does not produce as effective a trill as those on stopped notes.

It should be remembered that a string trill in the orchestra means a trill played simultaneously by a whole section. Sixteen first violins will not likely agree on the rhythmic quantities of a trill on a long note, and the effect will not have the clear articulation of the same trill given say to the first flute, played by a single player.

TREMOLO

A trill with a harmonic interval larger than a major second is a fingered tremolo. If a real tremolo is intended, rather than an alternation of two notes at a stipulated speed (sometimes called measured tremolo), it is advisable to write time values fast enough to insure a real tremolo, or to add the word *tremolo*, or *tremolando*. Slurs are necessary to show the legato movement of the bow.

EX. 30. Debussy—*L'Après-midi d'un Faune*   p. 28, ed. Kalmus

Permission granted by Editions Jean Jobert, Paris, copyright owners; Elkan-Vogel, Philadelphia, Pa., agents.

The division of the first violins in the first measure of Ex. 30 would seem on first glance to be only theoretical, but it is a way of making sure that both notes of the interval sound at each change of bow.

When the interval exceeds the limit of extension of the fingers on one string, the two notes are held as a double-stop; and the tremolo effect has to be made by an undulating motion of the bow, alternately touching the two strings. This type of tremolo is not the same as the true fingered tremolo, since it lacks the clear articulation of the finger strokes.

EX. 31. Brahms—*Symphony no. 1*   p. 102, ed. Kalmus

In the preceding example some of the groupings, such as Violin I, measure 4, can be played as fingered tremolo (measured), while others require two strings, like those in the first measure. On the other hand, all are possible as double-stops, with undulating bow.

The bowed tremolo is made with quick up- and down-bow strokes, the left hand holding the note or notes. It is a characteristic orchestral effect, capable of great dynamic range and variety of accentuation.

EX. 32. Debussy—*La Mer*   p. 18, ed. Durand

Equally idiomatic in orchestral writing is the continued repetition of bow strokes, *détaché*, on a series of notes, to give more energy and volume to the string tone.

EX. 33. Mozart—*Symphony*, K. 543   p. 8, ed. Philharmonia

MUTES

The mute is a three-pronged device made of wood, metal, bone, or other materials, which can be fitted onto the bridge for the purpose of absorbing some of the vibrations before they can be transmitted to the resonating body of the instrument. The tone quality of muted strings is difficult of description, but, once heard, its characteristic sound is easily remembered. While one of the results of muting is to reduce the dynamic power of the body of strings, the radical change in tone color is far more important. Muting should not be regarded as the primary means of getting the strings to play softly. A fine *pianissimo* can be achieved without mutes, and, furthermore, the special effect of *forte* with muted strings may sometimes be just what is wanted.

Time must be allowed for putting on and taking off mutes, at least a couple of measures in moderate tempo. The more time the better, to avoid confusion and disturbance. Numerous inventions to facilitate a quick change have appeared, such as mutes with a spring clip, or mutes permanently installed on the strings back of the bridge, to be pushed up against the bridge for muting. It cannot be said that any of these have met with complete acceptance by string players.

A gradual change to muted tone can be managed by directing the players to put on mutes one by one, or by desks, marking the point at which all are to be muted.

The indication to put on the mute is the Italian *con sordina*, or *con sordino*—plural *sordine*, or *sordini* (Fr., *avec sourdines;* Ger., *mit Dämpfer*, or *gedämpft*).

To call for removal of the mutes, the passage is marked *senza sordini* (Fr., *sans sourdines;* Ger., *ohne Dämpfer*), or *via sordini* (Fr., *ôtez les sourdines;* Ger., *Dämpfer weg*).

SCORDATURA

A change from the normal tuning of the strings is called *scordatura*. This has been employed to extend the downward range of basses and 'cellos on rare occasions. In *Don Quixote* Strauss asks the solo viola to tune the C-string to B, and a similar change is asked of the 'cellos in Casella's *Partita for Piano and Orchestra*. The strings do not give their best tone when altered more than a minor second, and the inconvenience and disturbance caused by retuning during performance seem to overbalance the slight advantage gained.

The use of *scordatura* for a change of tone color is another matter. In Mahler's Fourth Symphony the solo violin in the second movement has all four strings tuned up a whole tone, to make it sound "like a cheap fiddle." The concertmaster prepares a second instrument to use for this movement, so that retuning is avoided.

⇒》《⇐

THE VIOLIN

Fr., *violon;* It., *violino;* Ger., *Violine*

THE over-all length of the violin is 23⅜ inches. Minor variations in proportions and size are found in different models. The body is 14 inches long, the neck a little under 5¼ inches, and the sounding length of the strings—that is, from nut to bridge—is slightly over 12¾ inches. The length of the bow is 29 inches.

The top, or belly, of the instrument is usually of pine or spruce, the back of maple in one or two pieces. Ebony is used for the tailpiece, fingerboard, nut, and tuning pegs. Inside the body, the arched belly is reinforced by a strip of wood called the bass-bar, glued beneath the G-string edge of the fingerboard. A wooden sound post is held in place by tension between top and back at a carefully chosen spot near the E-string side of the bridge, having the double function of support and communication of vibrations. The *f*-holes are characteristic openings of traditional shape at either side of the bridge (Plate on page 38).

FINGERING

The violin is supported between the chin and the left shoulder. A chin rest attached at the left of the tailpiece helps hold the instrument so that the left hand is free to move up and down the fingerboard. The neck of the violin lies between the thumb and the palm of the left hand, and the left elbow is held far to the right, enabling the fingers to fall almost perpendicularly upon the strings.

The Violin

An important feature of articulation in string playing is that some notes are made by dropping the finger on the string, while others are made by lifting the finger. If the scale fragment in Fig. 15 is played in one legato bow, the ascending notes are articulated by striking and the descending notes by lifting. Also to be noted is that, after striking, the fingers remain on the string until there is necessity for moving them, as shown in the figure.

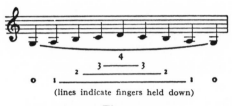

(lines indicate fingers held down)

Fig. 15

The manner in which the fingers are lifted or dropped affects the clarity, rhythm, and tone quality of the sounds produced. The finger action varies from exceedingly energetic strokes (Ex. 34) to an extremely light and fleet articulation (Ex. 35).

EX. 34. Schumann—*Symphony no. 2*   p. 172, ed. Philharmonia

EX. 35. Mendelssohn—*Italian Symphony*   p. 140, ed. Eulenburg

The following diagram gives the location of the fingers for all the natural notes in the first position.

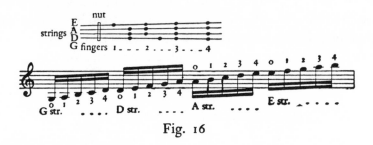

Fig. 16

Note that the first finger is drawn back close to the nut for F on the E-string, the interval being a minor second, instead of a major second as on the other strings. The diagram should be studied also for relationships involving more than one string. For example, from first finger on one string to second finger on the next higher string is a minor sixth; from first finger on one string to fourth finger on the next higher string is an octave; from second finger on one string to third finger on the next lower string is a perfect fourth, etc. Perfect fifths lie across the strings at right angles.

OPEN STRINGS

Duplication by the fourth finger of the open string notes A, D, and E is an advantage peculiar to the first position. There is, however, a marked difference in tone quality between the open string tones and those stopped by the fingers. The former sound clearer and richer in overtones, because the string vibrates between the bridge and the hard wood of the nut rather than the flesh of the fingertip. But without the control of the finger the open tone is susceptible to little modification by the bow, and it tends to sound with undue prominence. Furthermore, its pitch cannot be adjusted while playing (consider the note A as subdominant of E, and then as leading tone of B♭). These discrepancies of intonation are generally tolerated as a necessary evil, notably in the use of natural harmonics, whose pitch is dependent on that of the open string fundamental, and also in enharmonically notated passages. In

Ex. 36, open G is assumed to be a satisfactory equivalent of F double sharp.

EX. 36. Wagner—*Tannhäuser: Bacchanale*   p. 20, ed. Kalmus

Open string tones are usually avoided in expressive melodic phrases, but they are regularly employed in fast scales and figures. Their sound is characteristic of stringed instruments, and may even be exploited as such (Ex. 37).

EX. 37. Brahms—*Symphony no. 4*   p. 134, ed. Kalmus

ACCIDENTALS

A note affected by an accidental is played with the same finger as the natural note. On the G-string, the first finger plays A♭, A♮, and A♯. Also the first finger must play the sharped open string note G♯. The student should make a diagram similar to that in Fig. 16, marking the location of the fingers on the strings for the playing of the following passage.

Fig. 17

CHROMATIC PROGRESSION

Two notes in chromatic step relationship are by tradition played with the same finger. This requires a more or less rapid shift of the finger on the string; hence, with a legato bowing, a certain amount of portamento is unavoidable.

Fig. 18

Musically, the difference between (*a*) and (*b*), in Fig. 18 is one of tonality. The fragment (*a*) is understandable in the key of G, and (*b*) in the key of A♭, to mention two possible interpretations. The unorthodox fingering shown in (*c*) is entirely feasible, and the principle of using a separate finger for each chromatic step has in practice partially superseded the time-honored one, as by this means a more distinct articulation is obtained, without sliding or portamento.

There can be no doubt of the superiority of fingering (*c*) for rapid passages, but it should be recognized that at a slower tempo the differentiation in harmonic meaning suggested by (*a*) and (*b*) may be sacrificed, not to mention the elimination of certain slides firmly established in what we know as "violin style." It is true that harmonic developments in the twentieth century often demand complete acceptance of the enharmonic notation of the tempered scale, but the choice of fingering should be governed by musical rather than by mechanical considerations.

These two alternative fingerings are shown in the following scale. Obviously the sound of the finger slides is eliminated if a *détaché* bowing is used, but the lower, older fingering remains awkward even then.

Fig. 19

INTONATION

Good intonation (that is, playing in tune) is a perpetual preoccupation with all instrumentalists, wind as well as string players. It is not an absolute but a relative value, however. Observation and experiments have demonstrated that in practice performers do not adhere to any of the scientifically codified standards of pitch, such as equal temperament, Pythagorean, just, or mean-tone intonation. Nor does the player accept the tones he produces by using the proper fingering, etc., without subjecting them to constant control and correction through the ear (except, of course, in the case of instruments like the harp or the piano, whose pitch cannot be adjusted while playing). It can be said that leading-tones and chromatically raised notes are played sharp and very close to their melodic destinations, whereas flatted notes are played low in pitch, and that there operates a continual harmonic adjustment to the sounds of other instruments.

The peculiar vibrancy noticeable in the tone of a group of strings playing in unison is due in part to the minute differences in pitch that occur throughout the group.

POSITION TECHNIQUE

As the hand is moved to higher positions new groups of notes lie under the fingers.

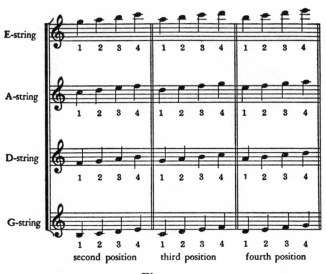

second position   third position   fourth position

Fig. 20

The series may be continued upward, with the qualification that on the lower strings high notes are increasingly difficult of production because of the shortness of the string in proportion to its thickness. On the E-string, tones can be played up to the end of the fingerboard, and even beyond, where diatonic intervals become smaller than the thickness of the fingertips. The G♯ written by Strauss in the following example lies in the thirteenth position, and has a sounding string length of a little more than an inch and three-quarters. It is played by two desks of violins, doubled at the unison by piccolo, and supported at the octave below by flute, E♭ clarinet, and two other desks of violins.

EX. 38. Strauss—*Also Sprach Zarathustra*   p. 57, ed. Aibl

Fingering at the top of the fingerboard is difficult not only because of the smallness of the intervals and the extended position of the hand, but also because the strings are spaced farther apart at the bridge than at the nut, to facilitate bowing.

The E two octaves above the open E-string may be recommended as a good practical upper limit, exclusive of harmonics, for orchestral violin parts.

HALF POSITION

The hand is said to be in half position when the first finger is a half step from the nut and the second finger plays notes usually played by the first finger. Certain combinations of notes are more conveniently fingered in this rather cramped position (Ex. 39).

EX. 39. Stravinsky—*Apollon Musagète*   p. 18, ed. Boosey & Hawkes

FOURTH FINGER EXTENSION

In the first position the left hand is capable of a stretch of an augmented fourth, and even a perfect fifth, from first to fourth finger. In higher positions, extension of the fourth finger beyond the range of the position is common procedure (Fig. 21).

Fig. 21

SHIFT OF POSITION

In changing from one position to another, a sliding finger acts as a guide to the interval of change. The hand may move to any of the positions, but the commonest shift is that from first to third, third to fifth position, etc., involving a slide of a third, usually for the first finger (Fig. 22).

Fig. 22

The guiding finger is not necessarily the stopping finger in the new position. Fig. 23 (*a*) is a characteristic position shift. The first finger slides from B to D, but the fourth finger stops G before D is heard. The slide can be made so quickly as to be inaudible, but it is often permitted to sound for expressive intensification. Other shifts are shown in (*b*), (*c*), and (*d*).

Fig. 23

When taste and the style of the music allow, the finger that is to play the second note may make a slight portamento on the string just before reaching the note. In a descending shift, the portamento on quitting the upper note is kept to a minimum, the thumb acting as a guide to the lower position.

The sliding sounds can be reduced to near imperceptibility, or they can be eliminated altogether, by skillful manipulation of the bow and fingers. However, they are idiomatic in string playing, and sometimes a particular fingering that will produce them is deliberately chosen.

Suppression of the portamento in the following example would certainly be inappropriate.

EX. 40. Strauss—*Der Rosenkavalier*   p. 330, ed. Boosey & Hawkes

GLISSANDO AND PORTAMENTO

A true glissando is made with one finger, on one string, with legato bow, and when it is properly executed all intervening stages of pitch are sounded between the indicated limits.

EX. 41. Ravel—*Daphnis et Chloé*   p. 297, ed. Durand

This glissando is scored as unison and octaves for first and second violins, violas, half the 'cellos, and basses, all on their open A-strings, sliding up and down two octaves in fast tempo.

In Ex. 42, G-string and A-string are designated, although the glissandos written could not be made on any other strings.

EX. 42. Bartók—*Dance Suite*   p. 8, ed. Philharmonia

It is evident that composers fail to distinguish between *portamento* and *glissando*, and it is unnecessary that a pedantic distinction should be made. Portamento seems to imply a manner of connecting melodic tones, and one thinks of a glissando as covering a fairly wide interval, but these conditions are not mutually exclusive. Care should be taken in the notation to show as accurately as possible the exact effect intended.

A straight line from one note to another is commonly used as a sign of portamento, although there is often doubt as to how complete a slide is wanted. In Ex. 43 a real glissando with one finger could be made where the lines are marked, but, on the other hand, the lines may be taken simply as suggesting a musical style in which more than usual emphasis is given to the portamentos associated with position shifts. Ex. 44 is more problematical. A complete portamento from the C down to the E is out of the question, since the upper note is too high to take on the G-string. The most the performer can do is to make a small slide at the beginning and end of the descent.

EX. 43. Mahler—*Symphony no. 4*   p. 118, ed. Philharmonia

EX. 44. Mahler—*Symphony no. 4*   p. 119, ed. Philharmonia

Likewise the glissando in the next example cannot be literally executed. After the open E is reached, something like a rapidly fingered chromatic scale or partial glissando on the lower strings must be substituted.

EX. 45. Ravel—*La Valse*   p. 39, ed. Durand

Permission granted by Durand et Cie., Paris, copyright owners; Elkan-Vogel, Philadelphia, Pa., agents.

WIDE SKIPS

To judge the degree of difficulty in fingering wide leaps one considers the strings involved and the position displacement necessary. The skip of two octaves and a major sixth in Ex. 46 passes from the G-string to the E-string, and the hand must move from first position (third finger C) to seventh position (fourth finger A). This is equivalent to a slide from C up to B for the third finger, an interval of a major seventh on one string.

EX. 46. Brahms—*Symphony no. 3*   p. 49, ed. Kalmus

Similarly, it is necessary to cross over two strings in the next example, but it happens that the left hand does not have to change position to play the two lower notes on the G-string. All are in the sixth position, except that the initial B is better played on the more brilliant E-string in third position.

EX. 47. Holst—*The Planets*   p. 29, ed. Boosey & Hawkes

Used by permission of J. Curwen & Sons, Ltd.

Skips made on one string are apt to demand more displacement of the hand. In the following example, the leap of a tenth from F♯ to A means a shift from first to seventh position, just as for the much greater interval in Ex. 46.

EX. 48. Mahler—*Symphony no. 9*   p. 118, ed. Boosey & Hawkes

Copyright 1912; renewed 1940, by Universal Edition A. G. Used by permission.

If the two notes are to be slurred, the interval must be arranged so that either a single string, or two adjacent strings, can be employed, since the bow could not play legato and at the same time jump over intervening strings.

EX. 49. Reger—*A Romantic Suite, op. 125*   p. 48, ed. Bote & Bock

With authorization of the original publishers Ed. Bote & G. Bock, Berlin, Wiesbaden.

A skillful player can give a fairly good impression of a legato skip across intervening strings by lightening and slowing the bow at the right instant. It must be admitted, however, that keen ears are not deceived.

EX. 50. Berg—*Lyric Suite*   p. 36, ed. Universal

Open strings may take part in passages in which the hand remains in a high position.

EX. 51. Hindemith—*Symphony in E Flat*   p. 126, ed. Schott

CHOICE OF FINGERINGS

More than one fingering is possible for any succession of notes, and the one selected is not always that which is most convenient for the fingers. Simplification of bowing, by eliminating string changes, is sometimes a predominant consideration. Often a fingering with more position shifts is adopted in order to preserve the unity of tone color and special quality of a single string, or to give a particular expressive turn to a melody. The student's attention is called to the importance of developing an appreciation of these differences in the sounds produced by stringed instruments.

In recent years one notes a strong tendency toward a liberation of violin fingering technique from the traditional system of positions. It cannot be denied that many forced and unnatural finger positions are the result of "correct" fingering, and that these produce bad intonation. Accomplished and experienced players find that they prefer to discover fingerings most suited to the shape of the hand, of their own individual hand, without reference to conventional patterns and positions, so that the notes to be played lie conveniently under the fingers that are to play them. Doubtless these principles will one day be incorporated into the teaching of violin playing.

CHARACTERISTICS OF THE STRINGS

While there is much more unity of timbre in a stringed instrument than in a woodwind, there exists in this respect within the homogeneity of the violin a striking variety and even contrast of colors and dynamic range. This is largely because of the differences in sound between the four strings. Since the pitch ranges of the strings overlap, the possibilities for variety are multiplied, and we cannot designate characteristics of low, medium, and high registers, as we do for wind instruments.

The E-string is made of steel. The radical change to this material from gut, in the interests of greater brilliance and durability, occurred in the first quarter of the present century and was felt by many to be a disaster because of the loss of a certain silky and mellow quality. A-strings are of gut, although some orchestra players now use a metal A. The D-string is either of gut or gut wound with aluminum wire. The G-string is always a wound string, silver or copper wire over gut being the commonest material. D- and G-strings entirely of metal are also used.

The tuning pegs to which the strings are attached are held in position by the friction of a good fit. A knot or a loop attaches the other end of the string to the tailpiece. Metal strings require a special screw device on the tailpiece for tuning fine differences.

The E-string has the most carrying power. Forceful and even strident at times, it is also capable of an ethereal quality, luminous and clear, when played softly (Ex. 52).

EX. 52. Milhaud—*Second Symphonic Suite*   p. 69, ed. Durand

The A-string is fairly strong in the first position, losing some brilliance and power as the string becomes shorter in upper positions. For a soft, expressive phrase in that range, it is generally preferable to move up the A-string rather than pass over to the E (Ex. 53).

EX. 53. Brahms—*Symphony no. 3*   p. 67, ed. Kalmus

The least powerful string is the D-string. It has a quiet, subdued quality in contrast to the G, and is especially suited to certain calm types of expression (Ex. 54).

EX. 54. Beethoven—*Piano Concerto no. 4*   p. 2, ed. Philharmonia

The G-string is next to the E-string in sonorous strength. It is excellent for broad melodies rising as high as the seventh or eighth position, although it has a tendency to hoarseness in the extreme high tones. A cautious limit for melodies on the G-string would be an octave and a fourth above the open string (Ex. 55).

EX. 55. Mahler—*Symphony no. 3*   p. 213, ed. Boosey & Hawkes

The next example illustrates a way of avoiding loss of volume and force by using the G-string instead of the weaker D.

EX. 56. Bartók—*Concerto for Orchestra*   p. 56, ed. Boosey & Hawkes

Loud accented notes on the G-string can be forceful to the degree of ferocity.

EX. 57. Roussel—*Symphony in G Minor*   p. 39, ed. Durand

To signify that a passage is to be played on a certain string, the passage may be marked *sul* G (or D or A), with a dotted line continuing as far as necessary. One should realize, however, that a violinist selects his fingering according to the musical and technical demands of the moment, and ordinarily such indications are needed only when a special effect is intended.

Most violin music will require the use of more than one string for a given phrase. The passing from one string to another is done in a way to reconcile their differences and as far as possible to preserve continuity of color and intensity.

DOUBLE-STOPS AND CHORDS

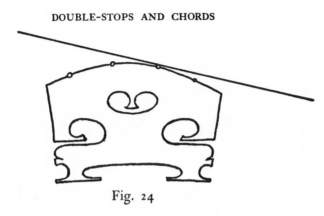

Fig. 24

The above representation of bridge, strings, and bow shows how little change in the elevation of the right hand is necessary for the bow to play on different strings. The bow can be drawn in a plane to engage two strings at once, whatever the position of the left hand (Fig. 25a). It cannot be drawn across three strings at once, unless enough pressure is put upon it to depress the middle string of the three into the same plane with the other two. This is done in three-part chords that are loud and of short duration (Fig. 25b). Otherwise, in both three-part and four-part chords, either the top note or the two top notes are held after playing the lower notes as grace notes (Fig. 25c and d). It is the custom to play the lower notes before the beat. If such anticipation is not desired, a notation like that shown in (e) should be employed.

Fig. 25

The notation in Fig. 25 (*e*) makes for fussiness in the score, and composers generally have been content to write the plain chord, relying on the musical intelligence of performer and conductor for a proper rhythmic execution. In the opening tutti chords of the *Eroica*, the first violins must sound the four strings as nearly simultaneously as they can, to match the staccato of the other instruments. (The example is given in condensed score. All instruments are notated at actual pitch.)

EX. 58. Beethoven—*Symphony no. 3*   p. 1, ed. Kalmus

The student can best determine the practicability of any multiple stopping by the method of making diagrams showing the location of the fingers, at least until he gains enough experience to be able to picture these positions in his imagination. The practice of making such diagrams will go far toward giving him that experience. The following points will be found useful in writing chords for the violin.

One finger can stop two adjacent strings at once (the interval of a perfect fifth), but it cannot stop three or four.

The less awkward and strained the hand position the better the chord will sound, and the less likely that it will be out of tune. One good rule is to try to have the higher-numbered fingers on higher strings. The following two contrasting cases will illustrate this.

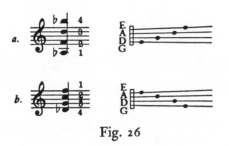

Fig. 26

The hand position for (*a*), with its outward slant, is practically that of the relaxed hand when the forearm is held upwards. In (*b*), not only must the hand be forced into a twisted position, but also the free vibration of the E- and A-strings is apt to be interfered with. It is not that the chord is unplayable but that (*a*) is much more certain and effective. Complex and awkward finger combinations need more time to set in place than simple and convenient ones.

Open strings are frequently used in chords and double-stops. They may be combined with stopped notes in higher positions (Fig. 27).

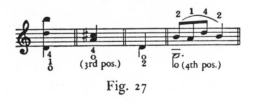

Fig. 27

The unison of stopped tone and open string is very resonant, especially in tremolo.

EX. 59. Prokofieff—*Chout*   p. 123, ed. Gutheil

The finger positions for three- and four-part chords are often the basis for arpeggio figures across the strings. The bow may play legato back and forth (Ex. 60), or it may bounce lightly by its own elasticity (Ex. 61).

EX. 60. Wagner—*Die Walküre: Siegmunds Liebeslied*

p. 15, ed. Eulenburg

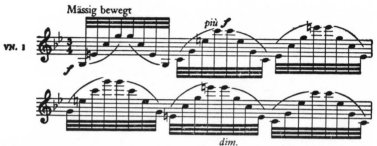

EX. 61. Rimsky-Korsakoff—*Capriccio Espagnol* p. 9, ed. Kalmus

HARMONICS

Although harmonics are primarily a coloristic resource, the octave harmonic is frequently employed as a normal tone in the melodic line, whether or not the composer has so indicated.

EX. 62. Schubert—*Symphony no. 5* p. 44, ed. Eulenburg

The upper limit for natural harmonics on the violin is generally placed at the fifth harmonic; that is, two octaves and a major third above the open string. In practice, the higher harmonics would probably be taken as artificial harmonics, up to the fourth or fifth position on the E-string, although still higher harmonics have been written (Ex. 63).

EX. 63. Copland—*Symphony no. 3*   p. 151, ed. Boosey & Hawkes

Examples are numerous of high pedal notes in harmonics, frequently with bowed tremolo. Their effect is enhanced by mutes; and in soft nuances chords in harmonics for divided violins, muted, make an attractive background of atmospheric color.

Artificial harmonics in quick succession, with either legato or détaché bow, involve continual shifting, much like playing a melody with one finger.

EX. 64. Milhaud—*Symphony no. 2*   p. 21, ed. Heugel

The glissando in natural harmonics is effective with a body of strings. The upper half of the string is brushed lightly with the third or fourth finger, the harmonics sounding at the nodes. There is no sound of portamento between the notes.

EX. 65. Stravinsky—*L'Oiseau de Feu*   p. 12, ed. Broude Bros.

An unusual, delicate effect is obtained with an arpeggio across the strings, in harmonics.

EX. 66. Ravel—*L'Heure Espagnole*   p. 121, ed. Durand

The artificial harmonic created by touching a perfect fifth above the stopping first finger sounds a twelfth above that fundamental. It is rarely used in orchestral scores, but some instances are found in modern music.

EX. 67. Bartók—*Dance Suite*   p. 31, ed. Philharmonia

FIRST AND SECOND VIOLINS

In score reading it is essential to bear in mind that a string part is played by a number of players, a whole section of sixteen first violins, for instance, as opposed to one player to a part in the case of woodwind or brass. The two sections of violins far outnumber any other group, while presenting on the printed page a look of equality.

The part for second violins, in a symphony orchestra, differs little in technical difficulty from that of the first violins. Indeed, one of the commonest functions of the second violins is to double the firsts at the unison or octave. This was necessary in the classical period because of the comparatively small number of violins available to balance horns and trumpets. But also in modern times we find that over twice as many violins are still not adequate to cope with the sonority of an enormously expanded brass section.

The first violin part is usually the top voice of the strings and carries the largest share of prominent thematic material. Seated on the left of the conductor, at the edge of the stage, the first violins play with their instruments in the most advantageous position relative to the audience. If the second violins are seated on the right, in traditional fashion, their instruments are turned away from the audience and some sound is lost. If they are massed with the first violins, as some conductors prefer, they are still dominated by the first violins who are between them and the listeners, and the effect of independence and antiphony often imagined by the composer is much reduced. This is one of the many acoustical problems standing in the way of an exact science of orchestration.

The second violins may have a secondary melodic part, or they may, for variety, be substituted for the first violins. They may engage in accompaniment figures of every sort, either by themselves or associated with first violins or other strings. In Ex. 68, in the first and third measures, the two sections alternately play figures from a single line, giving it more security and energy through the simplification of each part and the overlapping unisons at the joints.

EX. 68. Brahms—*Symphony no. 4*   p. 135, ed. Kalmus

Divided violins playing in parts may be employed unaccompanied by other instruments. In the following excerpt, the strings are reduced to four first violins, soli.

EX. 69. Liszt—*A Faust Symphony*   p. 148, ed. Eulenburg

Reprinted with the permission of the sole agents for Eulenburg Miniature Scores: C. F. Peters Corporation, New York.

SOLO VIOLIN

Many scores of the nineteenth and twentieth centuries contain parts
for solo violin, to be played by the concertmaster. These solo parts
vary in importance from the occasional phrases in Wagner and Mahler
to a developed obbligato of concertolike proportions and virtuosity, as
in *Ein Heldenleben,* by Richard Strauss. The reason for choosing the
sound of a solo violin is not merely that a reduction in volume is sought.
A single instrument possesses an intimate intensity in its tone quality
and expression; by comparison the complete section sounds formal and
impersonal. This is one of the motivating factors in the trend toward
the small orchestra in the twentieth century.

An acoustic phenomenon to be noted when the solo violin plays in
the midst of a large orchestra is its surprising ability to make itself
heard. It is well known that two instruments playing the same part do
not create twice the sonority of one. Their overtones are dulled by
minute pitch differences and, moreover, their individual expressiveness
is canceled in favor of a composite level. The solo violin, playing an
independent part, can in no way be looked upon as merely the sixteenth
part of the first violin section.

Performers are cognizant of three attitudes, or approaches, adopted
in the playing of music. These are the orchestral style, the chamber

music style, and the solo style. Playing in an orchestra, the individual allows himself to be absorbed in the mass. In chamber music style, the performer retains his individuality while sharing it on an equal basis with his associates. The soloist is properly assertive and aggressive, striving to project the music with all the vigor and authority at his command. This attitude contributes to the distinction of the solo violin part.

⇛ ⇚

THE VIOLA

Fr., *alto;* It., *viola;* Ger., *Bratsche*

THE proportions of the viola cannot be as nearly defined as those of the violin, which can be said to have a standard size within quite small limits of variation. Fine violas exist, and are being played, whose measurements show variations of 1½ to 2 inches in body length, and comparable differences in sounding string lengths. It seems that every imaginable combination of measurements has been tried in the as yet unfinished evolutionary process, the goal of which is to achieve an instrumental design that will answer to a common ideal of the viola's sound and capabilities. This common ideal is being delayed in its crystallizing by an unusual divergence of opinion among performers, composers, and listeners, both as to what kind of tone the viola should produce and what kind of music it should be expected to play. The viola presents an especially marked example of the continuity of the evolutionary process, which we cannot assume to be completed in the case of any of our instruments.

A hypothetical norm or average may be given for the principal measurements: length of body 16⅝ inches; length of neck 6¹⁄₁₆ inches; over-all length 27¼ inches; sounding length of strings 15¼ inches. Even the largest violas are not big enough in comparison with the violin to correspond to the pitch a perfect fifth lower, and this discrepancy is doubtless responsible in large part for the unique tone quality of the viola. The larger the instrument the more difficult it is to handle, especially when playing in upper positions.

The bow is somewhat thicker than the violin bow, and hence heavier.

The viola's heavier strings speak with more reluctance, and tone production requires a certain amount of "digging in." Light and airy types of bowing are therefore less natural to the viola than to the violin. They are not to be shunned, but one should realize that only skillful players with good instruments can make them sound effectively.

The two lower strings are wound with wire, the others being plain gut. Some players use wound strings for all four, and metal A-strings are also used.

FINGERING

The fingering system of the viola is identical with that of the violin. Since there is a difference of some 2½ inches in the two string lengths, the major and minor second intervals between the fingers are proportionately larger. Playing the viola requires a large hand and strong fingers, particularly the fourth finger, which is held in a more extended position than on the violin. The extension of the left forearm in the first position proves tiring after long playing. Positions above the third are inconvenienced by the awkwardness of getting around the shoulder of the viola with the left hand.

POSITIONS

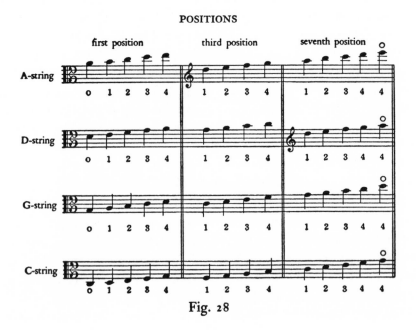

Fig. 28

The harmonic obtainable by extension of the fourth finger in the seventh position is shown in the diagram, as it represents a practical upper limit for orchestral writing. Except as harmonics, notes higher than this are rarely written, and nearly always they are doubled by violins.

EX. 70. Prokofieff—*Chout*   p. 53, ed. Gutheil

CLEFS

The normal clef for the viola is the alto clef (middle C on the third line). The treble clef (G clef) is employed when the part lies substantially above the range of the alto clef for a length of time. Too many clef changes should be avoided. A violist is quite accustomed to reading two or three leger lines above the staff, and he would prefer to do so rather than change clef for just a few notes.

HALF POSITION

Because of the wider spaces between fingers, the half position is more convenient on the viola than on the violin and is more frequently used.

EX. 71. Brahms—*Symphony no. 2*   p. 97, ed. Kalmus

CHARACTERISTICS OF THE STRINGS

Adjectives used to describe the tone of the viola, or of any other instrument, cannot do more than direct the student's attention to certain admittedly general and vague attributes. There is no way other

than actual hearing to store up the memory impressions that make possible the mental hearing ability indispensable for the practice of the art
of orchestration. One must develop the capacity to call to mind the
sound of each instrument, comparing it to other instruments, but it
is also important to distinguish differences in tone quality present in
each single instrument.

The top string of the viola presents a striking contrast to the other
three strings. Its timbre has been described as nasal, piercing, penetrating, and sandy. It has a tendency to sound unduly prominent, but it
goes without saying that a good performer keeps a smooth balance in
passing from the D-string to the A. The A-string's individuality is well
exhibited in the following example.

EX. 72. Shostakovich—*Symphony no. 5*   p. 12, ed. Musicus

Copyright 1945 by Leeds Music Corporation, New York. Used by permission.

The D-string is unobtrusive and gentle, although it has more tone-
weight than the D of the violin. It is, with the G-string, the best part
of the viola for the many kinds of accompaniment figure commonly
allotted to it, and it is excellent for melodies like the following. Here
the violas play in octaves with the oboe for two measures, and with the
flute for the rest of the phrase.

EX. 73. Brahms—*Symphony no. 3*   p. 9, ed. Kalmus

While the G-string is subdued in comparison with the A- and C-strings, it gives a richer and warmer tone than the violin's G.

EX. 74. Debussy—*Nocturnes: Nuages*   p. 10, ed. Jobert

The C-string of the viola is the only one beyond the range of the violin. It is powerful and distinctive in timbre. Although coinciding with part of the range of the 'cello, its tones are in sharp contrast to the sound of the D-string of the 'cello. Those who look for subjective qualities find it foreboding and menacing. In the following example, with vigorous détaché bowing, in the lower half of the bow, it gives much solidity and energy to the string unison.

EX. 75. Bartók—*Concerto for Orchestra*   p. 89, ed. Boosey & Hawkes

The C-string is also capable of soft, delicate tones, as in this accompaniment figure for divided violas.

EX. 76. Strauss—*Tod und Verklärung*   p. 41, ed. Kalmus

MELODIC USES

The situation of the viola in the middle of the pitch range of the strings seems to have made it the busiest member of the group. It is not only appropriate for melodies of its own, but it is constantly called upon to double violins at the octave or unison, or it may double the 'cellos or even the basses. The character and the sound of the viola are more suited to singing melody than to the performance of agile figuration.

DOUBLE NOTES

It has always fallen to the viola to perform a great deal of harmonic filling up. Viola parts in scores of the classical period and later abound with passages in double notes, often without indication as to whether or not these are to be played *divisi*. The fact that they are nearly always practicable as double-stops, by good players, suggests that this may have been optional, but it is certain that the result is neater and the intonation more secure when the part is divided. Example 77 shows that Mozart considered violas entirely adequate and suitable for the important accompaniment at the beginning of the G Minor Symphony.

EX. 77. Mozart—*Symphony in G Minor*, K. 550   p. 1, ed. Philharmonia

The absence of double notes in the viola part contributes to the transparency and fleetness of the orchestration of the Overture to *The Magic Flute*, whereas on the other hand the massive vibrancy of the Beethoven tutti shown in Ex. 78 is largely due to the violas' three-part

tremolo on the lower strings. Held chords for winds are omitted from the example.

EX. 78. Beethoven—*Violin Concerto* p. 8, ed. Eulenburg

When two notes lie both on the C-string, as in measure 2 of the next example, they must of course be played *divisi*.

EX. 79. Wagner—*Prelude to Parsifal* p. 23, ed. Eulenburg

In a modern orchestra there are usually twelve violas. In the period of Haydn, Mozart, and Beethoven, the number was at most five, with six to ten first violins and six to ten second violins. Violas have a heavier tone than violins, and in classical scores there is good evidence that the divided violas were thought a sufficient balance for the combined first and second violins.

Also, there are numerous instances in which these divided violas are combined with wind instruments, like the following.

EX. 80. Mozart—*Symphony in C Major*, K. 200 p. 3, ed. Philharmonia

The practice of dividing violas remains widespread to the present day, although one cannot say it is consistent enough to become the rule. There are many scores (*e.g.*, Ravel's *Daphnis et Chloé*) in which the violas are given regularly two lines in the score. There are likewise scores in which divided violas are a rarity (*e.g.*, Stravinsky's Symphony in C). It is now mandatory to mark clearly either *div.* or *non div.* when there are double notes.

VIOLAS AS BASS

A light bass situated in the octave below middle C is sometimes better given to violas than to 'cellos, in either *arco* or *pizzicato*.

EX. 81. Mahler—*Symphony no. 7*   p. 236, ed. Bote & Bock

With authorization of the original publishers Ed. Bote & G. Bock, Berlin, Wiesbaden.

DOUBLE-STOPS AND CHORDS

It is wise to adhere to the principle that the maximum stretch from first to fourth finger is the equivalent of a perfect fourth on one string, for chords and double-stops in the lower positions. The playability of any combination can be judged by making diagrams similar to those advised for the violin. Three-part chords will be found more generally useful than four-part chords unless a fairly heavy effect is wanted, and open-spaced chords sound better than those in close position.

In the following example of a viola passage in a full tutti, the double-stops and chords are skillfully chosen to give the maximum sonority. Notice the large number of open string notes employed.

EX. 82. D'Indy—*Symphony on a French Mountain Air*

p. 53, ed. Durand

Permission granted by Durand et Cie., Paris, copyright owners; Elkan-Vogel, Philadelphia, Pa., agents.

HARMONICS

All harmonics are good, as on the violin. Artificial harmonics are seldom written above the third position D on the A-string.

EX. 83. Schoenberg—*Serenade*   p. 40, ed. Hansen

Used by permission.

Several notes above this D are perfectly playable as artificial harmonics, but there is little occasion for their assignment to violas rather than to violins. The lower-pitched harmonics of the viola are in a more generally useful range.

For the glissando in harmonics, the longer string makes possible the extension of the natural series as far as the ninth partial. Notice the inclusion of the seventh harmonic in the following example.

EX. 84. Stravinsky—*Le Sacre du Printemps* p. 10, ed. Russe

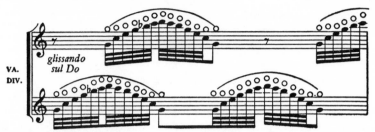

PIZZICATO

It is noticeable between the various stringed instruments that the greater the string length the more resonant are the tones played pizzicato. The viola pizzicato is slightly rounder, less dry and short, than that of the violin in comparable register. High notes on the A-string tend to sound hard and wooden above E or F. This quality may be turned to advantage in appropriate musical circumstances. In the next example the viola doubles the first oboe at the unison, the first flute playing an octave above.

EX. 85. Roussel—*Suite en Fa* p. 30, ed. Durand

An example of extreme high pizzicato is found in Alban Berg's Violin Concerto, where it is employed in unison with harp, two flutes, and two clarinets. It is interesting to note that whereas these instruments are playing *ff*, the violas are marked *f*.

EX. 86. Berg—*Violin Concerto*   p. 70, ed. Universal

At another place in this work, Berg indicates *pizzicato* to be played over the fingerboard (*Griffbrett*) and then at the bridge (*Steg*). These differences in the manner of plucking the string have been little studied by composers, although used by players to obtain variations of tone quality. The score also contains the following example of left-hand pizzicato on the open C- and D-strings, while the bow plays on the G-string.

EX. 87. Berg—*Violin Concerto*   p. 66, ed. Universal

(+ pizz. with the left hand)

PONTICELLO

The tone quality of the viola lends itself especially well to the effect of bowing close to the bridge. Examples are numerous, most often in bowed tremolo (Ex. 88) or fingered tremolo (Ex. 89).

EX. 88. Stravinsky—*L'Oiseau de Feu*   p. 14, ed. Broude Bros.

EX. 89. Debussy—*Gigues* p. 33, ed. Durand

The bow is frequently moved near to the bridge in the course of normal playing, in order to obtain more bite in the tone and a crisper rhythmic attack. This is doubtless the purpose of some uses of the indication *sul ponticello*. The mute is a practical obstacle to the proper position of the bow for a real ponticello effect.

EX. 90. Strauss—*Der Rosenkavalier* p. 109, ed. Boosey & Hawkes

SOLO VIOLA

The solo viola is not as frequently used in the orchestra as the solo violin, perhaps because its pitch and tone quality are such that it is easily covered by accompanying sounds. Nevertheless, there are many fine examples of successful writing for solo viola in symphonic scores. Example 91 is interesting for the rather lively type of melody given to the viola, in contrast to the more usual flowing, expressive kind of phrase, like that in Ex. 74. The very light accompaniment consists of a held D in the strings, the rhythm marked by staccato clarinets, harp, and two solo violins.

EX. 91. Enesco—*Roumanian Rhapsody no. 2*   p. 26, ed. Enoch

This striking passage for six solo violas occurs in *Le Sacre du Printemps*, accompanied by harmonics and pizzicato in 'cellos and basses.

EX. 92. Stravinsky—*Le Sacre du Printemps*   p. 80, ed. Russe

Division of the violas reaches its ultimate stage in the following example. Parts are written for six desks, all *divisi*, making twelve parts, or one for each player.

EX. 93. Strauss—*Don Quixote*   p. 53, ed. Philharmonia

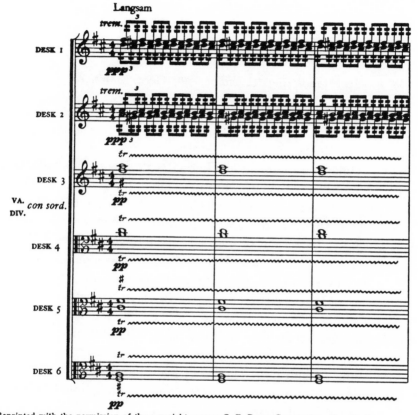

⇛ ⇚

CHAPTER FOUR

THE VIOLONCELLO

Fr., *violoncelle;* It., *violoncello;* Ger., *Violoncell*

THE violoncello is commonly known as the 'cello. It is pitched an octave below the viola, and although its general measurements are not proportionately large enough for its pitch, compensation for this is found in the greatly increased thickness from top to back. The main dimensions of the 'cello are approximately as follows: over-all length, 48 inches; length of body, 29 to 30 inches; length of neck, 11 inches; sounding string length, 27 inches; thickness at sides, 4½ inches; height of bridge, 3⅝ inches. In playing position, between the player's knees, the neck pointing over his left shoulder, the instrument is supported on the floor by means of an adjustable peg that slides out just below the end of the tailpiece.

Usually the A- and D-strings are of plain gut, the G and C being wire-wound. In recent times, however, there is a noticeable increase in the use of metal for all four strings.

FINGERING

Fig. 29

The patterns shown are the basic forms in the first position, on the C-string. The normal compass from first to fourth finger is a minor third. In (*a*) the minor third is made up of a major second followed by a minor second; hence the third finger for E. In (*b*), the minor second comes first, so E♭ is taken by the second finger. All four fingers fall into a sequence of half steps in (*c*). The pattern in (*d*) includes an extension based on the principle that a major second stretch is possible between first and second fingers.

Transposition of these patterns upwards by fifths will give the notes obtainable on the other three strings.

POSITIONS

The traditional diatonic basis for the numbering of the left-hand positions on stringed instruments becomes somewhat illogical when applied to the 'cello, since the spacing of the fingers would seem to suggest a progression by half steps. The following figure gives the pattern (*a*) from Fig. 29, as the hand moves diatonically in the direction of the bridge.

Fig. 30

As in violin fingering, these designations are retained even when the pattern is raised or lowered by chromatic alteration, involving on the 'cello a displacement of the entire hand. Some 'cellists have sought a more accurate terminology, using such terms as *raised first position, lowered second position, intermediate position,* and *one-and-a-half position,* the last two being applied enharmonically. The half position is used as on the violin.

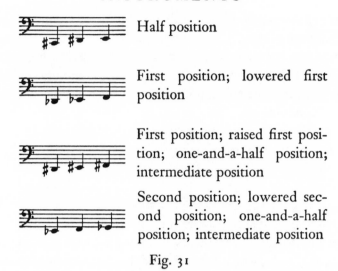

Half position

First position; lowered first position

First position; raised first position; one-and-a-half position; intermediate position

Second position; lowered second position; one-and-a-half position; intermediate position

Fig. 31

Because the compass of a third does not fill the interval of a fifth between strings, the 'cellist must shift position oftener than the violinist or violist. A few scales can be played in the first position with the advantage of open strings, while others call for several shifts.

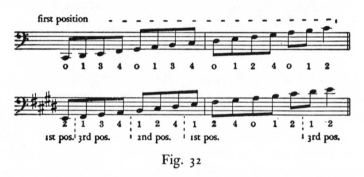

Fig. 32

The glide of the finger in shifting position is made in such a way that the slide is barely perceptible, although some portamento is purposely used when appropriate. The longer distances to be covered on the string lead easily to an exaggeration of portamento, the more pronounced when participated in by the entire group of ten 'cellos (Ex. 94).

EX. 94. Tchaikovsky—*Symphony no. 6*   p. 82, ed. Kalmus

Chromatic scales are fingered by repetition of the pattern 1 2 3.

Fig. 33

THUMB POSITION

The 'cellist's left hand has the advantage of great freedom of movement. The neck of the instrument being at the player's shoulder, all parts of the fingerboard are within easy reach, and since the weight of the 'cello rests on the peg the left hand is not called upon to assist in its support.

When the hand is advanced to the seventh position, an octave above the open string, it reaches the body of the instrument, and the thumb has to leave its position underneath the neck. The outer edge of the thumb may then be placed on the string, serving to stop the string as a kind of movable nut. With the hand in this position, the third finger will be found to reach a greater distance than the fourth finger, with the consequence that the latter is little used in the thumb positions. Occasionally the thumb position is employed at lower pitches when the longer stretch of the third finger is needed. Thumb notes cannot be suddenly introduced in a continuous passage of normal playing. An appreciable amount of time is necessary to place the thumb in its new position.

It is important to remember that the string length of a given interval diminishes as the hand moves to higher positions. On the 'cello, the span from thumb to third finger is easily equal to a quarter of an entire string length. This would be a diminished fifth in the half position, whereas in the seventh position it makes possible the stretch of an octave. The possibilities for extended finger patterns in the upper positions are numerous.

In Fig. 34 are shown a few combinations using the thumb.

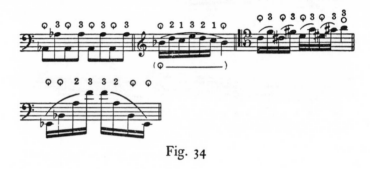

Fig. 34

CLEFS

The normal clef for the 'cello is the bass clef. The tenor clef (middle C on the fourth line) is extensively employed to reduce the number of leger lines in high passages, and the treble clef is used when the notes are too high to be easily read in the tenor clef.

Formerly, parts for the 'cello in the treble clef were habitually written an octave too high, except when the treble clef followed the tenor clef. This practice has been abandoned, and today all notes are written at their proper pitch. It is necessary to know that the custom was once prevalent, since examples of it may still be found in nineteenth-century editions.

RANGE

Orchestral parts may go as high as two octaves above the open A-string, without recourse to harmonics. This practical upper limit is exceeded by a fourth or a fifth in parts for solo 'cello, but instances like the following, for the 'cello section, are exceptional.

EX. 95. Britten—*Four Sea Interludes from Peter Grimes*

p. 65, ed. Boosey & Hawkes

HARMONICS

The following glissando, up to the twelfth harmonic on the D-string, can be taken as reaching the upper limit in the production of natural harmonics on any string.

EX. 96. Stravinsky—*L'Oiseau de Feu*   p. 12, ed. Broude Bros.

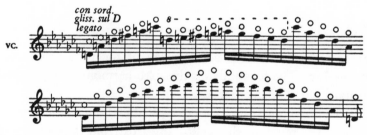

This is intended as a coloristic effect, the success of which does not require that every one of the notes shall be sounded by each individual player. The series is possible because of the progressive approach to the high notes. Ordinarily the eighth harmonic is rarely exceeded, and the 'cellist may prefer to play even that as an artificial harmonic from the fundamental two octaves below. The seventh harmonic is usually avoided as being too flat.

EX. 97. Mahler—*Symphony no. 1*   p. 3, ed. Universal

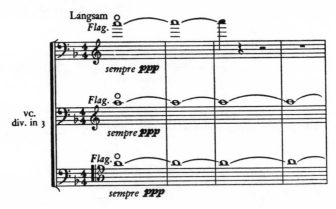

On the 'cello, the greater string length of the upper partials allows them to sound with more security than can be had on the violin or viola. The harmonic node a minor third above the nut can be used, although few instances of its notation are to be found.

EX. 98. Ravel—*Piano Concerto*   p. 29, ed. Durand

Permission granted by Durand et Cie., Paris, copyright owners; Elkan-Vogel, Philadelphia, Pa., agents.

Ravel's indication of the actual pitch of the tone produced is an octave too low. The E sounded is the sixth harmonic, two octaves and a fifth above the fundamental A.

Artificial harmonics are played with the thumb and third finger throughout the range of the 'cello, upwards from the low Db on the C-string. The third finger touches the node a perfect fourth above the fundamental stopped by the thumb. The harmonic sounded is two octaves higher than the thumb note.

ex. 99. Casella—*Pupazzetti*   p. 19, ed. Philharmonia

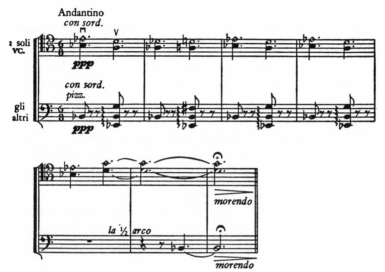

The artificial harmonic from the node a perfect fifth above the thumb can be sounded on the 'cello but is infrequently used, that of the fourth being easier to produce and of better quality.

This chord is for 'cellos and basses in harmonics, each section divided in four parts.

ex. 100. Ravel—*Rapsodie Espagnole*   p. 11, ed. Durand

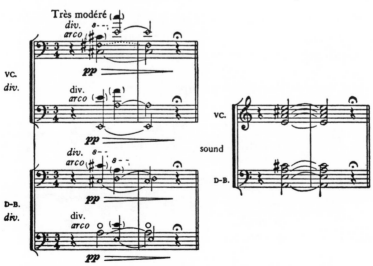

BOWING

The 'cello bow is a little shorter (28¼ inches) than the violin and viola bows, thicker and somewhat less springy. However, all the types of bowing previously mentioned are available to the 'cellist and are of excellent effect. The bow is held in the same way as for the other two instruments, except that it is turned so that the edge of the hair nearest the player is the first to engage the string. Another difference to be borne in mind is that the lower-pitched strings are nearest to the bow arm, on account of the playing position of the 'cello. The terms *up-bow* and *down-bow* continue to be used in the same sense as heretofore, although less accurately descriptive.

Bowing over the fingerboard, near the bridge, and with the wood, are effects in common use, as are all kinds of tremolo. Special mention should be made of the bowed tremolo *sur la touche* on the two lower strings of the 'cello. It has a mysterious quality unlike any other tremolo.

EX. 101. Debussy—*La Mer*   p. 105, ed. Durand

Permission granted by Durand et Cie., Paris, copyright owners; Elkan-Vogel, Philadelphia, Pa., agents.

A fingered tremolo with an interval larger than a major third can be played by using the thumb position. The amount of stretch possible varies according to the position on the string.

EX. 102. Schmitt—*Antoine et Cléopatre*   p. 78, ed. Durand

Permission granted by Durand et Cie.. Paris, copyright owners; Elkan-Vogel, Philadelphia, Pa., agents.

DOUBLE-STOPS AND CHORDS

Excepting seconds, all intervals within the octave are playable as double-stops in the lower positions without using the thumb. The major second can be reached, first to fourth finger, from the third position up, and the minor second from the fourth position up. The thumb is of course an additional resource, but one cannot usually introduce the thumb without a break in the music. Moreover, tones stopped with the thumb are comparatively less expressive in quality.

Chords found in scores should be studied by means of diagrams like those made for violin chords. In this way the mechanical problems in placing the fingers can be judged, and knowledge of writing chords for the 'cello acquired.

Chords containing one or more open strings are the most sonorous.

The thumb, as well as the other fingers, can stop a perfect fifth across two adjacent strings.

Three-part chords are more frequently used than four-part chords. The four-part chords are generally too heavy, but are sometimes appropriate. Arpeggio figures across the strings are best arranged to be fingered like four-part chords.

EX. 103. Strauss—*Symphonia Domestica*

p. 106, ed. Associated Music Publishers

With authorization of the original publishers Ed. Bote & G. Bock, Berlin, Wiesbaden.

Bowing of chords follows the conventions of violin chords, the lower notes being sounded first when no other indication is given. The direction may be reversed, shown by an arrow placed before the chord, in order to give emphasis to the bass.

EX. 104. Bartók—*Second Rhapsody for Violin and Orchestra*
p. 6, ed. Boosey & Hawkes

PIZZICATO

The 'cello pizzicato is especially sonorous and vibrant, and it finds frequent and varied employment in the orchestra. It is an everyday medium for the harmonic bass. The plucked bass tones give both body and transparency to the accompaniment. Another common use of 'cello pizzicato is in accompaniment figures like the following.

EX. 105. Brahms—*Symphony no. 2*   p. 80, ed. Kalmus

For the high notes, the tone quality in pizzicato remains good well over an octave above the open A. Then it begins to take on a rather wooden sound, suitable for special effects. High 'cello pizzicato is used effectively in this example.

EX. 106. Shostakovich—*Symphony no. 5*   p. 72, ed. Musicus

Harmonics, when plucked, sound not unlike those of the harp. They are best limited to the natural harmonics of the octave and the octave and fifth.

EX. 107. Moussorgsky—*A Night on Bald Mountain*

p. 81, ed. International Music Co.

By permission of the copyright owners W. Bessel et Cie., Paris.

Not all 'cellists have acquired the trick, borrowed from harp and guitar technique, in which the right hand touches the node and plucks the string simultaneously, allowing the left to stop tones other than open ones.

Chords in pizzicato may be arpeggiated upwards by using the thumb, or downwards with one or more fingers. The first way will be followed unless downward pizzicato is indicated by an arrow. Considerable variety of effect is to be had, from softly rolled four-part chords to short, abrupt chords on the three upper strings. The following example is taken from a passage in which the entire string section joins in an evocation of guitar playing.

EX. 108. Debussy—*Ibéria*   p. 104, ed. Durand

MELODIC USES

The A-string of the 'cello is characterized by much expressive
warmth and intensity, as well as dynamic power. Countless examples
show how often the 'cellos are given melodies in this register. The following excerpt gives only part of a remarkable passage for unaccompanied 'cellos; the entire melody extends over sixty-six measures.

EX. 109. Charpentier—*Impressions of Italy*   p. 3, ed. Heugel

The D-string is smooth and unobtrusive, less nasal than the A.

EX. 110. Wagner—*Siegfried Idyll* p. 46, ed. Eulenburg

There is little difference in timbre between the two lower strings. Their tone is full and rich in overtones, the C being slightly more ponderous than the G, in *forte*. In soft nuances, melodies lying in this range must be very lightly accompanied if they are not to be covered up.

EX. 111. Franck—*Variations Symphoniques* p. 38, ed. Enoch

In the score the only accompaniment is a delicate figuration in the solo piano part, marked *pianissimo*.

It is a regular duty of the 'cellos to play bass parts, either alone or with the double-basses. A common procedure is to write the same notes for 'cellos and basses. Since the latter sound an octave lower than written, the result is a bass part in octaves, in which the 'cellos act as reinforcement of the octave overtone of the double-basses. The 'cellos may occasionally be placed an octave lower so as to sound in unison with the basses, giving a more concentrated sonority.

ACCOMPANIMENT FIGURES

'Cello parts contain much passage work either of an accompanimental nature or designed to contribute animation to the general orchestral texture. A wide range may be covered, and elaborate figuration often calls for technical virtuosity. The student should look through numerous scores to observe the great variety in this kind of writing for the 'cello. Some examples are given here.

EX. 112. Beethoven—*Symphony no. 8*   p. 64, ed. Kalmus

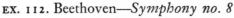

EX. 113. Ravel—*Rapsodie Espagnole*   p. 57, ed. Durand

Permission granted by Durand et Cie., Paris, copyright owners; Elkan-Vogel, Philadelphia, Pa., agents.

EX. 114. Dukas—*La Péri*   p. 46, ed. Durand

Permission granted by Durand et Cie., Paris, copyright owners; Elkan-Vogel, Philadelphia, Pa., agents.

Rapid passages in the low register, with staccato or détaché bowing, are difficult to make clear because of the inertia of the lower strings.

It takes good players to perform figures like the following without
scratchiness.

EX. 115. Stravinsky—*Le Sacre du Printemps*   p. 67, ed. Russe

DIVIDED 'CELLOS

The powerful sonority of the 'cello section and the intensity of the
'cello A-string combine to justify the frequent procedure of dividing
the group so that half play the melody. The other half play the bass
or a subordinate part, or they may even be divided further.

EX. 116. Mahler—*Symphony no. 4*   p. 115, ed. Universal

This Strauss example shows the division of the 'cellos carried to the point where each player at the four desks has a different part, eight in all.

EX. 117. Strauss—*Also Sprach Zarathustra*   p. 7, ed. Aibl

Reprinted with the permission of the copyright owners C. F. Peters Corporation, New York.

SOLO 'CELLO

One might describe the preceding excerpt as an instance of the use of eight solo 'cellos, although it is the result of progressive division of the strings to be noted in the scores of Strauss. In Rossini's Overture to *William Tell,* the opening is scored for five solo 'cellos in addition to a regular part for the remainder of the section. Tchaikovsky, in the *Ouverture Solennelle, 1812,* calls for four soli in conjunction with two solo violas. The most frequent and characteristic use of the solo 'cello is that in which a single player is given an outstanding melodic role.

EX. 118. Brahms—*Piano Concerto no. 2*   p. 125, ed. Simrock

Used by permission of the original publisher, N. Simrock, Hamburg.

CHAPTER FIVE

THE DOUBLE-BASS

Fr., *contrebasse;* It., *contrabbasso;* Ger., *Kontrabass*

OTHER English names for the double-bass are bass viol, contrabass, string bass, and bass. The last is the most common.

The double-bass presents a different appearance from the
other members of the string group because of its sloping shoulders
tapering into the neck, a characteristic of its ancestor the viol. Also
noticeable are the cogwheel tuning devices on the pegbox, replacing
the friction-held pegs of the other stringed instruments.

The bass stands on an adjustable peg, and is supported in playing
position by the body and left knee of the player. Bass players sometimes
sit on a high stool while playing.

Basses are of different sizes. For general orchestral use the size known
as three-quarters is preferred to the rather unwieldy full-sized bass.
Average dimensions of the three-quarter size double-bass are as follows:
over-all length, 73 to 74 inches; length of body, 44 inches; length of
neck, 17¾ inches; thickness at sides, 7¼ inches; height of bridge, 6⅝
inches; sounding length of strings, 42¾ inches; length of bow, 26 to
27 inches.

The G- and D-strings are normally of gut, the A and E of gut wound
with wire, but complete sets of metal strings are being adopted increasingly by bass players. Although they bring some modification in the
tone quality of the instrument, the metal strings seem certainly to be
superior to others in durability and dependability, and they respond
to the bow much more readily.

As previously mentioned, the double-bass sounds an octave below the written notes. Awareness of this fact should become a habit in reading or writing bass parts or playing them on the piano. In the examples of this book, all notes for double-basses sound an octave lower than printed, unless otherwise indicated.

Notes as low as C, below the E of the fourth string, are to be found in the scores of practically all composers. This is even more remarkable in the scores of Beethoven's time, when the three-string bass, now obsolete, was in common use. The lowest string of that instrument was tuned to A or G above the E of the modern four-string bass.

In performance the player simply plays an octave higher what lies below his range, trusting, no doubt, that the change of octave matters little at such low pitches. Granting that the octave difference will be noticed only by attentive and discerning ears, especially when the change is covered by doubling in the 'cellos, it must be realized that this procedure sometimes results in serious disfigurement of the musical idea. Compare, for instance, the following phrase with its shape as performed on the four-string bass.

EX. 119. Strauss—*Also Sprach Zarathustra*   p. 32, ed. Aibl

Reprinted with the permission of the copyright owners C. F. Peters Corporation, New York.

There are three ways to extend the range of the bass below E. These are the temporary tuning (*scordatura*) of the E-string to a lower pitch, the use of the five-string bass, and the adoption of a mechanical apparatus for extending the E-string to C. All three are employed.

The first of these is the least satisfactory because of the disturbance to the instrument by the change in tuning, and even more because a proper tone cannot be produced with a string whose tension has been reduced to the point of flabbiness. It is entirely practical, however, to tune to E♭ or even D. Such alterations are more easily accomplished with the tuning mechanism of the double-bass than with the pegs of other stringed instruments.

The five-string bass is not a common instrument, and some orchestras do not possess even one. Its fifth string is tuned to the low C, the body being correspondingly larger to favor the low pitches.

A marked increase in the use of the E-string extension attachment is apparent today. In some orchestras the whole bass section is equipped with the device. It consists of an arm acting as an extension of the fingerboard upward past the pegbox on the E-string side, and an ingenious arrangement whereby the notes C♯, D, D♯, and E are stopped by remote control, as it were, by means of keys at the side of the fingerboard, near the nut. In normal position the E remains stopped. Operation of the mechanism presents some fingering problems for the player, but the results on the whole are satisfactory.

Since there seems little doubt of the establishment of the four-string double-bass as the normal instrument, it follows that bass parts should be designed accordingly. If notes below E are felt to be indispensable, they should be regarded as exceptional, and it should be fully realized that they may be played by only one or two basses, or even not at all. The best procedure is to write the part in octaves where these low notes occur, showing clearly what is to be done by the player whose lowest note is E.

EX. 120. Moussorgsky-Ravel—*Tableaux d'une Exposition*

p. 133, ed. Boosey & Hawkes

Permission granted by Durand et Cie., Paris, copyright owners; Elkan-Vogel, Philadelphia, Pa., agents.

To prevent transposition of the low tones up an octave, a remark must be added, such as "five-string basses only," or "not an octave higher."

EX. 121. Mahler—*Das Lied von der Erde*   p. 126, ed. Universal

NB. only basses with low C

FINGERING

The compass of the hand, from first to fourth finger, is a major second in the lower positions. The third finger is not used independently but is placed on the string together with the fourth finger, until the sixth position is reached. Then the position of the hand and the lesser string length of the half step make it convenient to use the third and fourth fingers separately.

Some players develop a wider use of the third finger and of the extended position, stretching a whole tone from first to second finger; but the above are the basic principles of double-bass fingering.

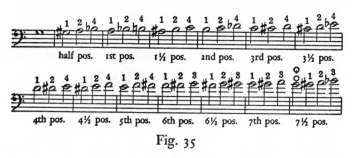

Fig. 35

Fig. 35 gives the notes playable in the positions of the first octave on the G-string. It will be seen that there are really twelve positions to the octave, one for each half step, but that the numbering 1st, 2nd, 3rd, etc., follows the diatonic steps on which the first finger is located, the positions in between being half positions. Just as in the case of the 'cello, there are other systems of designating the positions.

The thumb is brought into play above the seventh position.

To find the notes playable on the other three strings, the student should write out the transpositions of Fig. 35 down by fourths.

Scales containing open string notes can be played with fewer position shifts, as demonstrated by the following comparison of the scales of G major and B major.

Fig. 36

Chromatic scales are fingered by repeating the pattern 2 4 2 4 or 1 2 4 1 2 4.

CLEFS

The clefs employed are the same as for the 'cello; namely, bass, tenor (middle C on the fourth line), and treble (G clef).

RANGE

High notes for double-basses are very effective, and not of great difficulty except for intonation. They are safer when approached by step or by small intervals. The D an octave and fifth above the open G may be taken as a practical upper limit, exclusive of harmonics. This limit is exceeded in the following unusual example, in which the basses play in unison with violas, 'cellos, and bassoons.

EX. 122. Shostakovich—*Symphony no. 5*   p. 23, ed. Musicus

HARMONICS

Artificial harmonics are possible on the bass only in high positions and are impractical for orchestral purposes. Natural harmonics, on the other hand, are especially useful because of their medium pitch range. They are easily produced, because of the long strings, and are of excellent quality. Those available on the G-string are shown in Fig. 37. Transposition down by fourths will give the series on the other strings. Note that harmonics in the treble clef are notated at actual pitch, to save leger lines.

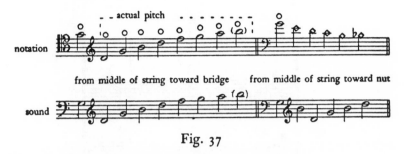

Fig. 37

The harmonic from the node located a minor third from the nut sounds more clearly on the bass than on any other stringed instrument.

EX. 123. Ravel—*Le Tombeau de Couperin*   p. 38, ed. Durand

Permission granted by Durand et Cie., Paris, copyright owners; Elkan-Vogel, Philadelphia, Pa., agents.

In the following chord of harmonics, one 'cello contributes the C♮, unobtainable on the bass at that pitch. The fourth bass part calls for a double-stop in harmonics.

EX. 124. Stravinsky—*Concerto en Ré*   p. 17, ed. Boosey & Hawkes

DOUBLE-STOPS AND CHORDS

The intervals playable on the bass as double-stops are thirds, fourths, and fifths, and any interval in which one of the notes can be taken on an open string. Double-stops, and chords of three and four notes, are rarely found in orchestral music, however. In general, small harmonic intervals do not sound well in low pitches because of the conflict of overtones, and even when used for special effect, better results are obtained by dividing the notes among two or more players. The following sequence of fifths is unusual.

EX. 125. Kodály—*Galánta Dances*   p. 53, ed. Boosey & Hawkes

BOWING

There are two distinct types of double-bass bow, usually referred to as the German bow and the French bow. The German bow is held with the thumb on top of the stick, the frog being shaped so that the fingers can grasp it as they might grasp a saw. The French bow is like a large 'cello bow and is held in the same way, except that some players place the thumb underneath the frog for certain strokes. It can be seen that the action of the wrist is quite different in the two hand positions, and that with the German bow the thumb exerts downward pressure on the stick, as opposed to the finger pressure with the French bow. There are advantages in both methods, and the choice depends upon the schooling and personal preference of the bass player.

All bow strokes employed on the other stringed instruments may be used on the bass, with the qualification that these must be thought of in terms of a shorter, heavier bow, thicker, heavier strings, and a much more cumbersome instrument—all factors in greater inertia to be overcome in the production of tones. Hence, too long slurs in legato bowing should be guarded against. The student will have to rely on observation and experience in this respect. It will help to remember that the aggregate sonority of the whole bass section tolerates a slower moving bow than does the tone of a single solo bass, and that longer tones are possible in soft nuances than in loud ones.

EX. 126. Wagner—*Tristan und Isolde*   p. 19, ed. Breitkopf

For the long held pedal notes, sometimes lasting for many measures and often seen in nineteenth-century scores, the basses are expected to change direction of the bow as often as necessary. Continuity of tone is preserved by seeing to it that all do not change bow at the same time.

Double-bass staccato is preferably of the on-the-string type, but the controlled bouncing bow is entirely feasible and often used. The modern bass section is capable of considerable delicacy in passages like the following.

EX. 127. Strauss—*Don Juan*   p. 58, ed. Kalmus

An example of fast detached bowing in a long, gradual crescendo:

EX. 128. Rimsky-Korsakoff—*Scheherazade*   p. 221, ed. Kalmus

Sul tasto and *sul ponticello* are regularly employed on the double-bass. The bass *col legno* staccato may be said to be more musical than on the other instruments because of the greater resonance of the bass. Bowed tremolo is very common in bass parts and is frequently called for *sul tasto* or *sul ponticello*.

The fingered tremolo is not practical in the lower positions. For most hands the minor third stretch becomes feasible above the second position. All major and minor trills are excellent, however.

EX. 129. Mahler—*Symphony no. 9*   p. 63, ed. Boosey & Hawkes

PIZZICATO

The bass player plays pizzicato much oftener than the other string players. This is not only because of the superior resonance of the bass pizzicato but also because it brings welcome relief and variety to the bass line, imparting lightness and transparency to the whole orchestral texture. Sometimes the basses double in pizzicato the part played arco by the 'cellos.

The string is usually plucked with the first finger, the other fingers holding the bow. The German bow hangs downward, held by the little finger hooked in the frog. Variations in tone quality and dynamic range can be obtained by plucking at different places on the string. The low tones in pizzicato demand care in their execution, to avoid a booming or dull, thudlike sound.

As for the high notes, one rarely exceeds the B shown in the following example.

EX. 130. Strauss—*Also Sprach Zarathustra*   p. 57, ed. Aibl

Reprinted with the permission of the copyright owners C. F. Peters Corporation, New York.

In the following example the bass pizzicato is not doubled by the 'cellos, but the bass clarinet underlines the accented measures.

EX. 131. Ravel—*Rapsodie Espagnole*   p. 12, ed. Durand

Permission granted by Durand et Cie., Paris, copyright owners; Elkan-Vogel, Philadelphia, Pa., agents.

MUTES

The double-bass mute has to be a heavy affair to be effective, since the vibrations of the large bridge are not easily damped out. Mutes are used for homogeneity of tone color when the rest of the string group is muted, and also for the peculiar veiled sonority they give to the basses. The mysterious measures at the beginning of Ravel's *La Valse* are scored for muted basses with no other instruments.

EX. 132. Ravel—*La Valse*   p. 1, ed. Durand

THE HARMONIC BASS

The commonest duty the basses have to perform is naturally that of supplying the harmonic foundation. This is accomplished in more than ninety per cent of all orchestral music by the double-basses playing in octaves with the 'cellos. When the latter are otherwise occupied, the function of octave doubling may be taken over by other instruments, such as bassoons or horns, or the violas. The clarity of the bass part seems to benefit greatly by this reinforcement, or confirmation, of the octave overtone of the deep fundamental of the basses, and the ear may also receive the impression of an even deeper octave by reason of the acoustic phenomenon known as the *difference tone*. The upper partials of this octave bass are an important source of enrichment of the entire orchestral sonority, although it must be added that they are very often in conflict with upper notes and may cause damage.

A common example of such damage is heard in a softly played minor triad, placed in such a way that the major third overtone from the bass may compete in strength with the minor third (Fig. 38).

Fig. 38

The above dilemma can be resolved only by reducing the dynamic level of the basses and strengthening that of the second violins.

The double-bass part is occasionally treated as an independent voice, without octave doubling, but it is significant that in the practice of composers this procedure is clearly exceptional.

EX. 133. Beethoven—*Symphony no. 9*   p. 165, ed. Kalmus

It is not out of place to caution the student that a common fault in writing for basses is excessive use of the lowest tones, a habit that tends to make the whole orchestra sound heavy and overponderous.

MELODIC USES

The harmonic bass may be a real melodic bass. Fine examples like the following are numerous.

EX. 134. Franck—*Symphony*   p. 117, ed. Eulenburg

Modern composers have exploited the possibilities of melodies in the high register for basses without doubling. In the following exposition of a fugue subject, the double-basses deliver the opening phrase quite unaccompanied, except for the group of eighth-notes at the start.

EX. 135. Riegger—*Symphony no. 3*

p. 81, ed. Associated Music Publishers

Prokofieff has suggested new possibilities for the double-basses, using them as melodic doubling of the solo violin (Ex. 136). The entire scoring of the six measures is given here. The clarinets are notated at actual pitch.

EX. 136. Prokofieff—*Violin Concerto no. 2*   p. 74, ed. Baron

The dexterity of bass players has reached a very high degree of virtuosity. The scores of Mahler, Strauss, Ravel, Stravinsky, and other modern composers should be studied to observe the demands made upon the basses for agility of bowing and fingering, wide skips, and complex rhythms.

EX. 137. Strauss—*Ein Heldenleben*   p. 20, ed. Eulenburg

DIVIDED BASSES

The double-basses are frequently divided in two parts. This practice is consistent with the tendency of modern French composers to divide each string section. The division in octaves furnishes the bass octaves within the double-bass part. Intervals smaller than fifths or fourths are less satisfactory in low pitches.

EX. 138. Debussy—*La Mer*   p. 83, ed. Durand

Permission granted by Durand et Cie., Paris, copyright owners; Elkan-Vogel, Philadelphia, Pa., agents.

Close intervals in the basses help to provide the dramatic, foreboding suggestion in the passage from which the next example is taken.

EX. 139. Debussy—*Pelléas et Mélisande*   p. 346, ed. Durand

Permission granted by Durand et Cie., Paris, copyright owners; Elkan-Vogel, Philadelphia, Pa., agents.

Basses are divided so that half can participate in a melody while half remain on the bass; and so that half can play pizzicato and half play arco on the same figure. Chords of three and four parts in low register are likely to have a percussive sound, especially if plucked (see the G minor chords in the *Marche au Supplice* of the *Symphonie Fantastique*, by Berlioz). To sound clearly, chords should be in open position, or located in the upper part of the range of the bass.

The following chord for basses ends an adagio movement, and is entirely unaccompanied. Although the notation indicates double-stops, in performance the chord is divided in four.

EX. 140. Dvořák—*Symphony no. 5*   p. 72, ed. Kalmus

A limitation in the number of basses ("*la metà*," "*4 bassi*," "1 desk only," etc.) is sometimes called for to secure a better balance.

THE SOLO BASS

The use of a single double-bass, solo, is not frequent. It is of novel effect because not often heard. The bass solo is surprisingly deficient in carrying power, considering the size of the instrument, and its accompaniment must be delicately adjusted. The following solo is written as for five-string bass but can be played using the E-string extension. It is unaccompanied.

EX. 141. Ravel—*L'Enfant et les Sortilèges*   p. 124, ed. Durand

※» «※

CHAPTER SIX

WOODWIND INSTRUMENTS

LOGICAL and convincing definition of the category we all know as *woodwind* is difficult to propose. It is easier to say which instruments are brass instruments. Woodwind instruments have been constructed of materials other than wood, and flutes are regularly made of metal at the present time. Rather than attempt to justify a nomenclature accepted by custom, let us distinguish the brass instruments as being those whose tones are produced by vibration of the lips held against a cup-shaped mouthpiece. Other orchestral wind instruments are woodwinds.

The woodwind section of the symphony orchestra is divisible into four family groups, as follows:

Flutes, piccolo, (alto flute)
Oboes, English horn, (oboe d'amore, heckelphone)
Clarinets, bass clarinet, (E♭ and D clarinets, basset horn)
Bassoons, contrabassoon

The instruments named in parentheses are only occasionally employed, while the others are standard equipment. This classification coincides with differences of tone color readily distinguishable by ear, brought about by differences of construction and method of tone production.

In the make-up of the woodwind section, three basic formulas, or types, exist:

(*a*) Woodwind by twos:
2 flutes
2 oboes

    2 clarinets

    2 bassoons

(*b*) Woodwind by threes:

    2 flutes and piccolo

    2 oboes and English horn

    2 clarinets and bass clarinet

    2 bassoons and contrabassoon

(*c*) Woodwind by fours:

    3 flutes and piccolo

    3 oboes and English horn

    3 clarinets and bass clarinet

    3 bassoons and contrabassoon

It will be found useful to regard departures from these three types as variations from the norm. The second type, woodwind by threes, is used so consistently in the twentieth century that it has become established as the normal woodwind section of the present day.

TONE PRODUCTION

The vibration of air enclosed in a pipe may be compared to the vibration of a string stretched between two points. One important difference is that whereas the pitch of a string is affected by length, density of materials, and amount of tension, the pitch of a vibrating air column depends upon its length alone. This rule is not perfectly accurate in a scientific sense, but it is the basis for the custom of speaking of pitches in terms of length. For example, the note produced by the C-string of the 'cello is identified as 8-foot C, being the note sounded by an open organ pipe 8 feet long. It is understood that this is a length adopted for convenience, and that a fractional correction would have to be made to bring it into agreement with whatever standard of pitch is being used.

Doubling the length of the air column lowers the pitch an octave, and halving the length raises the pitch an octave.

Fig. 39

These lengths will give the same pitches in all wind instruments, brass as well as woodwind, with one notable exception—the clarinet.

The clarinet is a cylindrical tube, closed at one end by the mouthpiece. Oboes and bassoons are conical, larger at one end than at the other. Flutes are in part cylindrical, but the open embouchure makes them open pipes. Now the stopped cylindrical pipe has properties unlike those of the open cylindrical pipe or the conical pipe, and one of these is that for a given pitch it requires but half as much length. In other words, if a flute and a clarinet employ the same amount of cylindrical tube length, the clarinet sounds an octave below the flute, only fundamental tones being blown.

THE SHORTENING-HOLE SYSTEM

Let us consider a primitive flutelike wooden pipe with six finger holes for the first, second, and third fingers of both hands. The fourth fingers are not used, since they do not naturally fall into a straight line with the others. The thumbs support the instrument in a horizontal position to the right of the player, and the left hand will be nearest to the embouchure, in this case a hole to be blown across. The left end of the pipe is tightly closed with a stopper. This six-hole tube is the basis for the fingering systems of all woodwind instruments.

All six holes must be closed by the fingertips to enable the pipe to vibrate through its entire length and sound its fundamental tone. For the sake of further similarity to the flute, let us say the length is a little over 21 inches, which is the length of the flute's low D.

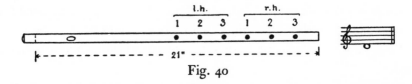

Fig. 40

If now the right third finger is raised, uncovering its hole, the sounding length of the pipe is shortened by the distance from the hole to the open end of the tube, much as though the tube were cut off at that point; and if the holes have been spaced for the intervals of a major scale, the note sounded will be E. All the remaining five holes must be kept closed.

The entire scale is obtained by successively raising the fingers, opening the holes from right to left, as shown here.

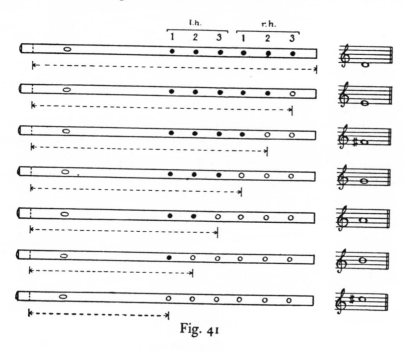

Fig. 41

FORK FINGERING

If the next hole to the right of the sounding hole is closed, the sounding note will be somewhat flattened, sometimes as much as a half step. This is the procedure called *fork fingering*, or *forked fingering*, and by its means the following in-between notes become available.

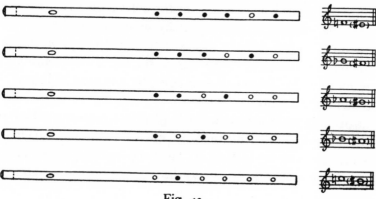

Fig. 42

There are now two ways to finger F♯, but E♭ cannot be obtained by fork fingering since there is no further hole to close.

KEYS

The acquisition of additional fundamental tones requires the boring of new holes and the invention of key mechanism. The left thumb is able to control a tone hole, leaving the supporting function to the right thumb. Both fourth fingers, however, need the help of keys in order to control properly located holes conveniently. The history of the development of key mechanism is one of increasing ingenuity in finding ways by which the fingers may cover and uncover holes beyond their reach through the use of keys, levers, axles, and springs. These also permit an extension in the length of the tube, with the added lower holes operated by keys.

The key systems of the various woodwind instruments will be described in succeeding chapters.

OVERBLOWING

In Chapter One, the harmonic attributes of a vibrating string were discussed. A vibrating column of air possesses these same characteristics, the over-all curve of the fundamental, and the subsidiary vibrations of the partials or harmonics that are present in the formant of the tone of the individual instrument. Just as a string harmonic is made to sound by lightly touching a node, so in a woodwind instrument a harmonic is produced by opening a hole located at or near a node. This hole is referred to as a vent. It may be one of the holes regularly used to sound fundamental tones, or a hole especially designed for the purpose and equipped with a key called a speaker key, register key, or octave key. On the flute, and with certain tones on the oboe, some harmonics can be produced without opening vent holes, by direction and shape of the air stream from the lips.

The production of harmonics in all wind instruments is called, rather loosely, overblowing. The tones so obtained are not usually called harmonics, as in string technique. They are regarded as normal tones, being the only tones possible above the range of the fundamental series.

The following figure shows how the octave D is obtained, by fingering for D and opening as a vent the hole from which C♯ normally sounds. Note that this hole is situated at a point marking one-half the tube length of the fundamental D, just where we know the node for the octave harmonic will be found.

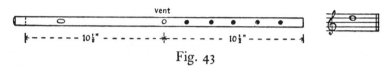

Fig. 43

Again the clarinet is exceptional, in the matter of overblowing. The physical properties of the stopped cylindrical pipe are such that the harmonics that divide the air column into even-numbered sections, requiring a node at the open end, cannot be sounded. The first overblown note on the clarinet is therefore the third harmonic, an octave and a fifth above the fundamental, vented by means of a register key.

EMBOUCHURE

The term *embouchure* refers to the apparatus for inducing sympathetic vibrations by resonance in the air column, and to the method of blowing. In playing the flute, the lips direct a concentrated stream of air to the opposite edge of an oval-shaped hole in the tube. For the oboe, two thinly scraped reeds are bound together and fixed to a small tube which in turn fits into a hole in the end of the instrument. This double reed is held gently between the lips, so as to avoid closing the tiny aperture between the reeds. The bassoon employs a similar double reed, larger than that of the oboe. It fits onto a curved metal pipe that leads to the smaller end of the wing joint. The clarinet has a single reed, held by a metal ligature to the open side of a mouthpiece fitting the end of the instrument. The reed is held against the lower lip, which covers the lower teeth, and the upper teeth rest on the beveled top of the mouthpiece.

Doubtless the principal factor in creating the characteristic tone color of a wind instrument is the embouchure, but it should not be forgotten that there are other important influences, such as the proportions between length and diameter of the bore, size and position of the tone holes, materials of construction, and of course the sound ideal and artistry of the player.

Tone quality varies with the player, and can be varied by him for expressive purposes. Human elements such as sensitivity, warmth, and natural vibrato are mysterious factors in musical performance that cannot be produced by mechanical means. The condition of the reed, its degree of pliability, has an effect on the tone of the reed instruments.

PITCH

Wind players are fully as much concerned with playing in tune as are string players. The pitch of the instruments can be altered slightly by modifying their total length through various manipulations of joints and fittings, but since the tone holes have been located with reference to fixed pipe lengths, any change in the latter will cause trouble. The control of intonation is managed by the lips. The wind player has not only to correct the pitch in terms of his own instrument (F♯ and G♭ have the same fingering, to mention one example), but he must continually adjust his pitch to the sounds of the other instruments of the orchestra. With good players, this is for the most part an instinctive and unconscious process.

All wind instruments are sensitive to changes in temperature. A cold instrument will be flat until warmed by playing, and a temperature above normal will cause a sharpness in pitch.

TONGUING

The tongue is held forward in a position to prevent the air, under pressure from the lungs, from striking the reed or passing through the lips until it is wanted. A tone is started by a sudden drawing back of the tongue, exactly as in speaking the syllable *tu*. This sudden action is necessary to overcome the inertia of the reed or air column. A wind tone cannot have an imperceptible beginning, like the gradual engaging of a string by the bow hairs, but certain variations in the attack can be made, such as *du* for *tu*, or even *htu*. The tone is ended by the return of the tongue to its original position.

When no slur, or other mark of articulation, appears over the notes, each note is articulated by the tongue with *tu*.

EX. 142. Brahms—*Variations on a Theme by Haydn*

p. 5, ed. Eulenburg

omitted: hns., trps., vc., d-b.

With practice these strokes can be repeated with considerable rapidity, although not for long periods of time without a chance to rest the tongue. If staccato is wanted, dots are placed over the notes, and the strokes are made as sharply as possible.

EX. 143. Berlioz—*Symphonie Fantastique*   p. 222, ed. Eulenburg

When the articulations demanded are too fast for the tongue to repeat the *tu* stroke, the formula *tu ku tu ku* is used. This is called double-tonguing. It is easily done on the flute, but while oboe, clarinet, and bassoon players employ it through necessity, it is not for them a wholly satisfactory tonguing because the *k* is formed back in the mouth, out of contact with the reed. An unevenness between the notes is sometimes to be detected.

EX. 144. Mozart—*The Marriage of Figaro: Overture*

p. 22, ed. Kalmus

omitted: hns., trps., timp., strings

In fast triple rhythm, still another formula may be used: *tu tu ku, tu tu ku,* or sometimes *tu ku tu, tu ku tu,* called triple-tonguing. Most players prefer the first way. There is also much to be said for the practice of applying double-tonguing to triple rhythms, so that the *t* and the *k* alternately begin the group of three notes—*tu ku tu, ku tu ku.*

EX. 145. Wagner—*Lohengrin: Prelude to Act III*   p. 20, ed. Kalmus

Brass and strings omitted

As a special effect, the tremolo made by rolling the tongue, as in the Italian or Spanish *r*, has been asked for by some composers. It is usually given the German name *Flatterzunge*, translated flutter-tonguing, and it is more practicable on the flute than on reed instruments. The whirring effect of a rapidly fingered chromatic scale, with flutter-tonguing, has a certain picturesque quality.

EX. 146. Ravel—*La Valse*   p. 8, ed. Durand

Flutter-tonguing is of rather poor effect on the oboe and bassoon, but somewhat better on the clarinet. In the score from which the following excerpt is taken, the clarinets are doubled by the harp, and also by bassoons and saxophone using ordinary tonguing. The clarinet parts are notated at actual pitch.

EX. 147. Berg—*Violin Concerto*   p. 12, ed. Universal

PHRASING

Two or more notes covered by a slur are played with an uninter-
rupted flow of air. It is important to realize that during the flow of
this continuous air stream the length of the vibrating air column is
continually changing with the fingering. Some notes are harmonics
and some fundamentals, some are more brilliant than others, so that
the embouchure has to be adapted to each new situation in order to preserve continuity of tone and intensity.

To slur a wide interval upwards, which involves increasing the tension of the embouchure, is easier than to slur the same interval downwards. A certain amount of reluctance has to be overcome when the
air column is suddenly lengthened or asked to return to its fundamental
after vibrating in partials. The inertia is more securely overcome by
tonguing. A tremolo between two notes a sixth or more apart runs the
risk of failure of the lower note to sound on repetition.

Phrases normally contain several slurs, or a mixture of slurs and single
notes. The player maintains a full and steady flow of air until a new
breath needs to be taken, and meanwhile the tongue articulates the
rhythmic pattern of the music. In the following phrase, the oboist will
probably not take a new breath until after the B♭ in the fifth full
measure.

EX. 148. Beethoven—*Symphony no. 3*   p. 155, ed. Kalmus

The function of the breath is to set up vibrations at the embouchure, not to blow into or through the instrument. Breathing indications are not written into the part, but good writing for wind instruments requires a sensitivity to this essential physical aspect of wind playing. Even though one doesn't play a wind instrument, one can learn much by alert observation and listening to good players. The art of breath control is a fine art of distribution of wind power according to the respective needs, both musical and mechanical, of the tones of the phrase. The dynamic design of the phrase has to be taken into account. Sometimes a new breath is taken to give sharper definition to a motive. The composer is advised to cultivate a feeling for the natural breathing quality in instrumental music, like that of singing. In fast passages it is better to sacrifice notes than to force the performer to snatch frantically at minute opportunities to replenish his wind supply.

REGISTERS

The woodwind instruments present a remarkable contrast to the strings, in that they possess far more pronounced individual sound characteristics; also each one has its peculiar variations within itself in tone color, intensity, carrying power, and tone-weight, depending on the part of its range being employed. Knowledge of these registers and their effect is an indispensable part of the technique of orchestration.

SCORE MARKINGS

The woodwinds are placed at the top of the score in this order:

piccolo
flutes
oboes
English horn
clarinets
bass clarinet
bassoons
contrabassoon

First and second parts for identical instruments, as two flutes, are written on one staff, except in cases where differences in rhythm and other complications might cause confusion in reading the two parts. Then a second staff is used temporarily for the second player.

When two parts are on the same staff, stems for the first part point up, those for the second part, down. Dots and accents are placed at the ends of the stems (Fig. 44*a*).

If both first and second players are to play the same part, double stems may be used (Fig. 44*b*), or the part may be written as for one player and marked *a 2* (Fig. 44*c*).

If the first player is to play alone, the second part may be represented by rests (Fig. 44*d*), or the single part may be marked 1, I, 1°, or I° (Fig. 44*e*).

If the second player is to play alone, the first part may be represented by rests (Fig. 44*f*), or the single part may be marked 2, II, 2°, or II° (Fig. 44*g*).

Fig. 44

The indications *divisi* and *unis.* are peculiar to string parts and are not used for winds.

CHAPTER SEVEN

THE FLUTE

Fr., *flûte, grande flûte;* It., *flauto, flauto grande;*
Ger., *Flöte, grosse Flöte*

T HE present century has seen the adoption of metal flutes and
the virtual obsolescence of the wooden flute as an orchestral
instrument, an event which cannot be reported without some
regret over the loss of the wooden flute's mellowness and beauty of
tone. It was to be anticipated that the evolution of musical taste toward
a predilection for orchestral brilliance and virtuosity would bring about
this radical change. Modern flutes are made of silver, gold, and even
platinum, and they surpass those of wood in ease of speaking, agility,
brilliance of tone, and security in the upper register. Their tone is pure,
clear, and serene, possessing beauty of a different quality from that of
their predecessors. Some wooden flutes with silver-lined head joint,
now in use, are evidence of a lingering wish to preserve qualities of
both types.

The over-all length of the flute is about 26½ inches. A cork stopper
with a screw tuning device is inserted in the end near the embouchure,
so that the sounding length of the tube is in the neighborhood of 24
inches. The lowest tone is 2-foot C. Some flutes are made with a low
B, necessitating lengthening of the instrument by about 2 inches. The
bore is cylindrical, with a diameter of ¾ inch, narrowed slightly at
the embouchure end in a parabolic curve.

The flute is made in three sections, the head joint, the body joint, and
the foot joint. The foot joint represents an extension to the six-hole
pipe envisaged in the preceding chapter, and it furnishes the additional

tones C♯ and C. A longer foot joint may be attached, giving the low B, for those rare occasions when that note is called for.

The modern flute embodies the revolutionary constructive principles introduced by Theobald Boehm in the middle of the nineteenth century, with a few subsequent improvements. What is known as the "Boehm system" is based on three main principles. First, holes were to be bored for all chromatic tones, and these holes were to be located in their acoustically correct positions. Second, the holes were to be as large as possible, for better tone and intonation, and they were to stand open. Formerly, the size of the holes depended on the ability of the fingers to cover them, and also on corrections in pitch necessitated by a compromise in the location of the holes. Third, the mechanism was to be arranged so that the fingers could control all of the holes, by means of keys, hole covers, axles, and springs. The following main features of this arrangement should be considered in relation to the basic six-hole pipe.

The right hand first finger now plays F♮ when depressed, instead of F♯, the second and third playing E and D, as before. By means of a rotating axle, the F♯ hole is closed when either the second or the third finger key is depressed. The right-hand first finger key also closes the B♮ hole above, providing an alternative fingering for B♭.

For the left hand, a finger plate enables the first finger to close the C♯ hole from a position an inch below the hole. A combination key and plate for the thumb allows closing either the C♮ hole or both C♮ and B♮ holes.

It was found inconvenient to keep two of the holes open, the G♯ and the low D♯. The G♯ hole is opened by the left little finger lever. A duplicate hole is bored, however, and this stands open unless the third finger is depressed for G♮. The right little finger opens the D♯ hole in the foot joint, and keeps it open for practically all notes above. The same finger controls a split key to play either C or C♯, the lowest notes.

The remaining keys are the high D and D♯ trill keys, operated by the right third and second fingers, respectively, and an added B♮ trill

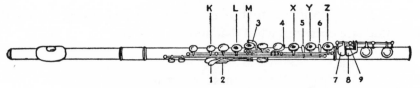

letters and numbers indicate keys to be depressed

fingers																				
left thumb	2	2	2	2	2	2	2	2	2	2	2 1	2	–	–	2	2	2	2	2
1st	K	K	K	K	K	K	K	K	K	K	K K	K	K	–	–	–	K	K	K
2nd	L	L	L	L	L	L	L	L	L	L	–	–	–	–	–	L	L	L	L	L
3rd	M	M	M	M	M	M	M	M	M	–	–	–	–	–	–	M	M	M	M	M
4th	–	–	–	–	–	–	–	3	–	–	–	–	–	–	–	–	–	–	–
right 1st	X	X	X	X	X	X	–	–	–	–	X	–	–	–	–	X	X	X	X	–
2nd	Y	Y	Y	Y	Y	–	–	–	–	–	–	–	–	–	–	Y	Y	Y	–
3rd	Z	Z	Z	Z	–	Z	–	–	–	–	–	–	–	–	Z	Z	–	–	Z
4th	9	8	–	7	7	7	7	7	7	7	7 7	7	7	7	7	–	7	7	7

left thumb	2	2	2	2 1	2	–	–	2	2	2	2	2 2	–	–	2	2	2	–	–	2
1st	K	K	K	K K	K	K	–	–	K	K	K	K K	K	–	–	–	K	K	–	–
2nd	L	L	L	–	–	–	–	–	L	L	L	–	–	–	L	L	L	–	–	L	L	–
3rd	M	M	–	–	–	–	–	–	M	M	–	M	M M	M	M	–	–	M	M	–	M
4th	–	3	–	–	–	–	–	–	3	–	–	–	–	3	–	–	–	3	3	–
right 1st	–	–	–	X	–	–	–	–	–	X	X	X	–	–	–	X	X	–	X	X	X
2nd	–	–	–	–	–	–	–	–	–	Y	Y	–	Y	–	–	–	–	5	–	–	Y
3rd	–	–	–	–	–	–	–	–	–	Z	–	–	–	Z	–	–	–	6	–	–
4th	7	7	7	7 7	7	7	7	7	7	7	7	7	7 7	7	7	7	–	–	–	9	9

Fig. 45. Fingering Chart for the Flute (Boehm System)

key for the right first finger, duplicating the action of the thumb plate.

Keys are named for the note sounding when the key is depressed. It is to be recognized, however, that whereas G♯ comes from the hole opened when the G♯ key is depressed, the effect of depressing the G♮ key is to close the hole from which A comes, the G hole being two holes farther down. The low C hole is the end of the flute.

Fingering a note involves not only pressing the key, but also closing all higher-pitched holes. The entire tube down to the note being fingered has to be tightly closed, except when vents are opened to produce upper partial tones.

In playing position, the flute is supported by the right thumb, the first joint of the left forefinger, and the player's chin. The lower lip partially covers the embouchure hole.

It is understood that enharmonic equivalents are fingered alike; *e.g.*, the fingering for G♯ and for A♭ is exactly the same.

OVERBLOWING

The fingering chart shows how the upper notes of the flute are obtained by fingering a fundamental and, except for the chromatic tones from E to C♯, inclusive, in the second octave, opening one or more holes as vents for the production of harmonics. This process is summed up in Fig. 46.

Fig. 46

TONE QUALITIES OF THE REGISTERS

The tones of the first half-octave, especially the foot joint notes, have a warm velvety quality of their own. The sound is deceptively heavy when heard alone, but it is easily covered by other instruments and by strong overtones from low bass notes. This is due, no doubt, to the weakness of the upper partials in the formant of the low register of the flute.

In the following example, the low C sounds clearly because it is the lowest of the three voices.

EX. 149. Stravinsky—*Symphony of Psalms*

p. 16, ed. Boosey & Hawkes

A gradual brightening of the tone takes place as the sounding length decreases through the first octave, although these fundamental tones do not achieve the clarity and serenity characteristic of the overblown notes of the second octave. This comparison can be noted in the next example, for two flutes.

EX. 150. Ravel—*Ma Mère L'Oye*   p. 1, ed. Durand

The third octave is brilliant, with much carrying power, without shrillness at least as far as A, or even B♭.

EX. 151. Schumann—*Symphony no. 1*   p. 140, ed. Philharmonia

The highest C♯ and D should be considered as extremely exceptional extensions of the flute's range. They can be included only in loud passages and it is advisable to double them with the piccolo. Instances of their use are quite rare.

EX. 152. Strauss—*Symphonia Domestica*

p. 18, ed. Associated Music Publishers

With authorization of the original publishers Ed. Bote & G. Bock, Berlin, Wiesbaden.

In the production of notes above the staff, various harmonics are employed (Fig. 46). The first C♯ is harmonic no. 2 (octave), the D no. 3 (octave and fifth), the D♯ no. 4 (double octave). These harmonics tend to differ in tone and brilliance. The top B♭ is a clearer, more manageable tone than the B♮, mostly because it is a harmonic no. 4 as opposed to a no. 5. The finger combination for high A sometimes proves awkward in passages. The reconciliation of these diversities is an essential part of the art of flute playing, and melodies may cover the entire range of the instrument, although it should be added that the dynamic range of the flute is not wide.

The following is a famous example of a modern solo for the flute.

EX. 153. Ravel—*Daphnis et Chloé*   p. 228, ed. Durand

AGILITY

No wind instrument surpasses the flute in agility, fleetness, and general virtuosity. Flute parts contain all manner of rapid scales, arpeggios, and brilliant passage work.

EX. 154. Strauss—*Elektra*   p. 186, ed. Boosey & Hawkes

Wide skips between registers are idiomatic for the instrument.

EX. 155. Strauss—*Ein Heldenleben*   p. 113, ed. Eulenburg

Loud passages in the high register require more wind. Opportunities should be provided for taking at least a quick breath, either in the phrasing or with a rest.

Two flutes may divide a passage in alternate motives, overlapping on the accented notes. This procedure makes breathing easier for both, and the result is a more rhythmic performance than if both flutes played the whole phrase in unison.

EX. 156. Stravinsky—*L'Oiseau de Feu*   p. 20, ed. Broude Bros.

Double-tonguing (Ex. 157) and triple-tonguing (Ex. 158) are both effective and efficient for fast staccato playing.

EX. 157. Tchaikovsky—*Nutcracker Suite no. 1*   p. 35, ed. Kalmus

EX. 158. Debussy—*La Mer*   p. 48, ed. Durand

Permission granted by Durand et Cie., Paris, copyright owners; Elkan-Vogel, Philadelphia, Pa., agents.

HARMONICS

We have seen that on the flute all normal tones above the first open C♯ are harmonics. But the term *harmonic*, in woodwind parlance, is used to denote a tone produced by using a harmonic different from that normally used.

Fig. 47

In Fig. 47 (*a*) are shown three ways to play the high D. First, the normal D as harmonic no. 3 from the fundamental G, with left first finger raised, opening the C♯ hole as a vent (see fingering chart); second, the same played with the vent closed; and third, the D as harmonic no. 4 from the low D, without vents.

Some flutists are able to produce the entire harmonic series (Fig. 47*b*) up to the seventh or eighth harmonic from low C, without opening vents.

Notes usually designated to be played as harmonics are those obtained unvented as harmonic no. 3 of the fourteen chromatic tones from low C up to open C♯, inclusive. They are marked with a small circle, like string harmonics. While they possess a certain veiled quality, it is generally admitted that they are inferior to normal flute tones both in clearness and intonation. In Ex. 159 is an extraordinary example of flute harmonics.

EX. 159. Ravel—*Daphnis et Chloé*   p. 60, ed. Durand

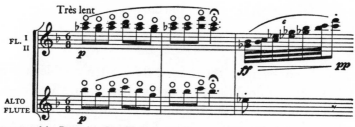

Permission granted by Durand et Cie., Paris, copyright owners; Elkan-Vogel, Philadelphia, Pa., agents.

Harmonics are useful as an added resource in the fingering of difficult passages. Sometimes the inclusion of one or two notes in "harmonic fingering" will simplify the execution without appreciably affecting the over-all sonority.

TRILLS AND TREMOLOS

The rapid alternation of two tones may present difficulties of fingering and also of embouchure. A trill may involve an exchange of finger combinations requiring the movement of several fingers, together with a quick adjustment of the embouchure to different harmonics. These difficulties can be smoothed out by the use of harmonic fingering or by the addition of extra keys to the instrument. The D and D♯ trill keys are examples of the latter expedient. In any case, the effectiveness of a given trill, or tremolo, depends upon the expertness of the performer. Practicability is a matter of degree rather than a subject for classification into possible and impossible.

The three keys in the foot joint being controlled by the right fourth finger alone, the trills C-C♯ and C♯-D♯, and the tremolo C-D♯, are not playable except rather slowly. The little finger has to glide from one key to the other.

The woodwind version of the bowed tremolo is the reiteration of a single note by means of flutter-tonguing, an effect not often used. The more usual tremolo is like the fingered tremolo of strings, a trill with an interval larger than a second. If the interval is too wide the lower note may fail to speak, owing to the inertia of the air column; and if harmonics are involved there is a risk that the fundamental may sound where it is not wanted. Within the first octave, tremolos having an interval greater than a perfect fifth are uncertain, whereas in higher registers a safer limit is the major third.

THE SECOND FLUTE

For added tone-weight, the second flute often doubles the first in unison. Less often it doubles at the octave below, in which case its octave overtone reinforces the first flute. The lower instrument is at a slight disadvantage, since the octave difference places it in a less brilliant register.

It is wise to assign some of the duties of the first player to the second player when both are not needed. This allows the first to rest, and tends to make the second part more interesting to play.

The two flute parts may be melodies of equal importance.

EX. 160. Stravinsky—*Orpheus*   p. 11, ed. Boosey & Hawkes

Light accompaniment figures may be arranged for two flutes.

EX. 161. Debussy—*Première Rhapsodie*   p. 28, ed. Durand

In the next example, an imaginative use is made of two flutes to supply two inner voices of a four-part texture, in which soprano and bass are played by strings in octaves.

EX. 162. Mendelssohn—*Italian Symphony*   p. 77, ed. Eulenburg

Another instance of inspired orchestration is the following chord from Mahler's Fourth Symphony. To be noted are the sudden change of mode in the harmonic progression, the unusual spacing of the chord in measure 5, and the placing of the perfect fourth in the two flutes. The effect is quite unexpected and magical.

EX. 163. Mahler—*Symphony no. 4*   p. 148, ed. Philharmonia

Combinations of flutes with other instruments should be studied through perusal of scores.

MORE THAN TWO FLUTES

The grouping of woodwinds by threes quite often includes three flutes instead of two flutes and piccolo. The more homogeneous color is preferred for purposes like the following.

EX. 164. Verdi—*Aïda*   p. 76, ed. Broude Bros.

A larger orchestra may call for four flutes. The following illustration is taken from the final measures of Berg's *Wozzeck*. In the score, the flutes are doubled at the unison by the celesta.

EX. 165. Berg—*Wozzeck* (*End of Act III*)   ed. Universal

THE PICCOLO

Fr., *petite flûte*; It., *flauto piccolo, ottavino*; Ger., *kleine Flöte*

In each of the four families of woodwind, there is one instrument that is regarded as the standard or normal instrument of the type. These four are flute, oboe, B♭ clarinet, and bassoon. They represent in each case the size and proportions found to give the most nearly characteristic tone color, as well as other features, answering to a more or less universal, albeit transitory, conception of how these instruments should sound. The other instruments in each group are auxiliary instruments, adjuncts to the normal types.

The auxiliary instruments have as their first *raison d'être* the extension of the pitch range of the families to which they belong. The piccolo extends the range of the flute family up to another octave C, the last note on the pianoforte keyboard. However, the top B♮ and C are quite difficult of production.

An auxiliary instrument, made for the purpose of playing higher notes than the normal instrument, is of smaller size, favoring the upper part of its range. The lower notes tend to be of less good quality. This is illustrated by the piccolo, whose low tones are decidedly inferior to those of the flute. Furthermore, the foot joint is lacking altogether, so that the lowest note of the piccolo is D.

Another principle of auxiliary instruments is exemplified in the piccolo, the principle of transposing instruments. The mechanism of the flute being reproduced in miniature (except for the missing foot joint), a flutist plays the piccolo with the same fingering to which he is accustomed. Since the instrument is but half the size of the flute (12⅝ inches), the notes sound an octave higher. The piccolo part in the score must be read as sounding an octave higher than written.

The interest of composers in the auxiliary instruments has given them positions of importance nearly equal to that of the standard types in each family. This development has been strengthened by advances, to the point of specialization, in the technique of playing these instruments, and still more by the realization that what were once considered defects are really qualities, to be studied for their advantages, and to be recognized as additions to the coloristic resources of the various families of woodwind. The peculiar hollow sound of low tones of the piccolo can be very effective in the right surroundings.

EX. 166. Shostakovich—*Symphony no. 7*   p. 13, ed. Leeds

The upper tones of the piccolo are bright and piercing, easily heard above the maximum sonority of the full orchestra. The instrument is here unsurpassed in penetrating power. Its highest octave should therefore be used sparingly. In high-pitched chords, the three upper notes may be given to two flutes with the piccolo on top. The piccolo adds highlights to the orchestral tutti, strengthening the upper partials of the harmony.

The piccolo will be found most useful in its medium range. Here it combines more flexibly with other instruments, and contributes less edginess to the sonority. It is often better, when doubling the flute with piccolo, to write the latter an octave below, so that the two will sound in unison, especially when the flute is in its upper octave. Solo parts for the piccolo in this register are numerous.

EX. 167. Milhaud—*Symphony no. 2* p. 1, ed. Heugel

Common errors in writing for the piccolo are the too consistent placing of the part in the highest octave, and the misconception that it is an instrument for loud music only. The piccolo is effective in inverse proportion to the amount of its use. It is capable of delicacy, and it can contribute much with a few notes skillfully placed.

Sometimes two piccolos are employed for the duration of a movement, or for a special passage. On these occasions, one of the piccolos is played by the second or third flutist.

THE ALTO FLUTE

Fr., flûte en sol; It., flauto contralto; Ger., Altflöte

The alto flute is an auxiliary instrument that has not yet become established as a regular orchestral instrument. Many orchestras do not even possess one. It is found in very few scores, but the significance of such works as *Daphnis et Chloé* and the *Sacre du Printemps* give the alto flute a certain standing and importance.

With a length of 34¼ inches, the alto flute is pitched a perfect fourth below the standard flute. It is therefore a transposing instrument, all notes sounding a perfect fourth lower than written. If the fingering for C on the flute is taken, the resultant sound will be G. It is also called the Flute in G, and sometimes called, erroneously, the Bass Flute.

The mechanism of the alto flute is the same as that of the regular flute, except for modifications due to its size. The left hand is placed so that it has to reach no farther to the right than on the regular flute, the holes being controlled by finger plates and axles. First and third fingers of the right hand are enabled to reach their key covers by means of discs placed at the near edges of the covers.

The range of the flute, up to the high C, is available on the alto flute, but the upper half-octave is lacking in brilliance, and suffers by comparison with the flute at the same pitch. The lower tones, on the other hand, are extremely rich and warm, and stronger than the low notes of the flute. The instrument is responsive even to active double- and triple-tonguing. It requires a little more breath than the regular flute.

In a grouping of four flutes, the alto flute is useful in extending the range downward.

EX. 168. Holst—*The Planets*   p. 131, ed. Boosey & Hawkes

Used by permission of J. Curwen & Sons, Ltd.

The most individual part of the alto flute's range is, of course, its lower octave. To be heard to the best advantage, it should be lightly accompanied, or, better still, not at all, as in the following example.

EX. 169. Ravel—*Daphnis et Chloé*   p. 243, ed. Durand

Permission granted by Durand et Cie., Paris, copyright owners; Elkan-Vogel, Philadelphia, Pa., agents.

In the medium register, the alto flute differs from the flute more subtly, in timbre. The comparison must be experienced by ear to be appreciated.

EX. 170. Stravinsky—*Le Sacre du Printemps*   p. 18, ed. Russe

Copyright 1921 by Edition Russe de Musique. Used by permission.

꧁ ꧂

CHAPTER EIGHT

THE OBOE

Fr., hautbois; It., *oboe;* Ger., *Oboe, Hoboe*

THE body of the oboe is a gently tapering conical tube, made in three sections, called upper, lower, and bell joints. The diameter of the bore measures ³⁄₁₆ inch at the top, and ⅝ inch at the beginning of the bell joint. The bell is flared a little and finished with a metal ring. In the small end is inserted the reed tube, or "staple," fitted with cork and the double reed, ¼ inch wide, bound to it by winding with thread. The length of the instrument, including the reed, is about 25½ inches, the reed and staple protruding 2½ inches, more or less. The pitch of the oboe can be varied but very slightly, only by pushing in or pulling out the reed tube.

Oboes are usually made of wood. Favorite woods are grenadilla, rosewood, and cocus wood. Some are of ebonite, which has at least the advantage of freedom from warping.

FINGERING SYSTEM

The fingering system of the oboe is based on the fundamental six-hole D major scale, described in Chapter Six. Unlike the flute, the oboe sounds F♯ when the right first finger is depressed, but the two instruments are similar in that the right fourth finger controls keys for low C, C♯, and D♯. The left fourth finger operates keys for G♯, a duplicate D♯ key, low C♯, low B♮, and B♭, the lowest note on the oboe. The right thumb supports the instrument, while the left thumb works an octave key and a B♭ plate.

146

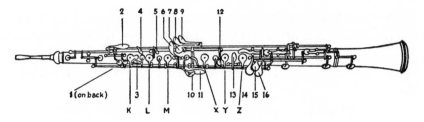

letters and numbers indicate keys to be depressed

fingers

left

	thumb	1st	2nd	3rd	4th

fingers																										
left thumb	–	–	–	–	–	– –	–	– – –	–	–	– –	–	– –	–	– – –	– – –	– –
1st	K	K	K	K	K	K K	K	K K	K	K	K K	K	K K	–	K K –	K/ꝏ – K	K K K	K/ꝏ K
2nd	L	L	L	L	L	L L	L	L L	L	L	L L	L	L L	–	– – L	L – 5	L 4 –	L L
3rd	M	M	M	M	M	M M	M M M	M	M M	–	– –	– – –	M – –	M – –	M M
4th	9	8	–	–	–	– 7	–	– – –	–	6 –	– – –	–	– – –	– – –	– 7

right

	1st	2nd	3rd	4th
1st	X	X	X	X	X	X X	X	X X X	X	–	– 11	–	X X	–	X 10	X X	X – X	X X
2nd	Y	Y	Y	Y	Y	Y Y	Y Y	Y –	–	– –	– –	–	– – –	Y – –	Y – 12	Y Y
3rd	Z	Z	Z	Z	Z	Z Z	–	13 Z	–	– –	– –	–	– – –	Z – –	Z – –	Z Z
4th	14	14	14	15	–	16 –	–	– – –	–	– –	–	– – –	15 – –	– – –	16 –

{K both with
3 1st finger

K/ꝏ = half-hole

left

	thumb	1st	2nd	3rd	4th
thumb	1	1 1	1	1	1 1	–	{2/K	{2/K {2/3	{2/K	{2/K	– –	– –	–	1 1	1 1	1	1	1	1
1st	K	K K	K	K	K K	{2/K	{2/K {2/3	{2/K	{2/K	K/ꝏ 2	K/ꝏ 2	K/ꝏ	K/ꝏ K/ꝏ	K/ꝏ K/ꝏ	K	K	K	–
2nd	L	L L	L	L	L L	L	L L	–	–	L –	L –	L	L L	L L	L	–	–	–
3rd	M	M M	M	M	M M	–	– –	–	–	M –	M –	M	M M	–	–	M	–	–
4th	–	– –	–	–	6 –	–	– –	–	–	– –	– –	8	6 {7/6	6 {7/6	–	–	–

right

	1st	2nd	3rd	4th
1st	X	X X	X	–	– 11	–	X X	–	X	X X	– X	–	– –	– –	X	X	X	X
2nd	Y	Y –	–	–	– –	–	– –	–	–	– –	– 12	Y	Y Y	Y Y	Y	–	–	–
3rd	–	13 Z	–	–	– –	–	– –	–	–	– –	– –	Z	Z Z	Z Z	13	–	–	⌒
4th	–	– –	–	–	– –	–	– –	–	–	14 –	14 –	–	16 –	16 –	14	–	–	–

Fig. 48. Fingering Chart for the Oboe (Conservatory System)

The tone holes are quite small compared to those of the flute. A feature of earlier types is still seen in some oboes, the tone hole under the left third finger consisting of two small holes bored close together. When one hole is closed the note sounded is A♭. With both closed, the note is G.

This half-hole principle is made permanent in the perforated key-cover on the C♯ hole, for the left first finger. A tab is provided onto which the finger may slide, leaving the key-cover down and the small perforation open for venting certain notes. Levers for upper B♭ and C♮, pressed with the side of the right first finger, a cross F♮ key, and the upper D and D♯ trill keys, are standard equipment. Further key work varies with different models. The French Conservatoire system, generally regarded as the best, has from thirteen to sixteen keys, in addition to plates or ring keys on the fundamental six holes. Special keys are added to individual instruments to facilitate the execution of this or that trill or figure. In consequence, a great many alternative fingerings exist. Only common fingerings are given in the chart, which cannot record all the variants in use, and hence must remain incomplete. It is intended to present a general view of oboe fingering.

OVERBLOWING

Keys 1 and 2 on the chart are called first and second octave keys. Like the half-hole device, their function is to induce the sounding of upper harmonics by venting. Some instruments have an automatic second octave key that goes into action when the first octave key is depressed and the fingering is taken for the A above the staff and upward.

Fig. 49

Figure 49 shows the scheme of harmonics employed for the higher notes. The last six harmonics are all sharp, relative to their fundamentals, by at least a half tone, high F being a whole tone sharp. The harmonics, numbers 3, 4, and 5, require further venting besides the half-hole and octave keys, and this venting is largely responsible for the sharpness of the harmonics, which necessitates the adoption of lower-pitched fundamentals to sound the notes wanted.

The octave and fifth harmonic (no. 3) can be produced from the notes of the first octave, up to and including B♭. F♯ and G are normally so overblown. Composers have not thus far made a practice of indicating these harmonics, but oboists sometimes use them as a means of achieving an especially fine pianissimo.

THE DOUBLE REED

An accepted part of oboe playing is the preparation of the reeds. A selected piece of cane is folded double when wet, the ends bound around a tube, the double reed cut to the desired length, and then the new ends are scraped with special tools to the required thinness.

The reed must be very thin to vibrate freely, but if too thin the tone is of poor quality. If the reed is too thick it is difficult to play staccato and the low tones do not speak easily. A stiff reed causes the tone to be harsh and strident.

The reed plays such a vital part in the tone quality of a reed instrument that the fact of the performer's preparing the reed makes of the oboe a peculiarly personal instrument. The sound reflects to a high degree the individual taste of the player.

EMBOUCHURE

Before playing, the reeds must be moistened. In playing position, the ends are held between the lips, which gently control the vibrations and prevent the teeth from touching the reeds. Because of the flexibility of the reeds, considerable variation in pitch can be obtained by the lips alone.

The tiny elliptical orifice between the reeds opens and closes with their vibrations, and these in turn set up vibrations in the air column of the instrument. The oboe requires by far the least amount of wind of any wind instrument. This means that long phrases may be played without taking a new breath, but it means also that the player is in a constant state of holding back the wind pressure. For this reason, as well as for the purpose of allowing relaxation of the lips and tongue, frequent rests should be provided in the oboe part.

TONGUING

The tongue controls the air stream at the orifice between the reeds. All the tongue articulations previously described are feasible on the oboe, with a few reservations. Double- and triple-tonguing are in the nature of emergency resources, used only when the tempo demanded is too fast for single-tonguing. They are not idiomatic features of the instrument, as they are in the case of the flute. On the other hand, the light oboe staccato in single-tonguing can achieve a surprisingly fast delivery.

EX. 171. Rossini—*La Scala di Seta: Sinfonia*   p. 3, ed. Eulenburg

The oboe staccato is superior to that of all the other winds for its sharp, dry, light quality, a point to realize when using woodwinds in combination.

Another important characteristic of the oboe embouchure is that tones have to be started with a definite attack, noticeable to the ear. If the reed is simply blown upon, without the *t* stroke of the tongue, the moment at which the tone begins to sound is unpredictable and impossible of control.

Flutter-tonguing has been employed on the oboe with no more than moderate effectiveness.

EX. 172. Stravinsky—*Le Sacre du Printemps* p. 88, ed. Russe

TIMBRE AND REGISTERS

The sound of the oboe has been called pungent, tangy, nasal, penetrating, biting, piercing, and raspy. These adjectives represent the more obvious qualities of double-reed tone, qualities that distinguish the oboe sharply from the flute, for example. There is a noticeable difference in the kind of tone produced by different schools of oboe playing, such as the French and the German, and by individual players. It is generally believed that the oboe tone of the present day is much thinner and much lighter than when the following melody was written.

EX. 173. Bach—*Brandenburg Concerto no. 1*   p. 15, ed. Kalmus

In direct contrast to the flute, the oboe increases in intensity as it descends through the lower fifth of its range, and the characteristics referred to become more pronounced. Here it is the problem of the oboist to subdue the natural tendency to loudness and even coarseness. The low B♭ is seldom found in scores. It cannot be attacked softly, and it is more appropriate for music of a robust character than for the nuance called for in Ex. 174. The B♮ is more manageable.

EX. 174. Prokofieff—*Chout*   p. 119, ed. Gutheil

Of the highest notes shown on the fingering chart, G♯ and A are impractical for orchestral writing. They are insecure of production and lacking in oboe quality. F♯ and G♮ are not often used, but they are more playable and they are considered a normal part of the range of the oboe. They had better not be approached by skip, and should not take part in active legato figuration. The following solo in the upper register is very difficult but very effective when well played.

EX. 175. Ravel—*Daphnis et Chloé*   p. 3, ed. Durand

Upwards from A above the staff the oboe tone gradually becomes thinner, and above D begins to sound less like an oboe. These high tones do not possess the warmth of the range below A, but they are very useful for adding brilliance to the woodwind and the upper strings. The oboe parts in Ex. 176 double the strings.

EX. 176. Chausson—*Symphony in B♭*

p. 93, ed. International Music Co.

The distinctive tone color and expressive capabilities of the oboe make it a favorite solo instrument. Below are two well-known oboe melodies.

EX. 177. Schumann—*Symphony no. 2*   p. 111, ed. Philharmonia

EX. 178. Brahms—*Symphony no. 2*   p. 80, ed. Kalmus

Melodies of folk-song character are especially well suited to the simple plaintiveness of the oboe. The following melody is contained within the range of an octave. The oboe repeats it several measures later an octave lower.

EX. 179. Bartók—*Concerto for Orchestra*   p. 68, ed. Boosey & Hawkes

Copyright 1946 by Hawkes & Son (London) Ltd. Used by permission.

The oboe intensifies the suggestion of a strange exotic pipe, imparted by the next example.

EX. 180. Falla—*El Amor Brujo*   p. 64, ed. Chester

AGILITY

Generally speaking, fast slurred arpeggios and figuration are not recommended for the oboe, unless a special effect is intended. It is not that the instrument is incapable of this kind of virtuosity, but rather that agility does not seem suitable to the double-reed tone, at least in comparison with flutes and clarinets. On the other hand, the oboe can articulate rhythmic patterns with superior neatness. The following quite difficult phrase proves eminently successful as oboe writing.

EX. 181. Ravel—*Le Tombeau de Couperin*   p. 1, ed. Durand

Permission granted by Durand et Cie., Paris, copyright owners; Elkan-Vogel, Philadelphia, Pa., agents.

TRILLS AND TREMOLOS

Even more than in the case of the flute, a tabulation of oboe trills and tremolos cannot be definitively made. There are the same variable factors of skill of the performer, and degree of rapidity in the alternation of the two notes, further complicated by differences in mechanism between individual instruments. Also, there is often more than one way to finger one or both the notes involved. It can be said that all major and minor trills are possible, and that most tremolos wider than a fourth are undependable. Tremolos on notes above the staff are apt to be of poor effect.

ORCHESTRAL USES

The oboe group commonly consists of two oboes, or two oboes and English horn, three oboes and English horn, or, less commonly, three oboes. Other combinations, like the four oboes and English horn in Stravinsky's *Symphony of Psalms*, are special and unusual cases.

Apart from the melodic uses described above, the oboes may reinforce violins or violas by doubling at the unison. In combination with other woodwinds they give incisiveness to wind chords and sharp definition to rhythmic figures. The unison doubling of oboe and clarinet is forceful.

A harmonic effect of extreme pungency is obtained by placing together three oboes and English horn, all in their low registers.

EX. 182. Strauss—*Till Eulenspiegel*   p. 8, ed. Philharmonia

Two oboes in thirds, or other close intervals, have a tangy quality of tone not possessed by the other woodwinds.

EX. 183. Debussy—*La Mer*   p. 82, ed. Durand

In the closing measures of Sibelius' Fourth Symphony, the oboe repeats a simple major seventh motive in diminishing nuances, with changing harmonies in flute and strings. With economy of means, a maximum effect is obtained.

ex. 184. Sibelius—*Symphony no. 4*   p. 68, ed. Breitkopf

Used by permission of the original publishers, Breitkopf & Härtel, Leipzig.

To obtain a more strident sonority, Gustav Mahler often directed the oboes and clarinets to raise the bell of the instrument so as to point straight at the audience. The instruction in German is *Schalltrichter auf!* a marking more usually seen in brass parts.

The opposite process is that of asking for muted oboes. Muting is accomplished by stuffing a handkerchief in the bell.

EX. 185. Stravinsky—*Pétrouchka*   p. 155, ed. Russe

THE ENGLISH HORN

Fr., *cor anglais;* It., *corno inglese;* Ger., *englisch Horn*

The mechanism of the English horn is similar in all details to that of the oboe, except that the low B♭ is lacking. It differs from the oboe in size (length 31½ inches, including reed), in the bulb-shaped bell, and in the bent metal crook extending from the top end of the instrument to hold the reed tube. The double reed is larger than that of the oboe. The weight of the English horn is supported by a cord around the player's neck.

The English horn is a transposing instrument, an instrument "in F." This designation means that when the player reads C, taking the fingering for C as on the oboe, the sound produced will be F, because of the difference in size of the two instruments. Since the English horn is larger than the oboe the sounds will be lower in pitch (it will be recalled that the piccolo sounds higher than the flute because of its smaller size). All notes written for the English horn, therefore, sound a perfect fifth below.

ORCHESTRAL USES

Although often used in eighteenth-century chamber music and the divertimento, the English horn has been a normal member of the orchestra, an auxiliary instrument of the oboe family, since the middle of the nineteenth century. It was at first introduced only occasionally for a featured solo melody, and was usually played by the second oboist, who resumed playing the oboe after performing the solo. This could be easily done, since the two instruments were identical in playing technique. As the importance of the English horn grew, and its individual capabilities were more appreciated, this process of interchange of instruments gave way to the establishment of the specialist on the English horn, who now occasionally plays third or fourth oboe.

As an auxiliary instrument, a primary function of the English horn is to extend the range of the oboe family downward. Since the instrument has no low B♭, the extension in sound is to E♮ below middle C. Its lower fifth does not have the tendency to coarseness noticed in the lowest notes of the oboe. The larger size seems to favor the low notes.

EX. 186. Bartók—*Second Rhapsody for Violin and Orchestra*

p. 3, ed. Boosey & Hawkes

Another service performed by the English horn is to play the notes of the oboe's lower fifth when a softer and less penetrating tone is desired. A three-part chord for three oboes sounds smoother and more homogeneous if the third oboe is replaced by the English horn.

For singing melodies the English horn brings a new tone color. It is closely related to the oboe sound, yet it possesses a quality that is highly distinctive and individual, owing, at least in part, to the peculiar bulb it has for a bell. Orchestral literature abounds in solo phrases for the English horn. Two of these are given below.

EX. 187. Berlioz—*Overture: The Roman Carnival*

p. 3, ed. Philharmonia

EX. 188. Strauss—*Ein Heldenleben*   p. 171, ed. Eulenburg

The English horn provides new coloristic resources in combination with other instruments, winds as well as strings. A perfect example of mixed timbre is seen in the following melody which is played in unison with a solo 'cello. The two instruments blend as one, and neither predominates at any time. The accompaniment consists of widely spaced harmonies in the strings, held pianissimo.

EX. 189. Debussy—*La Mer*   p. 28, ed. Durand

In common with all auxiliary instruments that are designed to extend the range downward, the upper tones of the English horn are the least effective part of its range. It is unwise to write above E in the orchestra, unless doubling by other instruments is provided. The **F** in the following example is produced by good players.

EX. 190. Roussel—*Bacchus et Ariane, Second Suite*   p. 16, ed. Durand

The English horn is equal to the oboe in agility and can participate in all active woodwind figuration.

THE OBOE D'AMORE

Fr., *hautbois d'amour*; It., *oboe d'amore*; Ger. *Oboe d'amore,*
Liebesoboe

Larger than the oboe but smaller than the English horn, the oboe d'amore is pitched in A, a minor third below the oboe. Its notes therefore sound a minor third lower than written. Its mechanism is like that of the English horn in that it does not possess the low B♭, and it also has the bulb bell. The tone is gentler than that of the other two instruments, and subtly different in tone color.

The oboe d'amore was a common instrument in the baroque period, and was much used by J. S. Bach. In modern orchestration it is known chiefly for its important part in Strauss' *Symphonia Domestica,* where its written range ascends to high F. Among other instances of its use are the *Bolero* of Ravel, and the following example by Debussy. The solo first appears unaccompanied.

EX. 191. Debussy—*Gigues*   p. 4, ed. Durand

THE HECKELPHONE

Ger., *Heckelphon*

Invented by Wilhelm Heckel, in 1904, the heckelphone was included in the scores of *Elektra* and *Salome* by Richard Strauss. It is a sort of baritone oboe, built to sound an octave below the ordinary oboe and furnished with an additional semitone taking it down to A. The keys are arranged high on the instrument, with the fingering of a German oboe. There is a bulb bell perforated on the side.

The heckelphone has a rich and full reedy tone in the lower octave, making an excellent bass for the oboe family. It can be played at least as high as E above the staff, although it would hardly be used for its upper tones. Instances of its use are so rare that few orchestras are prepared to supply the instrument.

The heckelphone is a transposing instrument sounding an octave below the written notes.

》》《《

THE CLARINET

Fr., *clarinette;* It., *clarinetto;* Ger., *Klarinette*

THE clarinet is a cylindrical tube, with a bell expanding slightly more than that of the oboe. It is most often made of grenadilla wood, less expensive kinds of ebonite, or metal. The key work is nickel silver. The body is in five sections, called mouthpiece, barrel joint, top joint, lower joint, and bell.

The clarinet mouthpiece is usually made of ebonite or crystal. It is sometimes referred to as a "beak" mouthpiece on account of its shape.

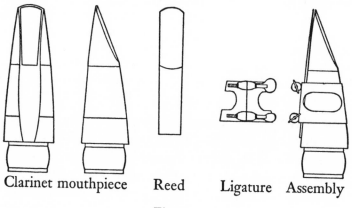

Clarinet mouthpiece   Reed   Ligature   Assembly

Fig. 50

The single cane reed is bound to the open side of the mouthpiece by means of a metal ligature with thumbscrews. Thus the flat side of the reed becomes part of the inner surface of the clarinet tube, and is in direct contact with the air column. The upper end of the reed is scraped very thin, and the orifice between it and the tip of the mouthpiece is carefully adjusted. A metal cap is placed over the reed when not in use.

In playing position, the reed is laid on the lower lip, which covers the lower teeth. The upper teeth rest on the bevel of the mouthpiece. Tone quality and volume are affected by the amount of reed within the mouth and the pressure of the lower lip on the reed. The tongue touches the tip of the reed with each articulation.

THE CLARINET FAMILY

The clarinet family is a large one. The list of its members, with approximate lengths and their transpositions, is as follows:

Instrument	Length in Inches	Actual Sound
(Sopranino) clarinet in A♭	14	minor sixth above written notes
(Sopranino) clarinet in E♭	19	minor third above written notes
(Sopranino) clarinet in D	20½	major second above written notes
(Soprano) clarinet in C	22¾	as written
(Soprano) clarinet in B♭	26¼	major second below written notes
(Soprano) clarinet in A	27½	minor third below written notes
Alto clarinet in E♭	38	major sixth below written notes
Basset horn (in F)	42½	perfect fifth below written notes
Bass clarinet in B♭	55	major ninth below written notes
Bass clarinet in A	55	octave and minor third below written notes
Contrabass clarinet in B♭	106	two octaves and major second below written notes

Of these, only four may be said to be regular members of the orchestra: the small E♭ clarinet, the pair of clarinets in B♭ and A, and the bass clarinet in B♭. The piccolo clarinet in A♭ is rarely seen even in bands. Parts written for D clarinet are most often played on the E♭. Many scores of the eighteenth and nineteenth centuries call for C clarinets, but today these parts are played on either the B♭ or the A clarinet. The alto clarinet is sometimes used to play basset horn parts, and it finds some employment in military and dance bands. The bass clarinet in A is virtually never seen except on paper, and the contrabass clarinet has yet to be adopted by composers. The alto and bass instruments are distinguished from the others by upturned bells, and bent metal pipes to which the mouthpieces are attached.

TRANSPOSITION

The clarinets furnish a complete object lesson in the evolution of transposing instruments. All of the instruments listed have the same fingering system, so that one who learns this system can play them all. In the act of playing any instrument there is automatic, instinctive translation of the printed note into the proper position of the fingers, and it would obviously be impractical to learn different fingerings for each of the pitches listed under the Clarinet Family. The player reads his part as though for C clarinet, and the instrument transposes according to its size. Since the C clarinet is now obsolete, a clarinet's notes are always different in pitch from those written.

In the discussion of fingering, registers, etc., the notes mentioned will be the notes as read, hence fingered, by the player. The normal, or standard, clarinet is the B♭ clarinet, corresponding to the flute and oboe, and exemplifying the ideal clarinet as preferred today. The A clarinet is somewhat less extensively used.

FINGERING SYSTEM

Referring to the elementary six-hole, six-finger scale described in Chapter Six, and used as a basis for studying the fingering of flute and oboe, we find that in the clarinet this scale starts on G instead of D, and gives the written notes shown in Fig. 51 (a).

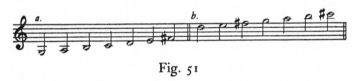

Fig. 51

The cylindrical tube of the clarinet produces only the odd-numbered harmonics, when overblown. The series shown at Fig. 51(b) represents the first notes available by overblowing from (a), at the twelfth above, leaving a large gap between the two series. This gap was filled by (1) boring a hole for the left thumb, giving G when open; (2) boring holes still higher on the tube, for G♯ and A, with keys operated by the left first finger; (3) utilizing the register key (provided for overblowing) to sound the B♭, this key being placed close to the G hole so that the thumb can depress the key and close the hole at the same

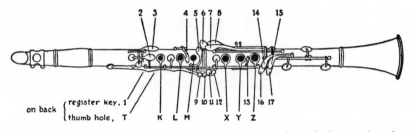

on back { register key, 1 / thumb hole, T   K L M   X Y Z

letters and numbers indicate keys to be depressed or holes to be closed

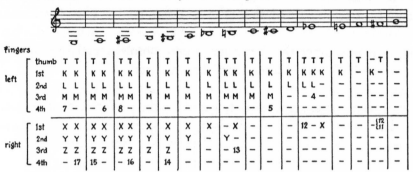

time; and (4) extending the downward range to E, with keys, so that the first overblown note is B♮. The last step involves the use of both fourth fingers. The right thumb supports the instrument.

The Boehm system and later improvements were applied with success to the clarinet, although some other systems are also in use. The Boehm clarinet has up to seven ring keys, and from seventeen to twenty-one other keys. Many alternate fingerings are provided, especially for duplicating the action of the fourth fingers.

Fig. 52. Fingering Chart for the Clarinet (Boehm System)   [*facing*]

It is to be noted that the thumb hole is kept closed, except for the so-called throat tones G, G♯, A, and B♭, and for one F♯ fingering; and that the register key, also called the speaker key, is depressed for all notes upward from the first overblown note, B♮.

Side keys 9 and 10 (right hand first finger) are used to trill B♭-C, and B♭-C♭, respectively.

Fingerings above F♯ are not standardized, except for A♮, and no attempt is made in the chart to list the many alternatives used by clarinetists. The practice is to discover by experimentation those finger combinations which produce the best results in terms of the individual player and the individual instrument.

REGISTERS

Fig. 53

THE CHALUMEAU

The low register of the clarinet is called the chalumeau register, from the name of one of its ancestors. The tone color in this part of the range has been called dark, menacing, and dramatic. There can be no doubt of its richness and individuality. It is unlike any other sound in the orchestra, and markedly different from other registers of the clarinet. It is often employed in effects of an atmospheric nature.

EX. 192. Respighi—*Fontane di Roma*p. 8, ed. Ricordi

Accompaniment figures of repeated notes and accented rhythmic patterns are of excellent effect in the chalumeau register.

EX. 193. Stravinsky—*Divertimento, Le Baiser de la Fée*

p. 18, ed. Boosey & Hawkes

The contrast between the low and high registers of the clarinet has suggested many passages in which first and second clarinets sound as two different instruments.

EX. 194. Mozart—*Symphony in Eb*, K. 543.   p. 45, ed. Philharmonia

THROAT TONES

As the upper part of the chalumeau register is approached, the sounding length of the tube is shortened and the characteristic tone quality is gradually lessened. The open tone G (thumb hole) has a sounding length of about 8¾ inches on the Bb clarinet, and the Bb a minor third higher sounds from a length just under 6 inches. Together with the G♯ and A, these are called throat tones. They are rather pale and less vibrant than other clarinet tones, but it is a mistake to regard them simply as inferior tones to be avoided. On the contrary, the throat tones should be recognized as a resource of the clarinet, to be employed appropriately. The slight awkwardness of fingering involving G♯ and A has been greatly overemphasized.

EX. 195. Debussy—*L'Après-midi d'un Faune*   p. 8, ed. Durand

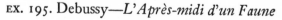

THE BREAK

The interval made up of the throat tones is often erroneously called the break. The break means more precisely the passage from B♭ to B♮, and vice versa, or, in other words, the point at which the highest fundamental tone, B♭, adjoins the lowest overblown note, B♮. Reference to the fingering chart will show that whereas B♭ is played with the entire tube open, B♮ requires the entire tube to be closed, with the exception of the vent hole opened by depressing the register key. It is true that this transition presents a difficulty of coördination for beginners, but it is made with perfect smoothness by good players.

EX. 196. Sibelius—*Symphony no. 3*   p. 40, ed. Kalmus

With permission of the original publisher, Robert Lienau, formerly Schlesinger, Berlin-Lichterfelde.

THE CLARINO REGISTER

The overblown notes from B♮ to the first C above the staff, inclusive, constitute the clarino register. Here the clarinet is bright, incisive, warm, and expressive.

EX. 197. Beethoven—*Symphony no. 7*   p. 75, ed. Kalmus

Above C, the high register tends to sound shrill and piercing in *forte*, and somewhat flutelike when played softly. A good tone quality is maintained up to high G, which may be taken as a safe top note for orchestral clarinet parts. Needless to say, the clarinetist exercises control over the different registers so that no lack of homogeneity is felt in widely traversing melodic lines like the following.

EX. 198. Stravinsky—*Symphony in Three Movements*

p. 30, ed. Associated Music Publishers

EXTREME NOTES

The clarinet can be played up to high C above the G just mentioned, but these extreme notes have little sonorous value. G♯ and A are occasionally found in scores, especially those of modern French composers, usually in tutti passages, or doubled by other instruments. Examples like the following are most exceptional.

EX. 199. Casella—*Puppazetti*   p. 48, ed. Philharmonia

Throughout its range, the clarinet has greater capabilities of dynamic variation than the other woodwind instruments. This is most remarkable in pianissimo. By subduing the reed's vibrations with the tongue, the tone can be reduced to virtual inaudibility. Sometimes the indication *subtone*, or *echo tone*, is given.

EX. 200. Berlioz—*Symphonie Fantastique*　　　　p. 117, ed. Eulenburg

USE OF THE A CLARINET

The A clarinet is not an auxiliary instrument like the piccolo or the English horn. It is paired with the B♭ clarinet for the position of normal or standard clarinet, although somewhat unequally. A clarinetist carries both as preparation for a playing engagement. He expects the music to be in part for B♭ and in part for A clarinet. Sometimes he is asked to make the change in the course of a movement, which he does by removing the mouthpiece from one instrument and connecting it to the other (to avoid playing with a dry reed).

Until recently, the reasons for using the A clarinet were three: (*a*) to simplify fingering in sharp keys by means of the added half tone transposition (B major would be written D major for A clarinet, C♯ or D♭ major for B♭ clarinet); (*b*) to give the less brilliant, slightly warmer tone of the longer instrument for certain expressive purposes; and (*c*) to gain the low C♯, sounding from the low E of the A clarinet.

These purposes now need to be further examined. In regard to (*a*), the assumption that some keys are easier to play in than others is misleading. The fact is that difficult passages may occur in C major, and easy ones may happen in F♯ major. In the chromatic harmony and shifting tonalities of the twentieth century, key signatures are unreliable indicators of fingering difficulties to be encountered. Furthermore, the perfection of mechanism and the enormous advance in playing technique have combined to minimize problems of execution.

As for (*b*), the difference in tone color between the A and B♭ clarinets is not striking. Indeed, it is often impossible to tell by the tone alone which of the two is being played. The size of the instrument is, however, unquestionably an aid to the performer in securing a desired tone quality.

And for (c), clarinet makers now supply B♭ clarinets having a low E♭ key (right hand fourth finger) to give the C♯. This addition has not been universally accepted. In order to sound this note the instrument has to be lengthened, and the question arises whether or not it remains a true B♭ clarinet. Writing for the A clarinet is the only sure way to obtain the low C♯.

As a matter of fact, the A clarinet has not fallen into disuse, despite a preference for the B♭ instrument and a tendency among clarinetists to play everything on the B♭, transposing A clarinet parts down a half tone. Sometimes that practice is reversed, the A clarinet being used to play the part written for B♭ clarinet to get a preferred fingering or a better tone on an important melody note. For example, the sound A♭, on the second space, would be written as throat tone B♭ for the B♭ clarinet, whereas on the A clarinet it would call for the full B♮, overblown from low E.

TRILLS AND TREMOLOS

All major and minor trills are good on the Boehm clarinet. Tremolos are of excellent effect, especially in the chalumeau, but should not be based on intervals wider than the major sixth in that register, or the perfect fourth above the break. Above the staff, the major third is a safer limit.

EX. 201. Kodály—*Psalmus Hungaricus*   p. 81, ed. Philharmonia

TONGUING

The clarinet staccato is much less pointed than that of the oboe, but it can be drier and sharper than the flute staccato. Fast passages of single-tonguing are better relieved by slurring two or three notes at appropriate places. Double- and triple-tonguing can be used as emergency expedients, as in the following instance where the clarinets are called upon to imitate the light triple-tonguing of the flutes.

EX. 202. Mendelssohn—*Italian Symphony*   p. 136, ed. Eulenburg

In variety of tongue attacks the clarinet is superior to the other reed instruments. The start of a tone can be controlled to give all gradations, from an explosive sforzando to a soft attack something like that of louré bowing in the strings.

EX. 203. Debussy—*Première Rhapsodie*   p. 7, ed. Durand

VIRTUOSITY

The clarinet is a close second to the flute in agility. Its tone quality, as well as its technical capacities, make it admirably suited for all kinds of rapid scales, arpeggios, and figuration calling for ease in mobility, and fluidity. Wide legato skips between registers are more easily accomplished when in an upward direction.

EX. 204. Schoenberg—*Pierrot Lunaire*   p. 13, ed. Universal

The following cadenza for two clarinets exhibits the flowing quality and flexibility of the clarinet legato.

EX. 205. Ravel—*Rapsodie Espagnole*   p. 8, ed. Durand

ORCHESTRAL USES

Besides the important melodic functions performed by clarinets, either as solo instruments or doubling other melodic voices, the harmonic and coloristic possibilities of the clarinet section are very numerous, as can be seen in almost any orchestral score. The unobtrusive nature of the clarinet's tone makes it extremely useful for doubling and for combination with practically all instruments. Clarinet accompaniment figures are common and often ingeniously arranged to contribute life and vibration to the background texture. The following is a good example of this use of clarinets, and should be examined in the full score.

EX. 206. Stravinsky—*Pétrouchka*   p. 37, ed. Russe

The evocative color of the chalumeau tones, combined with harp and solo violin, create a fascinating atmosphere in the opening measures

of Alban Berg's *Violin Concerto*. The clarinets are written at their actual pitch in the score, a practice adopted by a few modern composers, the parts being printed with the necessary transpositions. A footnote in the score explains that the first clarinet part is notated for B♭ clarinet, the second for A.

EX. 207. Berg—*Violin Concerto*
p. 3, ed. Universal

THE BASS CLARINET

Fr., *clarinette basse;* It., *clarinetto basso, clarone;* Ger., *Bassklarinette*

Although the bass clarinet in A exists, and some composers have called for it in their scores, few musicians have ever seen the instrument. Parts for it are practically always played on the bass clarinet in B♭, the player transposing the notes down a half tone. In most cases, the

composer's object in writing for the A instrument is to obtain the low
C♯, the actual pitch of the low E of the bass clarinet in A. This sound
is now available, however, through the addition of the low E♭ key
(right-hand fourth finger) to the B♭ bass clarinet. Because of this extension the length of the instrument is the same as that of the bass
clarinet in A. Since the bass clarinet is pitched an octave below the
ordinary clarinet, its lowest tone sounds a half tone above the open
C-string of the 'cello.

Bass clarinets have been made with a downward range to D, sounding C, and modern Russian composers give evidence in their scores of
the existence of bass clarinets descending to C, sounding B♭, the range
given by Rimsky-Korsakoff. A bass clarinet constructed by Rosario
Mazzeo, of the Boston Symphony Orchestra, provides two further
semitones, down to B♭, sounding A♭. At the present time, however, one
cannot with certainty count on having sounds lower than C♯ on the
bass clarinet.

The mechanism duplicates that of the standard Boehm clarinet, except that two register keys are provided. The throat tones may be
overblown at the twelfth, giving fuller tones from high D to F, but
few players take advantage of this, preferring to keep to the fingering
habits of the smaller clarinet. External features of the bass clarinet are
the upturned bell and the curved mouthpipe, both of nickel silver,
and the supporting neck-cord attached to two strap-rings.

NOTATION

There are two systems of notation in common use, called French
and German, terms that may have possessed logic when they originated. Subsequently both systems have been employed by French
and German composers interchangeably, but the names persist.

In the French system, the part is written throughout in the treble
clef, exactly as though for the ordinary B♭ clarinet, the sounds being a
major ninth lower.

In the German system, the bass is used as the normal clef, the treble
clef being employed only when the part lies so high that keeping to
the bass clef would require several leger lines. The sounds are a major
second lower than written, in either clef.

Fig. 54

The French system seems the more logical from the standpoint of fingering habits, whereas the German notation has the advantage of appearing more nearly where it sounds. Bass clarinetists, as a group, do not show a preference for either way. If the part begins with notes in the treble clef, ambiguity may exist as to which notation is to be followed. A footnote is sometimes given to make this clear, *e.g.*, "sounding a major ninth (or major second) lower."

TONE QUALITIES

The low tones are rich in their odd-numbered partials, and resultant major triads are often plainly audible when the instrument is playing alone. The bass clarinet makes an excellent bass for the woodwind group, with or without doubling by bassoons. Its pianissimo in the low register can be very much softer than that of the bassoons, and is a valued resource.

In the following expressive solo passage the bass clarinet is accompanied very lightly by flutes, with the harp placed above them. The written C♯ cannot be reached by most instruments.

EX. 208. Shostakovich—*Symphony no. 7*　　　　　p. 99, ed. Leeds

The low register is also effective for a kind of shadowy fleetness
characteristic of the clarinet family.

EX. 209. Milhaud—*Symphony no. 2*   p. 40, ed. Heugel

(German notation)

Reproduced by permission of Heugel et Cie., Paris, owners of the copyright.

It is important to form a mental picture of the sound of the clarino
register of the bass clarinet as compared to notes of the same pitch
played on the ordinary B♭ clarinet. There is obviously no way to do
this without actually listening to the two instruments, but some knowledge of what is involved in the way of fingering, overblowing, etc.,
helps the listener to know what to listen for, and to identify what he
hears. In this register the bass clarinet is paler and somewhat less incisive than its smaller prototype.

EX. 210. Strauss—*Ein Heldenleben*   p. 7, ed. Eulenburg

(French notation)

With the permission of the publisher F. E. C. Leuckart, Muenchen, Leipzig. Copyright 1899, renewed
1927, by F. E. C. Leuckart.

The bass clarinet is hardly less capable than the other clarinets of
a high degree of agility, despite the comparative cumbersomeness of
its mechanism, due to its size. The following example is the statement
of a fugue subject played alone by the bass clarinet, except for the sole
accompaniment of a snare drum. The high F is as high as it is advisable
to write for the bass clarinet.

EX. 211. W. Schuman—*Symphony no. 3*   p. 55, ed. G. Schirmer

(French notation)

THE CLARINETS IN Eb AND D

The small clarinets in Eb and D stand in the same pitch relationship to each other as the Bb and A clarinets. The D clarinet is little used. It is possible that in some instances the composer's choice of the D clarinet was motivated by considerations of fingering, but in any case parts for the D are nearly always played on the Eb clarinet, reading the notes a half tone lower.

Although the Eb clarinet has the same mechanism as the Bb, it is more difficult to play well, and in tune, especially if the performer is asked to change quickly to the smaller instrument from the larger. The small reed and the rather cramped finger position need time for adjustment. Usually one member of the clarinet section makes a specialty of playing the Eb clarinet.

The need for more strength in the high-pitched woodwind is often felt in the large symphony orchestra, and this the small clarinet can supply. It has a penetrating tone, an incisive staccato, brilliance and agility. It is used to reinforce violins and flutes, as well as the upper tones of the other clarinets; hence the most used part of its range is the high register. The high G, sounding Bb, can be considered a safe upper limit, although G♯ and A are written for the E♭ clarinet more frequently than for the B♭ clarinet.

The following is a characteristic E♭ clarinet passage.

EX. 212. Ravel—*Daphnis et Chloé*   p. 263, ed. Durand

The entire range is playable, down to the low E. The tone of the two lower octaves lacks the warmth and expressive quality of the B♭ clarinet, and the instrument has often been used here for purposes of parody and imitation. As in the case of the piccolo, however, it should be said again that auxiliary instruments bring new colors in their "weak" registers, additional resources needing only to be employed in the right way.

Below is a well-known solo for D clarinet.

EX. 213. Strauss—*Till Eulenspiegel*   p. 98, ed. Philharmonia

THE BASSET HORN

The basset horn may be described as a clarinet with extension to low C, pitched to sound a perfect fifth lower than written, *i.e.*, in F. Its lowest sound is therefore F, a fourth above the 'cello C-string. Its bore is narrower than that of the alto and bass clarinets, sometimes used as substitutes, and this gives the instrument a distinctive timbre.

In early forms of the basset horn, the tube made a sort of S-turn inside a box, as a means of gaining length of air column without lengthening the instrument. This device is not found in modern basset horns.

At present, the significance of the basset horn derives from a few notable instances of its use. Mozart wrote important basset horn parts in the operas, especially *Die Entführung* and *Die Zauberflöte;* also in the *Requiem* and in the *Serenade*, K. 361. Beethoven gave it a prominent solo in *Prometheus*. It has been revived by Strauss in the operas *Elektra* and *Die Frau ohne Schatten.*

Strauss writes the basset horn parts generally in the treble clef, even when it necessitates the leger lines for low C. Sometimes, however, the bass clef is used, and on these occasions the part is written to sound a perfect fourth higher. This is a practice that will later be seen in writing for the horn. The procedure is shown in the following example.

EX. 214. Strauss—*Elektra*   p. 252, ed. Boosey & Hawkes

Copyright 1916 by Adolf Furstner, assigned 1943 to Boosey & Hawkes, Ltd. Used by permission. (For Portugal, Italy, Germany, Danzig, USSR as of 1935: Furstner, Ltd., London.)

THE CONTRABASS CLARINET

Large clarinets have been constructed to sound in the octave below the bass clarinet, in E♭ and in B♭. The latter instrument is made of metal and folded upon itself after the manner of a contrabassoon. It has great dynamic variety, rich tone quality, and an astonishing pitch range, sounding from the D just above 16-foot C to the D just above middle C. The contrabass clarinet is as yet too great a rarity to be considered an available resource in symphonic composition.

LARGE CLARINET SECTIONS

The extent to which composers have expanded the group of clarinets in the large orchestras of the early twentieth century is shown by the following listing of the clarinets employed in some works.

Mahler—*Symphony no. 8*
    2 E♭ clarinets
    3 clarinets in B♭ and A
    1 bass clarinet

Strauss—*Elektra*
    1 E♭ clarinet
    4 clarinets in B♭ and A
    2 basset horns
    1 bass clarinet

Schoenberg—*Gurrelieder*
    2 E♭ clarinets
    3 clarinets in B♭ and A
    2 bass clarinets

Stravinsky—*Le Sacre du Printemps*
    1 D (E♭) clarinet
    3 clarinets in B♭ and A
    2 bass clarinets

THE SAXOPHONE

Fr., *saxophone;* It., *saxofono, sassofono;* Ger., *Saxophon*

Invented about 1840 by Adolphe Sax, the saxophone is classified as a woodwind instrument despite the fact that it is made entirely of brass. This is because its tones are produced with a mouthpiece and reed, almost exactly like those of a clarinet. It is commonly played by clarinetists without further training. The upturned bell of the saxophone is reminiscent of the bass clarinet, but its tube is widely conical, and the tone holes, increasing to very large size toward the lower end of the tube, present a contrast to the appearance of the clarinet family.

The tone holes have large brass padded key-covers, operated by rod-axles from keys which are arranged in two groups convenient for the hands. A cord around the neck supports the instrument when playing. The fingering is very much like that of the oboe, so that it need not be described in detail. Registers are as shown in the following figure. The scale is completely chromatic.

Fig. 55

Saxophones are made in a large variety of sizes and keys. All are written for in the treble clef, as in Fig. 55, their different sizes resulting in numerous transpositions for the sounds produced. The most common are the E♭ alto (sounding a major sixth lower), and the B♭ tenor (sounding a major ninth lower). Next to these in frequency of use are the E♭ baritone (sounding an octave and major sixth lower), and the B♭ soprano (sounding a major second lower). The soprano saxophone is usually made in straight form, without the upturned bell. The transpositions are shown in notation below.

Fig. 56

A large bass saxophone in B♭ is sometimes played; also soprano and tenor in C, and others in F. Ravel writes, in *Bolero*, for B♭ soprano and B♭ tenor, and also for a small sopranino in F (sounding a fourth up). The part for the latter, however, can perfectly well be taken over by the less rare B♭ soprano, since it does not go too high.

The saxophone possesses the agility of the clarinet, except in the matter of fast tonguing, which is hindered by a slightly slower response in the embouchure.

Modern developments in saxophone playing have completely changed the nature and sound of the instrument from what it was when melodies were assigned to it by Bizet and other European composers before 1920. From a pure, steady tone, partaking of both horn and reed instrument qualities, its tone has become, coincident with its ascendancy in the field of popular dance music, tremulous, oversweet, sentimental; and it is almost invariably played out of tune. The saxophone as played today cannot be used successfully in instrumental combinations, and it is perhaps for this reason that it did not, as seemed likely twenty-five years ago, become a member of the symphony orchestra.

The numerous instances of the use of the saxophone in symphonic music have been chiefly as a special instrument introduced to play a featured solo (see Moussorgsky-Ravel—*Tableaux d'une Exposition*). In the following example, the soprano saxophone is employed to impart a flavor of the jazz style of the 1920's.

EX. 215. Copland—*Concerto for Pianoforte and Orchestra*

p. 36, ed. Cos Cob Press

(pizzicato accompaniment omitted)

The following legato, expressive solo passage for alto saxophone represents a rather unusual use of this instrument in a work of religious character.

EX. 216. Britten—*Sinfonia da Requiem; Dies Irae*

p. 38, ed. Boosey & Hawkes

CHAPTER TEN

THE BASSOON

Fr., basson; It., *fagotto;* Ger. *Fagott*

THE bassoon is picturesque in appearance as well as in sound. Its air column is about 9 feet 2 inches long, sounding the B♭ just below the open 'cello C-string, and the instrument is rendered manageable by being folded in two, so to speak. The bassoon is usually made of maple, in four sections—the bell joint, the bass (or long) joint, the butt, and the wing (or tenor) joint. The butt and the wing joint are lined with rubber, against moisture. A double reed ½ inch wide, quite like a larger English horn reed, is fitted onto a gracefully curved metal mouthpipe called the crook, or bocal, and this fits into the top end of the wing joint. A neck-cord, attached to a ring at the top of the butt, provides support so that the hands are free. Some bassoonists use a hand rest, fixed to the butt and bracing against the palm of the right hand.

The right hand holds the butt close to the player's right hip, the left hand grasping the bass and wing joints together. In this position, the thumb keys are on the side toward the player (called the back), and the fingers find their positions on the front side, out of sight of the player. Since the tube makes a sharp U-turn inside the butt, the left hand controls at once the lowest notes, on the bass joint, and the highest notes, on the wing joint.

The bore is conical, from ⅛ inch at the small end of the crook, to about 1½ inches at the bell. The pitch of the bassoon can be altered only by changing the position of the reed on the end of the crook. It is not a transposing instrument.

The wing itself is a device for adding thickness to the wall of the tube, in order that tone holes, bored on a slant, may be spaced properly for pitch on the inside, yet close enough together on the outside for the fingers to reach (Fig. 57).

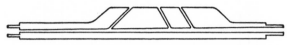

Fig. 57. Cross Section of Bassoon Wing

Some holes in the butt are also bored slantwise. This peculiarity and the situation resulting from the folding of the tube create an external aspect of confusion and complexity in the fingering system.

FINGERING SYSTEM

Bassoons in use at the present time are of two main types, the French (*Buffet*), or the German (*Heckel*). Most German bassoons can be identified in the concert hall by the white ivory ring at the top end of the bell joint. Some, however, do not possess this distinguishing feature.

Modern improvements, such as the Boehm principles that revolutionized the mechanisms of other woodwind instruments, have not been successfully incorporated into the bassoon. It seems that practically all devices for improving the instrument's purity of intonation and capabilities of execution inevitably destroy just those characteristics of tone quality and delivery which go to make up the cherished individuality of the bassoon. Some key work was indispensable in order to cover the extraordinarily wide range, and modern bassoons are equipped with seventeen to twenty-two keys.

The fundamental six-finger-hole series gives a scale just an octave below the written clarinet scale, starting on G. In the butt are G, A, B♮, covered by right third, second, and first fingers—the G with the aid of a key, as the hole is beyond reach. On the wing are C, D, and E (left third, second, and first fingers), and the open note, F♮.

The downward extension of this series uses the rest of the butt (F right fourth finger, E right thumb), and the bass and bell joints. The left thumb controls a nest of four keys (D, C, B, and B♭), as well as four other keys on the wing joint that lie within its reach.

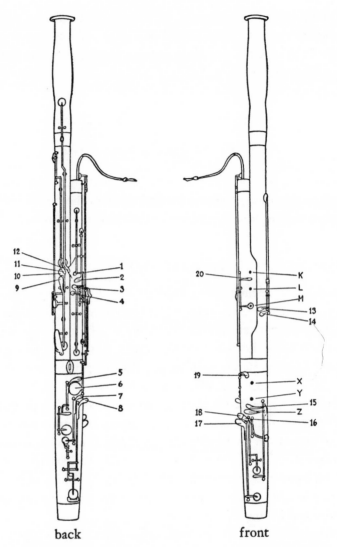

back   front

Fig. 58. Fingering Chart for the Bassoon (Heckel System)

There are three speaker keys and several chromatic keys, and in the crook there is a tiny hole called the pinhole, controlled by the crook-key. This hole is a vent, which the crook-key automatically closes when the right thumb depresses the key for low E. Overblowing is accomplished by using the half hole (for F♯ and G), speaker keys, and venting.

Some differences exist between the fingering systems of French and German bassoons, such as the slightly different arrangement of the *letters and numbers indicate keys to be depressed or holes to be closed*

	fingers														
left	thumb	{12/4	{11/4	{10/4	{10/4	{9/4	{9/4	4	4	4	4	4	4	4	4
	1st	K	K	K	K	K	K	K	K	K	K	K	K	K	K
	2nd	L	L	L	L	L	L	L	L	L	L	L	L	L	L
	3rd	M	M	M	M	M	M	M	M	M	M	M	M	M	M
	4th	–	–	–	14	–	13	–	–	–	–	–	–	–	–
right	thumb	6	6	6	6	6	6	6	–	–	–	–	–	5	–
	1st	X	X	X	X	X	X	X	X	X	X	X	X	X	X
	2nd	Y	Y	Y	Y	Y	Y	Y	Y	Y	Y	Y	Y	Y	–
	3rd	Z	Z	Z	Z	Z	Z	Z	Z	Z	Z	Z	–	–	–
	4th	18	18	18	18	18	18	18	18	16	–	17	–	–	–

left	thumb	4	{4 3/9	4	4	4	4	4	4	–	–	–	–	–	{1 3	–
	1st	K	K	K	K	K	–	Ǩ	Ǩ	K	K	K	K	K	K	K
	2nd	L	L	L	–	–	–	L	L	L	L	L	L	L	L	L
	3rd	M	M	–	M	–	–	M	M	M	M	M	M	M	M	–
	4th	–	–	–	–	–	–	–	–	–	–	–	–	–	–	–
right	thumb	–	–	–	–	–	–	–	–	–	–	5	–	–	–	–
	1st	–	–	–	–	–	–	X	X	X	X	X	X	–	–	–
	2nd	–	–	–	–	–	–	Y	Y	Y	Y	Y	–	–	–	–
	3rd	–	–	–	–	–	–	Z	Z	Z	–	–	–	–	–	–
	4th	–	–	–	–	–	–	16	–	17	–	–	–	–	–	–

Ǩ = half-hole

left	thumb	–	–	–	–	–	–	{2 3	{2 3	1	1	1	1	3	3
	1st	K	K	K	K	Ǩ	K	K	K	K	K	K	–	Ǩ	Ǩ
	2nd	L	–	–	–	L	L	L	L	L	–	–	L	L	L
	3rd	–	M	M	M	M	M	M	M	–	M	M	M	M	M
	4th	–	13	13	13	13	13	13	13	13	13	13	13	13	13
right	thumb	–	–	–	5	–	–	–	–	5	5	5	5	–	6
	1st	X	X	X	X	X	–	–	X	X	X	X	–	19	–
	2nd	Y	Y	Y	Y	–	–	–	Y	Y	Y	–	–	–	Y
	3rd	Z	Z	–	–	–	Z	Z	–	–	–	Z	Z	–	15
	4th	–	–	–	–	18	–	–	18	18	18	17	17	17	–

Fig. 58 (*Continued*)

left-hand thumb keys, and the position of other keys (low Eb on the French bassoon is for the left thumb instead of the right fourth finger), but since the German type is much more commonly used at the present time, the chart of fingerings is given for the Heckel bassoon.

The four left-hand thumb keys for the lowest notes are arranged so that pressing key 12 also closes 11, 10, and 9; pressing key 11 also closes 10 and 9; and pressing 10 also closes 9.

Special trill keys are 8 (G-A♭), 15 (A-B♭), 19 (C-D♭), and 20 (F-G♭).

The half hole is used for venting, but the half closing has to be done by the finger alone, without the help of a half-hole key like that on the oboe. Fork fingering is normally used for middle E♭.

For the high notes, there are various fingerings other than those given in the chart. Some instruments have high D and E keys, in addition to the high A (key 2) and C (key 1), on the wing joint. Variations in the bore, and in the size of the tone holes, affect pitch, and individual players find combinations of vents to correct this.

Many awkward situations confront the performer on the bassoon, and these he overcomes with more or less deceptive skill. An illustration is furnished in the following apparently simple phrase.

EX. 217. Tchaikovsky—*Ouverture Solennelle, 1812*   p. 45, ed. Kalmus

Reference to the fingering chart will show that moving from A♭ to E♭ requires the coördinated movement of both thumbs and both fourth fingers, the right fourth finger having to move off key 17 onto key 18. All must be accomplished without the slightest break, because the two tones are slurred.

REGISTERS

Fig. 59

It is hard to say whether the complex fingerings in the upper register affect the pitch of the fundamentals chosen, or that of the harmonics produced. For the bassoonist, as for the players of other woodwind instruments, the production of high notes is a matter of experimentation to find the most workable combination of open and closed holes. The solution may vary with the instrument as well as with the player.

There is no dividing line of contrast to be drawn between the registers of the bassoon, as far as sound is concerned. Low merges into medium and medium into high.

The lowest fifth or sixth of the range is sonorous and vibrant, with a little roughness. It is rich in audible overtones. It is not easy to attack softly, and it is incapable of anything like the pianissimo of the bass clarinet. Sometimes the instrument is muted by a handkerchief in the bell in an effort to reduce the tone. The B♭ gives a softer *piano* than the B♮.

EX. 218. Milhaud—*Second Symphonic Suite*   p. 46, ed. Durand

Low A for the bassoon may be seen in the scores of Wagner and Mahler. This note can be played by replacing the bell joint with a longer one made for the purpose. Modern bassoons extending to low A can be purchased, but the extra semitone cannot be considered within the normal range of the instrument.

The middle register, sometimes called the baritone register, includes the notes of the fundamental six-hole scale, on the smaller half of the butt and the wing joint. Here the tone is smoother and more subdued in expressive character than in the lower part of the range. It is easily covered or absorbed if too thickly accompanied.

EX. 219. Moussorgsky-Ravel—*Tableaux d'une Exposition*

p. 23, ed. Boosey & Hawkes

Permission granted by Durand et Cie., Paris, copyright owners; Elkan-Vogel, Philadelphia, Pa., agents.

The two bottom octaves are shown to advantage in the following example, for solo bassoon, in three-part melodic writing with solo violin and oboe. The passage should be studied in the full score.

EX. 220. Hindemith—*Concerto for Orchestra*   p. 8, ed. Schott

Copyright 1925 by B. Schott's Soehne; renewed 1952 by Paul Hindemith. Used by permission.

The gentlest and most delicate part of the bassoon's range is the upper middle register, from F♯ to D, the first overblown notes. These harmonics have the least intensity and carrying power, and are softly expressive.

EX. 221. Brahms—*Symphony no. 3*   p. 50, ed. Kalmus

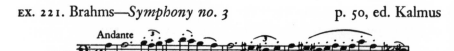

Solo passages in louder nuances passing through this register must be lightly accompanied. The following phrase sounds over soft staccato chords for three trombones, in their low register.

EX. 222. Stravinsky—*Symphony in C*   p. 55, ed. Schott

Ascending the high register from D up to about C, the tone of the bassoon becomes more tense and penetrating, although it can be well modulated up to A or B♭.

EX. 223. Beethoven—*Symphony no. 9*   p. 136, ed. Philharmonia

The extreme high register extends to E.

EX. 224. Wagner—*Tannhäuser: Overture*   p. 48, ed. Kalmus

Approached by skip, this note is hazardous and uncommon. In this instance it is somewhat safer because of unison doubling by violas and 'cellos, but the highest notes are always better approached by step. High F has been written, by Alban Berg in the opera *Lulu,* and still higher sounds can be forced from the bassoon. The smaller bore of the French bassoons favors the production of these upper notes. However, such extreme tones are strained and pinched, and unreliable.

The following melody employs the high register effectively up to C♯, the bassoons being doubled at the unison by the bass clarinet. The composer acknowledges the difficulty of its performance by cueing in the part for alto saxophone and two clarinets, explaining in a footnote that these instruments are to play only in case the "purposely exposed" passage cannot be played by the bass clarinet and the two bassoons.

EX. 225. Berg—*Violin Concerto*　　　　　　p. 61, ed. Universal

It is to be noted that the tenor clef is used for high notes. The treble clef is rarely used.

The attempt will not be made here to describe the difference in sound of these melodies as played on French or German instruments. It is an interesting fact that, although their tone qualities are indisputably very different, both are accepted as sounding like bassoons. Mechanical considerations aside, the choice of one or the other type is dependent on personal taste. A performer, through training and experience, develops an ideal of tone toward which he strives, and he chooses the instrument with which he can best approach that ideal. French and German bassoons are both widely used, and one sometimes sees them side by side in the same orchestra.

EMBOUCHURE

Like the oboist, the bassoon player fashions his own reeds. The double reed and the technique of tone production are similar in both instruments, qualified, of course, by the fact that the bassoon reed is larger and heavier. The bassoonist does not have the oboist's problem of holding back the breath; in fact, the low notes require much breath, especially for loud and long tones. As in all wind instruments, slurs over wide intervals are good ascending and risky descending.

TONGUING

Tonguing is like that of the oboe, but a little less light and active. The bassoon staccato is especially effective and examples are numerous.

EX. 226. Beethoven—*Symphony no. 4*   p. 7, ed. Kalmus

Passages like that in Ex. 226, if long continued, present breathing problems. A short, quick breath can be taken at almost any point, but the process is likely to disturb the rhythm of the staccato. It is better to provide a musical break, or else to arrange the two bassoons in some such manner as the following.

EX. 227. Prokofieff—*Symphony no. 5*   p. 52, ed. Leeds

Single-tonguing can be executed with remarkable rapidity, although if unrelieved by slurs or rests the tongue will become fatigued. Double-tonguing, and even triple-tonguing, can be employed as a last resort.

It is doubtful if the passage shown in Ex. 228, occurring in an orchestral tutti, is ever accomplished by single tonguing, without slurring or omitting some notes.

EX. 228. Mozart—*Così Fan Tutte*p. 431, ed. Broude Bros.

TRILLS AND TREMOLOS

A tabulation of the relative merits of all bassoon trills would be impractical and of limited usefulness. Each trill has its own peculiarity as to mechanical feasibility and effect in sound. Short of consultation with a good player, the best approach to the subject is to attempt as far as possible a diagnosis of each situation by study of the fingering chart, remembering that it cannot take into account special trill keys that may exist on individual instruments.

The best trills are those made by the up and down movement of a single finger (Fig. 60a); those requiring two fingers are not as easy (*b*). The more fingers in motion, the more difficult the trill, especially if some are raised while others go down (*c*). It is impossible to trill if the fourth finger is required to move back and forth between two keys (*d*), or if both notes are played with the left thumb (*e*).

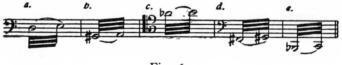

Fig. 60

The same observations apply to tremolos. Also, they should not cover an interval wider than a fourth.

Besides serving as the natural bass of the woodwind section, with or without bass clarinet, the bassoons perform an everyday function of doubling the bass part of the strings, either at the octave or unison. They not only reinforce the double-bass and 'cello tone, but give point and clarity to staccato and rhythmic figures, without noticeably affecting the string tone quality.

Inner harmonic and contrapuntal voices are likewise often strengthened or taken over by bassoons. In the following example, the two bassoons play the two inside parts in a four-part texture, blending perfectly with the string octaves.

EX. 229. Brahms—*Piano Concerto in D, op. 15*   p. 76, ed. Eulenburg

The bassoon merges unobtrusively with other woodwinds and horns in all kinds of accompaniment figures. Melodic doubling is especially well suited to it. Composers of the classical period were fond of placing the bassoon in the octave below a first violin melody.

EX. 230. Haydn—*Symphony in G (Paukenschlag)*   p. 38, ed. Kalmus

An extraordinary effect of mixed tone colors is created by Berlioz with the unison of four high bassoons, English horn, and horn (Ex. 231). In the concert hall one is impressed by the fact that the English horn, far from being lost in this combination, is distinctly heard as an ingredient in the composite timbre.

EX. 231. Berlioz—*Roméo et Juliette*   p. 255, ed. Eulenburg

The following solo passage for three bassoons shows to advantage their capacity for music in neat, rhythmic style, combining staccato and slurred notes.

EX. 232. Bartók—*Concerto for Orchestra*   p. 37, ed. Boosey & Hawkes

THE CONTRABASSOON

Fr., *contrebasson;* It., *contrafagotto;* Ger. *Kontrafagott*

The only auxiliary instrument of the bassoon family is the contrabassoon, also called double-bassoon, an instrument with a vibrating air column 18 feet 4 inches long. It duplicates the technique and range of the bassoon an octave lower, reaching the B♭ a whole tone below the lowest pitch of the five-string double-bass. Strauss has written a half tone still lower, and extensions for the low A are made, although rarely seen.

This huge instrument, as designed by Heckel, is folded so that there are four parallel wooden tubes, connected by the butt and two U-joints, and terminating in a brass bell pointing downwards. Other styles exist, with the bell pointing up in the air, and some French contrabassoons were made entirely of brass. The weight is supported by a peg to the floor.

Despite some notable exceptions, *e.g.*, Debussy—*Iberia*, and Wagner—*Parsifal*, the contrabassoon is properly written as a transposing instrument, sounding an octave lower, like the double-bass. In this way a bassoonist can play the larger instrument, using the accustomed fingering for the written notes.

For playing works requiring no notes below C, the extension pipe and bell may be removed, considerably lightening the instrument.

LOW REGISTER

The tone of the contrabassoon is a little rougher than that of the bassoon, and in the low register the buzzing sound of the slow vibrations is often audible. The lower octave is its most useful range. There was real need of a deep and heavy bass for the woodwind, more than could be supplied by bassoons and bass clarinet, to balance the modern string and brass sections, and in recent times the contrabassoon has become established as a standard member of the orchestra. In octaves with the bassoons, it makes a full, sonorous, woodwind foundation in soft or loud nuances. It is often used to reinforce and give point to the double-bass part, and it may also serve as a deep bass for brass groupings. The low tones require much breath, and the part should contain frequent rests.

HIGH REGISTER

The quality of the upper tones varies with the player, but in any case they are the weak part of the contrabassoon, from the first overblown note, F♯, upwards. The F above the staff is a wise limit for high notes, although Mahler takes the contrabassoon to the A beyond, and Ravel asks for B♭, in *Ma Mère L'Oye*. These notes can be played, but are of poor quality compared to the same pitches on the ordinary bassoon. In the doubling of double-basses the contrabassoon is often carried higher than it would be taken alone.

AGILITY

Theoretically, anything playable on the bassoon is playable on the contrabassoon, but the slow vibrations and inertia of the large instrument prevent anything approaching nimbleness or easy agility. A certain clumsy impression is inevitable. It may be covered by doubling.

EX. 233. Ravel—*La Valse*   p. 51, ed. Durand

Permission granted by Durand et Cie., Paris, copyright owners; Elkan-Vogel, Philadelphia, Pa., agents.

STACCATO

The staccato is dry and heavy. Fast repeated tonguing is difficult because of the slow response of the air column. The following example is taken from a general tutti of a rather noisy character, not too fast for the tongue, and in characteristic style for the contrabassoon.

EX. 234. Strauss—*Till Eulenspiegel*   p. 90, ed. Philharmonia

Reprinted with the permission of the copyright owners C. F. Peters Corporation, New York.

SOLO USE

The contrabassoon has proved to be a solo instrument of novel effect, for purposes of characterization and descriptive suggestion, but also in

phrases of purely musical intent. The next example, from a typical
Mahler *Ländler*, is especially interesting for the coloristic touches, as
horn and bassoon unison, different dynamic markings, subtle interruption in the bassoon part, open strings for the 'cellos, and the harmonies
created by the double pedal point.

EX. 235. Mahler—*Symphony no. 9*   p. 104, ed. Boosey & Hawkes

The following long pianissimo legato melody sounds an octave below the unison of two Wagner tubas and a contrabass tuba. The brass instruments are muted.

EX. 236. Strauss—*Elektra*   p. 122, ed. Boosey & Hawkes

THE SARRUSOPHONE

Some French composers, dissatisfied with the contrabassoon as they knew it, preferred in its place an instrument called the sarrusophone. The family of sarrusophones, used in European military bands, is a large one, comprising nine members, from the sopranino in high E♭ to the contrabass in B♭. The contrabass in C is the only sarrusophone ever used in the orchestra, and parts designated for it are now played on the contrabassoon. This is partly because of great improvements in the contrabassoon, and partly because the tone of the sarrusophone is more suitable for playing out-of-doors than in a concert room.

The sarrusophone is entirely of brass, with large tone holes and hole covers similar to those of the saxophone, and it is played with a double reed like a bassoon reed. It has a wide conical bore. The contrabass is folded after the manner of the contrabassoon, except that its flaring bell points straight upwards. The keys are arranged in two groups convenient for the fingers. The fingering system resembles that of the flute, oboe, and saxophone.

CHAPTER ELEVEN

BRASS INSTRUMENTS

THE student of orchestration is faced with a difficult situation in attempting to form a mental image of the sound of music written for brass instruments. The absence of standardization in the types of brass instruments leaves him on far more insecure ground than in the case of woodwinds. Not only do the types themselves show important differences in different countries, but instruments other than those designated in the score may be regularly used by custom. Furthermore, the student listening to a performance of one of the great works of symphonic literature, let us say Beethoven's Ninth Symphony, must continually remind himself that the sound of the brass, especially, does not truly represent the sound as conceived by the composer.

Three principal objectives are necessary for the study of brass in orchestration. First, the student should learn all he can about the basic principles of construction and playing technique common to all brass instruments. Then, he should proceed with the examination of the types of instruments that have been, or might be, used to play the parts he sees in scores. This includes natural horns and trumpets and other obsolete instruments, understanding of which is indispensable to an understanding of the orchestration by composers of the classical period, as well as of later periods. Finally, it is of great importance that he keep abreast of his own time by seeking all available information about contemporary practices in orchestral brass playing.

In a modern symphony orchestra the brass section consists of four subdivisions—horns, trumpets, trombones, and tubas. Auxiliary instruments do not exist in the same family relationships to these four groups as were observed in the woodwind section. The horns (French horns) are always written today as horns in F, although in practice B♭ horns or double horns in F and B♭ may be used to play the parts. Trumpets are either B♭ or C trumpets, the D trumpet and the bass trumpet appearing rarely. Cornets can hardly be considered members of the trumpet family. Trombones are regularly tenor trombones, except that one of them may be a bass, or a combination tenor-bass instrument. The tuba is a bass tuba, generally speaking, the tenor tuba (euphonium) being only occasionally employed. The Wagner tubas are special instruments, more like horns than tubas.

The average brass section in a score employing woodwind by threes is as follows:

> 4 horns
> 3 (or 2) trumpets
> 3 trombones
> 1 tuba

This will be found convenient to adopt as a standard, to which may be related the numerous variations in the make-up of the brass section. Personal taste and the character of the particular composition are the chief deciding factors in the adoption of variants by the composer. The variants range from the classical convention of two horns and two trumpets to the expanded forces called for in scores of the late nineteenth and early twentieth centuries.

The following are illustrative examples of differently constituted brass:

> Berlioz—*Symphonie Fantastique*
> 4 horns
> 2 cornets
> 2 trumpets
> 3 trombones
> 2 bass tubas

Holst—*The Planets*
6 horns
4 trumpets
3 trombones
1 tenor tuba
1 bass tuba

Wagner—*Die Götterdämmerung*
8 horns
4 Wagner tubas
3 trumpets
1 bass trumpet
3 trombones
1 contrabass trombone
1 contrabass tuba

Schoenberg—*Gurrelieder*
10 horns
4 Wagner tubas
6 trumpets
1 bass trumpet
1 alto trombone
4 tenor-bass trombones
1 bass trombone in E♭
1 contrabass trombone
1 contrabass tuba

TONE PRODUCTION

The function of sound generator, performed by reeds in oboe, clarinet, and bassoon, is fulfilled in a brass instrument by the player's lips, held against a more or less cup-shaped metal mouthpiece fitted to the small end of the main tube of the instrument. As the air stream is forced through the lips, they are set in vibration, and these vibrations are communicated to the column of air enclosed in the brass tube.

The size and shape of the interior of the mouthpiece has a vital influence on the tone quality of the instrument, and also on the relative ease of production of lower or higher notes in its range. A shallower cup, or bowl, adds brilliance and force, bringing out the higher partials of the tone, whereas the cone-shaped opening of the horn mouthpiece, merging gently into the bore, produces tones characterized by softness and mellowness.

Individual taste and changing styles make it impossible to describe accurately a universal standard shape of mouthpiece for the various brass instruments. The forms shown in Fig. 61 are average types.

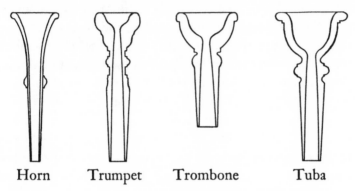

Horn   Trumpet   Trombone   Tuba

Fig. 61. Mouthpieces of Brass Instruments (Cross Section)

OVERBLOWING

By means of lip tension, the harmonics of the tube's fundamental tone are isolated and made to sound individually. The pitch of the fundamental tone being determined by the length of the tube, a tube 8 feet long is theoretically capable of sounding the following harmonic series from 8-foot C.

Fig. 62

These harmonics represent vibrations of the air column in fractions, after the manner of fractional string vibrations (see Chapter One, page 29. For the second harmonic the air column vibrates in halves, with a node at the halfway point. For the next tone, G, the whole 8-foot length vibrates in thirds, and so on. It will be noticed that the ratio between successive pairs of tones shows intervals of steadily diminishing size. Hence the minor third between sixth and seventh harmonics is bound to be smaller than the minor third between fifth and sixth harmonics. It follows that the seventh harmonic, B♭, will always sound too flat. For this reason, the use of the seventh harmonic is regularly avoided in brass playing.

There are other tones in this "chord of nature" that are out of tune with our tempered scale. Those usually mentioned are numbers 7, 11, 13, and 14, but if we examine numbers 8, 9, and 10, we find that these two major seconds are intervals of unequal size. In short, the performer on a brass instrument, practically all of whose tones are harmonics, as opposed to fundamentals, can never relax his vigilance as to the intonation of notes as they come from his instrument.

Pitch can be modified by the lips, within small limits. Other means exist, such as the mobile slide of the trombone, or the right hand inserted in the bell of the horn. Here it is well to repeat that in practice, pitch is not absolute, and that playing in tune involves continual adjustment to the sounds of other instruments.

RANGE

The range of a brass instrument should be thought of in terms of the length of its tubing, and the portion, or number, of partials of its harmonic series it can produce.

The length of the tube, regardless of its diameter, is a reasonably accurate gauge of the pitch of its fundamental tone. Length is also a factor in the availability of upper harmonics, because the shorter the tube the more difficult it becomes to sound the highest partial tones. Two tubes of equal length may differ in range because of different diameters. A wider bore facilitates the production of lower harmonics, whereas a narrow bore is better for the higher ones. To these considerations we must add the width and depth of the mouthpiece used, and the aptitude and skill of the player.

Tones higher than the sixteenth harmonic can be sounded by some players but they are not practical because of their difficulty and insecure pitch. Fundamental tones are called pedal tones. They are not always obtainable, or they may be of such poor quality that they are not used. Instruments that do not sound their fundamental are called half-tube instruments, in contrast to whole-tube instruments, which give the pedal tone.

CROOKS AND SLIDES

In the classical period, horns and trumpets played only notes in the harmonic series of the fundamental to which they happened to be tuned. This tuning was accomplished by fitting different-sized sections of tube, called crooks, to the instrument, an operation requiring a certain amount of time. Further adjustment was made by means of a tuning slide. This was a U-shaped bend somewhere in the tube, designed so that the two prongs of the U fitted like sleeves over two ends of the tube. By sliding this U in or out, the total tube length could be carefully regulated.

The principle of changing the sounding length of a tube by means of a slide is the principle of the trombone (Fig. 63), dating at least as far back as the fifteenth century.

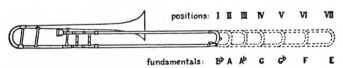

Fig. 63. Positions of the Trombone Slide

The fundamentals given in the diagram are those for the tenor trombone. The seven positions of the slide, shown by dotted lines, provide seven different series of harmonics, moving down by half steps a diminished fifth. Change of position cannot be effected instantaneously, so that there are problems of playing technique to be mastered, but the slide system is ideal for perfection of intonation, since the slide may be moved at will to satisfy the ear.

Although invented fairly early in the nineteenth century, the valve system was slow in gaining acceptance among musicians, and it was well after 1850 before instruments equipped with valves could be said to have become established in the orchestra.

The operation of a valve opens the way for the air column through an extra loop of tubing, at the same time blocking the original path, so that the total tube length is greater than before, and therefore lower in pitch. Depressing the piston or lever accomplishes instantaneously what was previously done by changing crooks.

Two types of valve mechanism are used, the rotary valve and the piston valve. Their method of operation may be seen in Fig. 64.

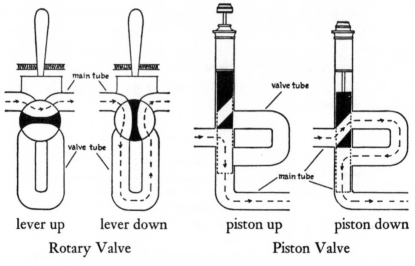

lever up   lever down   piston up   piston down

Rotary Valve   Piston Valve

Fig. 64. Valves (path of air column is shown by broken line)

The drum of the rotary valve is wound with linen fishline or gut, attached to the connecting arm of the finger lever in such a way that depressing the lever gives the drum a quarter turn. This aligns the openings inside the drum in the manner shown in the diagram. The piston valve works up and down within a cylinder. Both are provided with springs, which return the valve to its original position when the pressure of the finger is released.

The basic valve system employs three valves, operated by the first three fingers of the right hand, except on the horn, where the left hand is used for fingering. The valves are arranged so that the first valve (the one nearest the player, and played by the first finger) lowers the pitch of the tube a whole tone; the second valve lowers the pitch a half tone; and the third valve lowers the pitch a tone and a half. Two valves, or three, may be depressed at the same time. The following table gives the possible valve positions and combinations. These are sometimes identified by number with the trombone positions having a corresponding effect.

Valves Depressed	Interval by Which Pitch Is Lowered	Corresponding Trombone Slide Position
None	none	first
No. 2	semitone	second
No. 1	whole tone	third
No. 3, or nos. 1 and 2	minor third	fourth
Nos. 2 and 3	major third	fifth
Nos. 1 and 3	perfect fourth	sixth
Nos. 1, 2, and 3	augmented fourth	seventh

The use of valves in combination presents difficulties of intonation. The length of each valve tube is that proportion of the whole tube length (without valves) necessary to lower the pitch by the desired interval. If, however, one valve is depressed, the other valves do not then add tubes sufficiently long to meet the proportional requirements of the new total length. This is less serious where the shorter tubes of first and second valves are concerned, but the discrepancy is pronounced when the third valve is used in combination.

In order to compensate for this deficiency in the third valve, its tube, in trumpets and cornets, is generally made a little longer, with the result that notes played using the third valve alone are flat, and have to be played sharp by the lips. For this reason, the combination of first and second valves is preferred to the third alone.

The valve tube can be pulled out a bit by the hand not engaged in fingering, and instruments are often equipped with rings or levers to facilitate this means of pitch adjustment. Some instruments have automatic compensating devices. Finally, extra valves may be added, on the larger instruments, for the purpose of correcting pitch.

Other reasons for adding more valves to the three-valve system are to extend the range with lower tones, and to effect the transposition of the entire instrument to a new pitch. These devices will be described in connection with the individual instruments concerned.

It is to be noticed that whereas in the woodwind instruments the process of changing the pitch of fundamental tones is one of shortening the air column by opening holes, in brass instruments it is one of lengthening the air column by adding tubing. The ascending valve found on some horns of French manufacture is an exception. Mention should also be made of the technique of hand stopping, by which tones of the horn can be flattened without lengthening the tube.

FINGERING

If the student will take the trouble to write out the harmonic series of 8-foot C, transposing it six times downward progressively by half steps, he will have before him the notes theoretically obtainable in the seven valve positions, or combinations, as shown in the table. It will be at once apparent that in the upper part of the range the same note can be found in more than one series. Many of these will be harmonics known to be out of tune, and so avoided. Others will be occasionally chosen for their special sound, or because of their fingering in relation to that of preceding or following notes, as in trills, for instance. In principle, however, that fingering is chosen which involves the addition of the least amount of tubing, the purest tones being those nearest to the open series, without valves.

The simplest view of the fingering is had by considering a descending chromatic scale in the performance of which the valves are employed for their original purpose of lowering the pitch of open tones progressively by half steps.

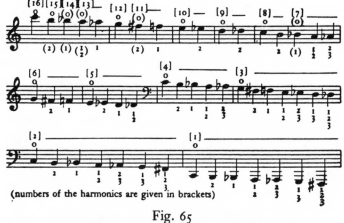

Fig. 65

The proximity of the uppermost open tones (nos. 12 to 16) suggests the possibility of playing with the lips alone in that register, but using the valves helps intonation and articulation.

As the scale descends, the intervals between the open tones grow larger, and the necessity for the use of the third valve increases. This means that the attendant pitch defect is more pronounced in the range of the bass instruments, and it accounts for the presence of extra valves on instruments like the tuba.

Since the total lowering of pitch by the three valves combined is a diminished fifth, no tones are available between the fundamental and the F♯ above it. Extra valves are needed if this gap is to be filled in.

The total (theoretical) extension of the pedal tones down from 8-foot C, as given in the figure, would necessitate the sounding of the fundamental of a tube nearly 12 feet long.

No brass instrument can encompass this entire scale. In studying each instrument, the scale should be transposed to fit the individual tube length, and the instrument's capabilities and limitations should be learned.

EMBOUCHURE

In general, the lips are loose for low tones and tight for high ones. Considerable muscular development in the lips is needed for the production of high notes and for control of tone. The conformation and

texture of the lips is very important, some persons possessing more natural capabilities than others in this respect. It is interesting to note that
horn players become specialists in either low notes or high, and are not
expected to change that specialization. Often long study and experimentation are necessary to discover just the right shape of mouthpiece
to suit the individual mouth.

The lips must be able to pick out accurately the right harmonic in
the series, and make the proper adjustment where valve changes are involved. Following are some technical details of embouchure, based on
the 8-foot scale.

Fig. 66

In (*a*) the three intervening harmonics must not be accidentally
sounded, and if too much tension is given for the upper C, the next
harmonic, D, may sound.

In (*b*) the problem is that of slurring from one tone to a second tone
which is a lower-numbered harmonic, but with a higher fundamental.
D is the fifth harmonic from the fundamental B♭ (first valve), while
C is the fourth harmonic from the fundamental C (open).

Slurring between adjacent harmonics in the same series, (*c*), gives
the best legato on brass instruments. If the harmonics are not adjacent
(*d*), more skill is called for to avoid sounding intermediate tones, and
to minimize any possible break between the two tones.

TONGUING

Tonguing on brass instruments employs all the various tongue
strokes used by the woodwinds. The *tu* of the woodwind attack is more
like *ta* in the upper brass and like *dü* (French *du*) on trombone and
tuba. More variety in soft and sharp attacks can be had with brass than
with woodwinds. Example 237 is an illustration of soft attacks in extreme pianissimo; Ex. 238, of sharp attacks in forte.

EX. 237. Dvořák—*Symphony no. 5*   p. 55, ed. Kalmus

Used by permission of the original publisher, N. Simrock, Hamburg.

EX. 238. Strauss—*Don Juan*   p. 9, ed, Kalmus

Reprinted with the permission of the copyright owners C. F. Peters Corporation, New York.

The *sforzando*, sharp accents, and *forte-piano* are especially well suited to brass. Care should be taken to write the exact kind of accent desired.

Fast staccato in single-tonguing can be used for all brass instruments, but it is to be expected that tubas, and the low registers of horns and trombones, will respond less promptly than the smaller tubes. For lightness in fast tonguing, the trumpets, or cornets, are the best in the brass group.

EX. 239. Debussy—*Jeux*   p. 98, ed. Durand

The following is an instance of the use of double-tonguing for the entire brass section.

EX. 240. Rimsky-Korsakoff—*Scheherazade*   p. 209, ed. Kalmus

Brass players are not in agreement as to the relative merits of *t-t-k* and *t-k-t* in the articulation of triple-tonguing. The majority seem to favor *t-t-k*. Double-tonguing can also be used for triple rhythms, alternating the *t* and the *k* as the initial stroke of each triplet, thus: *t-k-t*, *k-t-k*, etc. In any case the effect of triple-tonguing is best on the high-pitched instruments.

EX. 241. Debussy—*La Mer*   p. 51, ed. Durand

Permission granted by Durand et Cie., Paris, copyright owners; Elkan-Vogel, Philadelphia, Pa., agents.

Flutter-tonguing is easy on the horn or trumpet, less easy on the trombone or tuba. It is sometimes indicated for brass as a tremolo, like a bowed tremolo for strings.

EX. 242. Strauss—*Don Quixote*   p. 55, ed. Philharmonia

Reprinted with the permission of the copyright owners C. F. Peters Corporation, New York.

BREATHING

More wind is required in brass playing than in woodwind playing. It is essential that a reserve of wind is kept available to the embouchure at all times. The air is blown into the tube of the instrument, where some of it condenses, making it necessary to drain the tubing from time to time, either by means of a water key or by pulling out the valve slides.

Phrase markings are like those for woodwind. It is unfortunately not general practice to mark the places where breath is to be taken, as opposed to tongue articulations. These are often very important for the correct phrasing and dynamic emphasis of the music. The difference between an interruption for breathing and the effect of tonguing is especially noticeable in the brass, most of all in chord progressions such as those in Ex. 237 and Ex. 238, where all the voices are in the same rhythm. Composers should study this detail of phrasing, which ought not to be left to the decision of the individual player or the conductor.

The wind is controlled by the diaphragm. It is not permitted to puff out the cheeks, a condition under which command of the tone would be impossible.

DYNAMIC RANGE

The full dynamic power of the brass is a dominating force capable of obliterating the sound of the rest of the orchestra, and it is often allowed to do so by conductors lacking either authority or discrimination. The limit of loudness and tone-weight of strings and woodwinds is a physical fact. Forcing them to compete with the brass simply results in disagreeable sounds, with the brass still far in the lead. Orchestral balance in great climaxes is an impossibility unless the brass volume is measured by the sonorous capacity of strings and woodwind.

This problem of balance is a besetting one for the composer and orchestrator. Its solution lies mainly in the understanding of the music by the conductor and the orchestra. The first performance of a new and unfamiliar score is seldom a satisfactory test of the merits of the orchestration, and, on the other hand, it must be recognized that many well-known and well-loved symphonic masterpieces are made to sound well orchestrated only through sympathetic and understanding adjustment of the written parts in performance.

The practice of marking the brass at a lower dynamic level than strings and woodwind should be reserved for special purposes, and not resorted to as a corrective for faulty balance due to the lack of understanding referred to above, or to unskillful scoring. Good brass players know that dynamic indications do not signify absolute, but relative, values. It goes without saying that the orchestrator strives to place the various instrumental voices so that the effect will be as near as possible to that imagined.

At the other end of the dynamic scale, the brass cannot match the softness of a string or woodwind pianissimo. It provides, however, a real pianissimo in terms of the brass itself, and this is a valuable resource in orchestration.

MUTES

Muted brass is of course still softer, and it can be reduced to inaudibility. A vast array of mutes, of every conceivable shape and tone color, have been invented in the twentieth century, products for the most part of the enthusiastic interest in new sounds in the field of popular music. Thirty years ago it was believed that the new mutes would be introduced into the symphony orchestra, but at the present writing it cannot be said that standard equipment of the symphonic brass section includes such coloristic resources as Solo-tone, Harmon, Whisper, Tonalcolor, Vocatone, or cup mutes, to name but a few.

The mutes ordinarily used are cone-shaped air chambers of cardboard, wood, fiber, or aluminum, with small blocks of cork to prevent too tight a fit when one is inserted into the bell of the instrument. The usual sound of muted brass is somewhat metallic, more akin to the oboe sound than to any other in the orchestra. It can be cutting and strident when attacked with force. Loud muted brass is a common orchestral effect. Mutes are used on all brass instruments, and a similar muted sound can be obtained on the horn by hand-stopping.

SCORE MARKINGS

Horns are placed above the trumpets in the score, just below the bassoons. If there are four, two staves are used, with two horns on each staff.

Three trumpets may occupy one staff, unless the parts are so different in rhythm as to cause confusion in reading, in which case a second staff is allotted to the third trumpet.

First and second trombones are on one staff, usually in the tenor clef. The third trombone is placed on the same staff as the tuba, in the bass clef.

The custom of omitting key signatures for horns and trumpets is fairly universal, although some composers prefer to include them. Originally the parts for these instruments were always in C, with an indication of the proper crook to sound in the key of the piece. Modern players often express a preference for this freedom from key signatures, especially when they may be using an instrument in a key other than that prescribed, and transposing the part. Trombones and tuba are given the same key signature as the strings.

The directions given in Chapter Six (page 126) are equally applicable to brass parts.

CHAPTER TWELVE

THE HORN

Fr., *cor;* It., *corno;* Ger., *Horn*

THE horn is often called in English the French horn, but it is significant that it is not so called by the French. The term is supposed to have originated in England in the eighteenth century. However, the horn as we know it today has been developed mainly by Germans, and it could with more justification be called the German horn.

A true French horn does exist, almost exclusively in France. It is an instrument of small bore, equipped with piston valves instead of the rotary valves generally used on the horn. Its tone is of a light, brilliant, and open quality, quite different from the warm, rich, and rather dark tone of the German horn, used practically everywhere.

The horn without valves is called the natural horn, or hand horn (Fr., *cor simple;* It., *corno naturale;* Ger., *Waldhorn*). Earlier names, such as hunting horn, *cor de chasse, corno da caccia, Jagdhorn,* are not found in scores of the period we are studying. The horn with valves is called the valve horn (Fr., *cor à pistons, cor chromatique;* It., *corno ventile;* Ger., *Ventilhorn*).

THE NATURAL HORN

In its eighteenth- and nineteenth-century shape, the natural horn is an open hoop or coil of brass tubing, a quarter of an inch in diameter at the small end holding the mouthpiece, expanding gently to a diameter of 3 inches at the throat of the bell. The bell flares widely, measuring about 11 inches across. This wide bell is considered to favor the lower partials in the make-up of the tone of the horn.

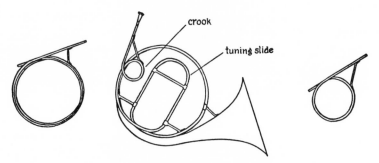

Fig. 67. Natural Horn with Crooks

A tuning slide in U-shape is located within the circle of tubing. This part of the bore is necessarily cylindrical so that the slide may be moved in and out.

Crooks of various sizes can be fitted onto the end of the tube, the mouthpiece being inserted in the end of the crook. Some crooks were later made with slides, enabling them to be attached in place of the tuning slide.

The crooks most used were those which pitched the horn in the following keys: B♭ alto, A, A♭, G, F, E, E♭, D, C, and B♭ basso. The total tube lengths, when crooks are added to a horn pitched in 8-foot C, measure from approximately 9 feet 3 inches for the horn in B♭ alto to 18 feet 6 inches for the horn in B♭ basso. The following are the intervals of transposition, shown by the effect on one note of the harmonic series, the eighth harmonic.

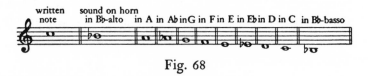

Fig. 68

Higher pitches than B♭ alto have very rarely been prescribed. In the Haydn symphonies may be found horns in B♮ alto and C alto. The C alto appears to be the horn without crooks. "Horn in C" always means a horn with C crook, sounding an octave lower than written.

As for low pitches, the horn in A basso is seen in Italian opera scores, the B♮ basso crook is called for in Brahms' First Symphony, and the D♭ crook in *Roméo et Juliette*, by Berlioz.

RANGE

The range of the horn is from the second harmonic to the sixteenth inclusive, with some qualifications. The shorter tubes, from F up, sound with difficulty above the twelfth partial, whereas these upper harmonics are more easily produced on longer tubes. On the other hand, the pedal tone comes out well on the short B♭ alto horn, poorly on the F horn, and hardly ever on lower-pitched crooks.

The separation of horn players into "high" and "low," together with the evolving of taste in quest of the ideal horn tone, brought a preference for the lower-pitched horns, and a great development in the technique of tone production in the lower part of the range. For a time, the keys of E, E♭, and D seemed the most preferred, and more interesting and important parts were written for the second player, or for the fourth if there were four horns. In the nineteenth century, the preference turned to the middle pitch of the F horn, and the F horn became the standard horn, to which the valve system was applied. The principle of high and low hornists persisted and became permanent. In the usual quartet of horns, first and third are high, and second and fourth are low.

The low players of the natural horn used a larger mouthpiece and developed a different embouchure. They also added to the horn's available notes by the discovery that the second harmonic can be lowered as much as an augmented fourth by the lips alone. These tones are called artificial, or factitious, tones. Figure 69 shows their place in the harmonic series. Modern horn players do not make a practice of using these tones.

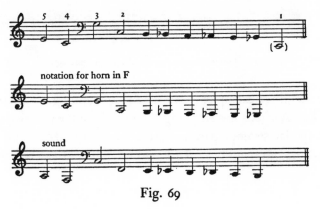

Fig. 69

BASS CLEF NOTATION

When the bass clef is used for the horn, the notes in that clef are by custom written an octave too low. Hence the part for horn in F in Fig. 69, sounding a perfect fifth lower than written in the treble clef, sounds a perfect fourth higher than written in the bass clef. Modern composers have tried to correct this illogical notation by writing notes in the bass clef in their proper octave, but when this is done a note should be given in the score—"horns in the bass clef sound a fifth lower than written," to avoid misunderstanding.

STOPPED NOTES

It was discovered that if the natural horn were held so that the right hand could be inserted in the bell, the hand could, by partially closing the throat of the horn, not only control the quality of the tone, but also correct the pitch of those harmonics that were out of tune. Furthermore, by lowering the pitch of the harmonics in this way, many new notes were made available. Half to three-quarters closing of the tube lowered the note a half tone, full stopping a whole tone.

The stopped tones, however, had a decidedly dull and subdued sound in contrast to the open tones, and great skill in embouchure and right-hand technique was required to achieve equality in tone in melodic passages containing stopped notes.

EX. 243. Schubert—*Symphony no. 7*   p. 1, ed. Eulenburg

In the Schubert example, notes requiring stopping are marked with a cross. The A needs less stopping than the B, since it is stopped from the already flat seventh partial. The F is stopped from the eleventh partial, whose pitch lies between F and F♯. The passage is successful in

piano, but would be unconvincing in *forte*. The problem does not arise, of course, when the phrase is played on the valve horn.

Orchestral composers were sparing in their use of new notes available as stopped tones. Instances like the fourth horn part in the *Adagio* of Beethoven's Ninth Symphony are exceptional. But the hand technique proved subsequently most valuable as a means of tone control and correction of intonation on the valve horn.

The natural horn, with all its limitations, had a vital and lasting influence on melody and harmony. Melodic turns of phrase for all sorts of instruments, even the pianoforte, often show characteristics of natural horn music. The following is an illustration of this universal quality in simple horn melodies.

EX. 244. Beethoven—*Piano Concerto no. 5*   p. 11, ed. Eulenburg

Reprinted with the permission of the sole agents for Eulenburg Miniature Scores: C. F. Peters Corporation, New York.

CHOICE OF CROOKS

In general, the crook chosen was that of the key of the movement, as being the one that would give the most notes of the scale. Exceptions to this rule might be prompted by a planned modulation to a related key in which horns were to be given a prominent part, or by a preference for low-pitched horns when the key is high, *e.g.*, E horns for a piece in A major.

When four horns were used, they were most often crooked in pairs in two different keys. Berlioz frequently wrote for four horns crooked in four different pitches, ingeniously chosen to provide certain combinations of notes.

EX. 245. Berlioz—*Roméo et Juliette*   p. 12, ed. Eulenburg

THE VALVE HORN

The stage of transition from natural horns to valve horns was longer for the composers than for the players. The new instrument had to prove its value and overcome much prejudice and nostalgic feeling for the natural horn, as well as general mistrust as to the future of valved instruments. The horn without valves was used, at least occasionally, up to the beginning of the twentieth century; on the other hand, many composers wrote as though for natural horns even when they knew the valve horn would be employed.

In *Rienzi, The Flying Dutchman*, and *Tannhäuser*, Wagner specified two valve horns and two natural horns.

EX. 246. Wagner—*Tannhäuser: Bacchanale*   p. 14, ed. Kalmus

The following example shows the much-discussed experimental crook markings used by Wagner in *Lohengrin*.

EX. 247. Wagner—*Lohengrin: Prelude to Act III*   p. 17, ed. Kalmus

The indications call for instantaneous changes in the key of the horn, to be accomplished by valves instead of crooks, as formerly. With the horn crooked in F, as was the case, "in E" could be met by depressing the second valve and playing as on the natural horn in E. In the same way, for "in D" one could use the third valve, or valves 1 and 2. But no combination of valves can put the F horn "in G," so here it was necessary to transpose up a major second and play as for the F horn with valves. Perhaps Wagner had in mind the system of crooks as applied to the C horn, but at any rate the notation was abandoned after *Lohengrin.*

Much fine horn music is contained in the works of Brahms, usually in the style of hand horn music, and mostly playable on that instrument. There is no doubt, however, that it sounds better on the valve horn, if only because of the elimination of stopped notes.

EX. 248. Brahms—*Symphony no. 3*   p. 75, ed. Kalmus

THE MODERN HORN

In the present century the valve horn in F (tube length including valves about 17 feet) continued to be regarded as the standard horn, but increasing demands in the high register led to the adoption by first and third players of the high B♭ horn (tube length including valves under 13 feet). They were attracted by its brilliant tone, and the ease with which it produced tones of the same pitch as the highest partials of the F horn. While the F horn was playable up to the sixteenth harmonic and beyond, the top notes were difficult and tiring to the embouchure. To obtain the same sounds on the B♭ horn, the notes were transposed down a perfect fourth, so that the sixteenth harmonic of the F horn became only the twelfth harmonic of the B♭ horn.

It became apparent, however, that the most valued attribute of the horn—its characteristic warmth and dark beauty of tone—could not be supplied by the high-pitched B♭ horn, whatever else it had to recommend it. Today this problem seems to have reached a workable solution with the invention of the double horn.

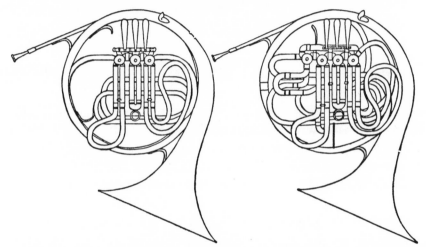

Fig. 70. (left) Single Horn in F; (right) Double Horn in F and B♭

The double horn is fast replacing the single horn in orchestras. As its name implies, it is actually a combination of the F and B♭ horns into one instrument. The valve tubes are duplicated and operated from a single set of rotary valves, with a fourth valve, for the thumb, to switch from F horn to B♭ horn, and vice versa. The switch can be made at any time and in any part of the range.

RANGE

Music for the double horn is always written as for F horn, whether played on the F or on the B♭ division. The choice is left entirely to the player, and is not indicated in the part.

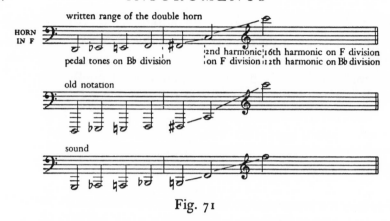

Fig. 71

On the double horn of the usual type, the two divisions can be used separately as single horns in F and B♭, but players of the double horn have come to regard it as a single instrument. When using the B♭ division to play parts written for horn in F, the mental process is not the same as when using the single B♭ horn—namely, to transpose the written part down a fourth and then finger for the resulting notes. It is rather to employ directly a new set of fingerings for the notes as written. This involves learning a new set of fingerings for the double horn. The steps in this procedure are compared in the following figure. (See Chapter Eleven, Fig. 65, for the normal fingering on the single horn.)

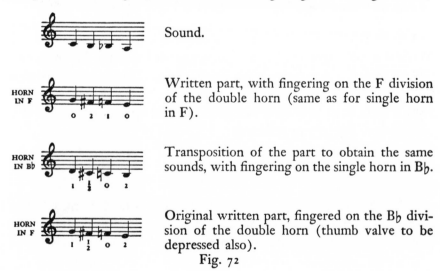

Sound.

Written part, with fingering on the F division of the double horn (same as for single horn in F).

Transposition of the part to obtain the same sounds, with fingering on the single horn in B♭.

Original written part, fingered on the B♭ division of the double horn (thumb valve to be depressed also).

Fig. 72

The B♭ division is used not only for the greater facility gained in the upper register, and the prompter response of the shorter tube's low register, but also for the alternative fingerings made available in all parts of the range.

The double horn combines the good qualities of the F and B♭ horns while making it possible to avoid their defects. Its own peculiar problem for the horn player is that of equalizing the tone between the two divisions. The B♭ division tends inevitably to have a certain hardness characteristic of the B♭ horn, in comparison to the tone of the F division, but this is successfully overcome by good players. The function of the right hand in the bell becomes of prime importance in controlling the tone quality of the double horn.

STOPPED TONES

Although the technique of the hand horn is no longer necessary for completing the chromatic scale of the horn, the hand is constantly engaged in refining the pitch of most notes. Stopped tones in the modern sense are, however, quite different from those used on the natural horn. The hand is inserted far enough to close the tube completely. This produces tones of muted quality, and since it is necessary to force the wind a little these notes have the metallic vibrancy characteristic of muted brass.

EX. 249. D'Indy—*Istar*   p. 1, ed. Durand

The act of full stopping cuts off enough of the tube's vibrating length to cause all stopped notes to sound a half tone higher. It is therefore necessary for the player to transpose them down a semitone to compensate for this. Some horns are equipped with an extra half-tone valve, operated by the thumb, to effect the transposition automatically. This valve is called the stop valve, or transposing valve. It is found commonly on the B♭ horn, but not often on the double horn because of the added weight of the extra valve.

Mutes, of metal or cardboard, are also used on horns. They are so constructed that they do not alter the pitch, except for some types of metal mutes that require the same pitch correction as stopped notes. Stopped notes are apt to be unreliable below middle C (written), and mutes are often used for these lower notes in preference to stopping. Although the muted horn does not sound quite like the stopped horn, in usage the two terms are sometimes carelessly interchanged.

Despite the fact of their occasional misuse, the terms should be used in their true meaning. For brass instruments, the directions for inserting and removing mutes are the same as for using them on stringed instruments, in all languages. The word *stopped* (Fr., *bouché*; It., *chiuso*; Ger., *gestopft*) means hand stopped, canceled by *open* (Fr., *ouvert*; It., *aperto*; Ger., *offen, nicht gestopft*). Single stopped notes are sometimes marked by a cross, canceled if necessary by *o*, for open.

EX. 250. Falla—*El Amor Brujo*   p. 61, ed. Chester

Copyright for all countries J. & W. Chester Ltd., London.

Horn players often ignore the direction to play with mutes, preferring the less bothersome and quicker hand stopping. In their defense it must be added that the practice is abetted by composers who are indifferent to the distinction between the two effects.

The metallic sound of stopped tones is less noticeable in soft playing, more pronounced in forte. Frequently this kind of sound is called for in exaggerated form by the word *brassy* (Fr., *cuivré*; Ger., *schmetternd*). It is obtained by lip tension and hard blowing, causing the metal to vibrate. The degree of brassiness can be varied, and the sound can be made on open notes as well as stopped and muted. The usual marking is *stopped*, with a sforzando or forte sign (Fr., *bouché-cuivré*; Ger., *gestopft-stark anblasen*).

EX. 251. Mahler—*Das Lied von der Erde*   p. 49, ed. Universal

In the following passage written for natural horn, the sudden piano and the rise of a half tone on the last note will be obtained simultaneously by keeping the G fingering and playing the Ab as a stopped note. It is believed that this method was not used in Beethoven's day, when the Ab would have been partially stopped, from the thirteenth harmonic.

EX. 252. Beethoven—*Symphony no. 3*   p. 35, ed. Kalmus

TRILLS

On the horn, trills are played either with valves or by the lips alone. The lip trills are possible only where two harmonics lie a second apart, so their range is limited, as is also their chance of good intonation. In effect they can be compared to vocal trills. Trills made with valve action suffer from the inertia of the valve tubes when called upon to speak quickly. The second valve being the shortest, half tone trills are likely to work better than whole tone trills, although there are exceptions. Horn trills never escape a certain sluggish quality, especially in comparison with woodwind trills, and they are not among the best features of the horn.

In the following example, the trill is used in music suggesting a rustic dance.

EX. 253. Mahler—*Symphony no. 9*   p. 65, ed. Boosey & Hawkes

TONGUING

All types of tonguing are used in horn playing. The articulations cannot be as sharp and crisp as on the trumpet, because of the length of the tube. Care should be taken to provide rest for the tongue in long passages in fast tempo. The following is very difficult.

EX. 254. Moussorgsky-Ravel—*Tableaux d'une Exposition*

p. 87, ed. Boosey & Hawkes

An arrangement like that in the next example would produce a more rhythmic result, being more playable.

EX. 255. Strauss—*Don Quixote*   p. 48, ed. Philharmonia

The following is an instance of effective and delicate use of both double- and triple-tonguing.

EX. 256. Ravel—*Rapsodie Espagnole*   p. 69, ed. Durand

GLISSANDOS

A quick slurring upwards over the harmonics of any given finger position produces the horn glissando.

EX. 257. Stravinsky—*Le Sacre du Printemps*   p. 91, ed. Russe

CAMPANA IN ARIA

When the horn is in its usual playing position the bell is pointed down and away from the listener, in addition to its being partially closed by the right hand. Occasionally the player is directed to play with the bell up (Fr., *pavillon en l'air;* It., *campana in aria;* Ger., *Schalltrichter auf*). The right hand is taken out of the bell, and the horn is raised into a horizontal plane, so that the sound may come free and unobstructed from the bell. The effect is lusty and blaring. Without the control of the hand in the bell, the notes may not always be in tune.

EX. 258. Mahler—*Symphony no. 4*   p. 121, ed. Philharmonia

MELODIC USES

The horn has always been a favorite solo instrument. Its most comfortable harmonic range is from the third or fourth harmonic to about the twelfth. The following solo calls for fine breath control to achieve a perfect legato. A note in the score directs that the high B is to be taken only if it can be played piano. The horn plays in canon an octave and fifth below the flute. Harp chords and pulsating strings form the accompaniment.

EX. 259. Shostakovich—*Symphony no. 5*   p. 46, ed. Musicus

It is usually advisable to double extreme high notes in loud passages, to assure volume and security of attack.

EX. 260. Copland—*Symphony no. 3*   p. 70, ed. Boosey & Hawkes

It is likewise advisable to double extreme low notes, even when very soft; in fact, low tones in pianissimo gain much in steadiness and tone quality, and need not sound any louder when played by two horns instead of one. In the following example, three horns are used on the bass part.

EX. 261. Mahler—*Symphony no. 1*   p. 89, ed. Universal

Melodies played by horns in octaves are rich and sonorous.

EX. 262. Debussy—*La Mer*   p. 6, ed. Durand

The unison of the entire horn group, usually four horns, is frequently employed when breadth and force are desired. If the score calls for more than four, all can be united on the melody. Example 263 is for six horns.

EX. 263. Holst—*The Planets*   p. 83, ed. Boosey & Hawkes

The low horns, second and fourth, may be taken up to the top of the horn range occasionally, and especially when they participate in this type of doubling. The classification of low and high horns remains in force, however. Second and fourth players cultivate the lower notes, for which they are more talented by nature, but all four can play the entire range.

AGILITY

Although technical improvements in the horn and in horn playing have made possible the execution of music of considerable virtuosity, it remains true that agility is not in the nature of the instrument. It is an interesting fact that the style of horn music is still under the influence of the principles of the natural horn, and that the best writing for the instrument carries the suggestion that it might be playable on the hand horn. This is of course not literally so, but passages like the following, even though effective and successful for their special purposes, cannot be said to be idiomatic horn music.

EX. 264. Strauss—*Elektra*   p. 187, ed. Boosey & Hawkes

HARMONIC USES

For many years, from the mid-nineteenth century on, it was a common habit of composers to use the four-part harmony of horns as a foundation for orchestral writing. This "blanket of horns," as someone has called it, could be so unobtrusive as to be unnoticed by the lay listener, and it offered a sure means of obtaining continuity and fullness of sound. The growth of interest in contrapuntal voices and in clarity led away from this procedure, with the result that it is unusual today.

The harmonic background can be presented by horns in all kinds of figuration and rhythmic division. As in the next example, it can be skillfully arranged to have contrapuntal interest and transparency.

EX. 265. Stravinsky—*Divertimento: Le Baiser de la Fée*

p. 70, ed. Boosey & Hawkes

Horn tone combines well with that of all instruments. The horns therefore form an important link between brass and woodwind. Indeed, they seem to be as much a part of the woodwind section as of the brass, to which of course they belong by nature. This perhaps accounts for their being placed in the score above the trumpets, so they are near the woodwinds.

In respect to tone-weight, horns are unmistakably weaker than what is called the heavy brass—trumpets, trombones, and tuba—whereas the horns in turn are stronger than the woodwinds. When in combination with other brass they must be carefully placed, and sometimes doubled, if balance is to be maintained.

The larger symphony orchestras possess eight horns, but lesser ones cannot be expected to have more than four or five. A fifth player may be given the duty of assisting the first horn, playing his part in the less important measures, so that he may save himself for prominent solo passages. Extra players may be engaged for works requiring six or eight horns. Even more than for the performance of scores calling for these, the eight horns are a great advantage in that the players may change about, affording rest for fatigued embouchures.

CHAPTER THIRTEEN

THE TRUMPET

Fr., *trompette;* It., *tromba;* Ger., **Trompete**

THE trumpet as known to Haydn, Mozart, and Beethoven was a slender brass tube, folded twice, with a flaring bell of moderate size (about 4 inches across), and fitted with a cup mouthpiece. The bore, measuring under half an inch in diameter, was cylindrical except for the last foot and a half or so, which became conical as it approached the bell.

In the eighteenth century, trumpets were made in various sizes, and these could be lengthened by adding crooks. The C trumpet was an 8-foot tube, and its harmonic series was therefore the same 8-foot series presented in Chapter Eleven, Fig. 62. This series is the written series playable, with restrictions to be noted, on the natural trumpets of the classical period. Just as in the case of the horn, the sounds produced will be transpositions of the series according to the tube lengths of the various instruments. It is to be noticed that this is the same series as that of the "horn in C alto," to which the different horn crooks were added. Also, the series is an octave lower than that of our contemporary C trumpet, which is a 4-foot instrument.

Near the beginning of the nineteenth century, the choice of pitches had settled on the F trumpet as the standard instrument, having a tube length of about 6 feet. It was equipped with a tuning slide, and crooks could be applied to put the instrument in E, E♭, D, and C. The lower pitches of B, B♭, and even A and A♭ could be obtained by combining crooks.

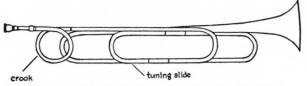

Fig. 73. Classical Trumpet, Crooked in E♭

Trumpets pitched higher than F were rarely called for. In pieces written in G major, for example, C trumpets might be used, or none at all. In Beethoven's Seventh Symphony in A major, D trumpets are chosen rather than the heavily crooked A trumpets.

TRANSPOSITION

The C trumpet sounds as written. The shorter trumpets sound higher than written, the longer ones lower.

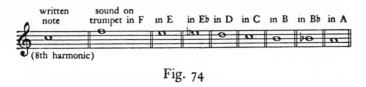

Fig. 74

RANGE

In the early eighteenth century trumpeters had developed the art of playing very high harmonics, even going as high as the twenty-first partial (a perfect fourth above the sixteenth partial). This technique, known as clarino playing, was acquired through long practice and specialization, aided by natural ability, and a shallow mouthpiece. In comparison with trumpeters of today, the player had also the slight advantage of a lower pitch, requiring less lip tension for a given harmonic.

Examples of these high trumpet parts may be seen in the works of J. S. Bach, but after the middle of the century the art of clarino playing appears to have suddenly declined and to have become lost completely, doubtless because of the change in musical style from the linear to the symphonic idiom. Composers of the classical period almost never wrote for trumpets above the twelfth partial, although higher harmonics were obtainable on the trumpets with lower-pitched crooks.

The pedal tone was playable only on the F trumpet, the second harmonic was of uncertain pitch on most trumpets, and the third harmonic poor on the low crooks. In short, the range of the classical trumpet, with few exceptions, was restricted to the harmonics numbered three to twelve, inclusive, giving the following written notes:

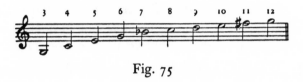

Fig. 75

Among these tones, the seventh was too flat, but it was nevertheless occasionally written.

EX. 266. Beethoven—*Symphony no. 9*   p. 27, ed. Kalmus

The eleventh harmonic, F♯, lay in pitch between F♯ and F♮, and if used, required correction with the lips. No hand stopping, like that on the horn, was physically possible.

In the following example, it might seem that a pedal tone is indicated for the second trumpet. It is an unusual instance of the appearance of the bass clef in trumpet parts, and it is reasonable to suppose that the practice, followed in writing for the horn, of placing notes in the bass clef an octave too low, has been followed here. That would give the second trumpet not a pedal tone but the second harmonic, even that being an unreliable note on the D crook.

EX. 267. Mozart—*Don Juan: Overture*   p. 2, ed. Kalmus

This extremely limited repertoire of notes remained in force until the middle of the nineteenth century, when valves were incorporated into the trumpet. The ingenuity and adaptability shown by the composers of the period in their efforts to make the most of such small resources attests to the need they felt for the sound of trumpets in the orchestra. One cannot study the orchestration of these important composers intelligently without a knowledge of the technique and limitations of the classical trumpet.

ORCHESTRAL USES

The most familiar trumpet effect in the classical orchestra is probably the traditional flourish of trumpets and drums, usually in the tutti, with horns.

EX. 268. Mozart—*Symphony in C major*, K. 551

p. 84, ed. Eulenburg

Reprinted with the permission of the sole agents for Eulenburg Miniature Scores: C. F. Peters Corporation, New York.

When trumpets were used harmonically, for loud tutti chords, or for dynamic accents, they were often doubled on whatever note of the chord was available to them. The composer evidently preferred to risk a badly balanced chord rather than lose tone-weight by omitting one trumpet. This is doubtless the reason for the occurrence of trumpet parts like the following.

EX. 269. Beethoven—*Symphony no. 6*   p. 143, ed. Kalmus

The three chords of the tutti from which this is drawn are the triads
F major, D minor, and G major. The C trumpets can contribute only
one note of the D minor triad, hence the doubling of D, and the unorthodox voice leading of the second trumpet part. The two trumpeters
probably played the note somewhat less than fortissimo. Furthermore,
the long classical trumpet must have been less piercing in tone than our
present-day instrument.

Long held notes in octaves, rhythmic punctuation, and patterns on
one or two notes, are other characteristic features of trumpet parts.
Also an occasional solo phrase of short duration might occur. Themes
were often constructed on the harmonic series, so that the trumpets
could play at least part of the melody in the tutti.

EX. 270. Beethoven—*Symphony no. 5*   p. 33, ed. Kalmus

The trumpets were not assigned loud passages exclusively. The following entry is an example of delicacy in the use of trumpets and drums.

EX. 271. Beethoven—*Symphony no. 1*

p. 31, ed. Kalmus

THE VALVE TRUMPET

When the valve trumpet was introduced, in the middle of the nine-teenth century, it was the same standard trumpet in F with a 6-foot tube, now lengthened by the three-valve system to nearly 8½ feet. Its written chromatic range, from third to twelfth partial was, then, as in Fig. 76, sounding a perfect fourth higher on the F trumpet.

Fig. 76

The lowest tones were probably of useless quality. Examples of these low notes written for the trumpet in F cannot be regarded as proof of their playability on the F trumpet, because of the likelihood of the part having been played on a differently pitched instrument.

Composers continued to write for trumpets in the keys of the various crooks, such as E, E♭, and D, and even C and B♭. One concludes either that the parts were transposed and played as for F trumpet, or that trumpets of larger sizes were used.

Richard Strauss, in his revision of the *Treatise on Instrumentation* by Berlioz, advises as the best procedure the writing for trumpets in a variety of keys, choosing those keys which will cause the written part to appear as far as possible in C major. This will make it convenient for the trumpeter to transpose the part and play it on the instrument of his individual choice. The advice is based on the knowledge that performers will not necessarily use the instrument designated, and that diverse practice makes it impossible to predict what their choice will be.

These remarks by Strauss are of great importance to the student of the orchestration of the last half of the nineteenth century, and, as we shall see, of our own century. A part marked *trumpet in F* may not have been played on that instrument, and, what is even more significant, the composer may not have expected that it would be.

Reports of the tone quality of the F trumpet, its nobility, its heaviness, its tendency to dominate, its superiority over the modern trumpet, all doubtless contain a part of truth, as can be ascertained by playing on the original instrument. Nevertheless, there is nearly always a question whether or not the testimony is based on actual hearing of the F trumpet.

We may exercise our imagination as to the effect of the following, if played on the instruments indicated.

EX. 272. Bruckner—*Symphony no. 7*   p. 28, ed. Philharmonia

THE MODERN TRUMPET

The trend toward greater use of the high register, and preference for more brilliance and agility, led to the adoption of smaller instruments, and in the twentieth century the standard trumpet is either the C or the B♭ trumpet, in their modern forms. These trumpets have tube lengths one-half as long as the classical trumpets of the same keys. The tube of the C trumpet measures 4 feet, not counting the valves, and that of the B♭, 4 feet 6½ inches. The B♭ trumpet can be changed to an A trumpet, ordinarily by pulling out a specially designed slide at the first U-bend and adjusting the valve slides for the new pitch. Some trumpets with rotary valves exist, but piston valves are the universal standard for the trumpet, in contrast to the horn.

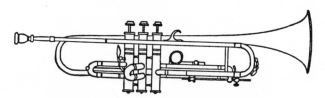

Fig. 77. Modern Trumpet in B♭ and A

The written series of harmonics we have used thus far must now be replaced by one an octave higher.

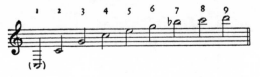

Fig. 78

The fundamental tone can sometimes be produced, with extraordinarily flexible lips. Its sound is of such poor quality that its playability has not been cultivated, and it should not be included in the range of the trumpet. Harmonics above the eighth are more easily obtainable on the Bb trumpet than on the C, and as usual the flat seventh harmonic is avoided.

The C trumpet sounds as written, the Bb trumpet a major second lower than written.

FINGERING

The notes playable in the seven valve positions are as follows:

Fig. 79

As previously noted, the use of the third valve presents intonation difficulties. The Ab series can be corrected by the lips, but the last two series cannot. Low F♯ and G, and their fifths C♯ and D, not being duplicated in another series, can be fingered only as in Fig. 79, and are therefore bound to be out of tune. These pitches are corrected by mechanical devices. The first valve is lengthened by a spring trigger for the left thumb, and the third valve by means of a ring for the left third finger. These devices may be operated while a note is sounding. High Ab is another note to which special attention must be given for intonation.

Lower sounds than the F♯ can be obtained by such drastic expedients as pulling out the valve slides and the tuning slide as far as possible.

EX. 273. Ravel—*Rapsodie Espagnole*   p. 35, ed. Durand

TONE QUALITY

The trumpet possesses carrying power sufficient to sound with authority over the full orchestra. The volume and tone quality depend somewhat on the bore, whether small, medium, or large, and on the width and depth of the mouthpiece employed. These factors are decided by individual taste. The B♭ trumpet preserves a little more of the fullness of tone characteristic of the older trumpets, whereas the C trumpet has more intensity and at the same time more delicacy. There has been a noticeable increase in the use of C trumpets in the last twenty-five years. They are often played when B♭ trumpets are specified in the score. On the other hand, many trumpeters prefer to play the C parts on the B♭ trumpet.

In the low register the trumpet sounds full, and with much solemnity.

EX. 274. Shostakovich—*Symphony no. 5*   p. 14, ed. Musicus

The normal comfortable range for melodies lies between middle C (written) and the G a twelfth above. High and low points in the melodic curve may exceed these limits, if desirable.

EX. 275. Hindemith—*Concerto for Orchestra*   p. 6, ed. Schott

In the high register, from G to C, the tone is naturally most penetrating. These upper notes have a beautiful quality in *piano*, but they are difficult to play softly.

EX. 276. Stravinsky—*Symphony in C*   p. 65, ed. Schott

EXTREME HIGH NOTES

The ninth harmonic is often played by those trumpeters who make a practice of playing C trumpet parts on the B♭ trumpet, since they must play D when the high C is written. A written high D is much more difficult on the C trumpet, however. A part like the following would most probably be played on the D trumpet.

EX. 277. Bartók—*Concerto for Orchestra*

p. 107, ed. Boosey & Hawkes

Copyright 1946 by Hawkes & Son (London) Ltd. Used by permission.

The production of higher notes is a matter of lip tension, aided by the kind of mouthpiece and the bore of the instrument. Dance band trumpeters frequently play up to G, the twelfth harmonic, and even further, but it is noticeable that this is accomplished at a sacrifice of quality, especially in the medium and low registers. The situation is reminiscent of the clarino playing of the eighteenth century. But whereas the clarino player was admittedly a high register specialist, the orchestra trumpeter of today is expected to be at his best in the medium part of the range. It would be folly for him to weaken this more valuable aspect of trumpet playing for the sake of extending his range upward.

MUTES

Muted trumpets can give forth the most piercing sound in the orchestra (Ex. 278), and on the other hand they can be used softly for a kind of echo effect, a sound as of an instrument played at a distance (Ex. 279). At one time in the early twentieth century, muted trumpets were so much in vogue that they were heard almost as frequently as open trumpets.

EX. 278. Stravinsky—*Pétrouchka*   p. 65, ed. Russe

EX. 279. Berg—*Violin Concerto*   p. 45, ed. Universal

TONGUING

Separately tongued notes on the trumpet are more incisive than on the horn. They are especially forceful when accented.

EX. 280. Stravinsky—*L'Oiseau de Feu*   p. 129, ed. Broude Bros.

Compared with the horn, the trumpet responds more quickly to the various tongue strokes. Its staccato is extremely crisp and pointed. Double- and triple-tonguing are performed on the trumpet with a lightness and neatness unsurpassed by any other wind instrument.

EX. 281. Debussy—*La Mer*   p. 122, ed. Durand

Permission granted by Durand et Cie., Paris, copyright owners; Elkan-Vogel, Philadelphia, Pa., agents.

TRILLS

A few lip trills are possible in the high register, but trills on the trumpet are ordinarily made with valves. Most are very good, but some are awkward in effect because of awkwardness in the fingering. The following examples show fingerings that do not produce good trills.

Fig. 80

Fast running figures are quite playable, although perhaps not in the best trumpet style. The following gives a dazzling splash of color, the trumpets sounding with a loud tutti for the first two beats, then with only the marking of the beats by pizzicato strings and timpani.

EX. 282. Ravel—*Daphnis et Chloé*   p. 269, ed. Durand

Music of a fanfare or pronouncement character falls naturally in the trumpet's sphere.

EX. 283. Copland—*Music for the Theater*   p. 3, ed. Cos Cob

Combinations of other than brass instruments in unison with the trumpet are usually not successful. The trumpet is too assertive and

preponderant. When muted, however, it blends especially well with the English horn.

EX. 284. Debussy—*La Mer*   p. 25, ed. Durand

(English horn doubles an octave below)

When the brass section includes three or four trumpets, a parallelism of chords suggests itself, and this effect has been widely used. The following passage is accompanied by full pizzicato chords on each eighth, kettledrum on each quarter, and arpeggio figures for two clarinets and bass clarinet.

EX. 285. Casella—*Partita for Piano and Orchestra*   p. 29, ed. Universal

The auxiliary instruments of the trumpet family are the small trumpets in D and E♭, and the bass trumpet.

The modern D trumpet is not to be confused with the earlier D trumpet, which had a tube length of about 7½ feet. The small D trumpet measures 3 feet 5 inches, not including the valves. It should be remarked here that all comparisons of measurements between new and old instruments should take into account the fact that the eighteenth-century pitch was not only variable but was, in a general way, about a half tone lower than the pitch of the twentieth century.

Small trumpets in E♭ and D exist as separate instruments, but the D trumpet is now equipped with a device for changing to E♭, thus combining the two into one instrument. This is a great convenience for the player, who may find it advantageous to play an E♭ part on the D trumpet, or vice versa. Some players like to use a smaller mouthpiece, others use the same as for the C trumpet. The technique and the written range are the same as those of the C instrument. The D trumpet sounds a major second higher than written, the E♭ trumpet a minor third higher than written.

The tone of the small trumpets has a tendency to shrillness, especially in the high register, where they are most used. Following are examples of parts for each.

EX. 286. Britten—*Four Sea Interludes from Peter Grimes*

p. 28, ed. Boosey & Hawkes

EX. 287. D'Indy—*Symphony in B♭*   p. 186, ed. Durand

The bass trumpet, as written for by Wagner and Strauss, in the keys of 8-foot C and the B♭ below, is to all intents and purposes a valve trombone. It is played by trombonists, using the trombone mouthpiece. The bass trumpet in E♭, however, preserves a trumpet quality with a large trumpet mouthpiece, and it sounds especially well in the register where the standard trumpet is not at its best. It is supplied with a fourth valve, by means of which it may be changed to a bass trumpet in D. This adds a half tone to the downward range of the E♭ instrument, so that its lowest written note is F, sounding the A♭ a major sixth lower.

EX. 288. Stravinsky—*Le Sacre du Printemps*   p. 104, ed. Russe

The bass trumpet may be used to play melodies written for B♭ or C trumpets in the low register, when a more resonant tone is desired. Also it is the best instrument on which to play parts for the older trumpets, if they happen to descend too low for the modern trumpet.

EX. 289. Strauss—*Ein Heldenleben*   p. 220, ed. Eulenburg

In modern Russian scores a *tromba contralta* may be found, an instrument described by Rimsky-Korsakoff as having been invented by him. Although it has the same fundamental as the nineteenth-century valve trumpet in F, its bore and mouthpiece give it a range from the second to about the ninth partial, whereas the older F trumpet played from the third partial up to the twelfth.

The small D and E♭ trumpets are used in the performance of clarino trumpet parts by Bach, Handel, and others. Special instruments for this purpose have been constructed in high F and G, sometimes called Bach trumpets. This is of course a misnomer. The instruments do not furnish the harmonics originally played, from eighth to sixteenth, but their harmonics from fourth to eighth sound just as high, since they are but half the length of the original trumpets. The gaps between partials are filled in by means of the valve system.

Highest of all trumpets is the B♭ sopranino, with a main tube length of 2 feet 3¼ inches. It is used in some military bands.

THE CORNET

Fr., piston, cornet à pistons; It., cornetta; Ger., Kornett

The cornet originated in France about 1825. It is not a trumpet but a descendant of the post horn, and thus it has more family ties with the horn. Formerly its rather squat, compact appearance was in contrast to the streamlined trumpet, but the modern cornet has come to resemble the trumpet more and more, both in external shape and in tone quality.

First made in a variety of pitches, the standard cornet is now in B♭, with a slide change to A. It has the same tube length and range as the B♭ trumpet. Its bore is two-thirds conical and one-third cylindrical, and it is played with a cup mouthpiece.

The cornet tone shares characteristics of both trumpet and horn. The heroic quality of the trumpet is lacking, but, on the other hand, the cornet is capable of a warmth and mellow smoothness associated only with the horn. It must be added that the cornet is rarely well played, so that its good qualities are not often to be appreciated.

An outstanding feature of the cornet is its superiority over the other brass instruments in ease of performance in music requiring fluent agility and virtuosity.

Long used in bands and theater orchestras, cornets were first introduced into the symphony orchestra to supplement the trumpets and fill out the brass harmony, a usage seen in French scores well after the valve trumpet had become established. Cornets were found to combine more sympathetically with other instruments than did the trumpets, and to be more appropriate for melodies in a style like the following.

EX. 290. Tchaikovsky—*Capriccio Italien*   p. 49, ed. Kalmus

The cornets are nevertheless not regular members of the symphony orchestra. Rather, they are adjuncts, to be employed on special occasions. This is perhaps a result of the circumstance that cornets and trumpets have grown to be so nearly alike that the distinguishing characteristics of the cornet are scarcely noticeable.

The following example is in typical cornet style.

EX. 291. Stravinsky—*Pétrouchka*　　　　　　　　p. 83, ed. Russe

꘏꘏꘏ ꘏꘏꘏

CHAPTER FOURTEEN

THE TROMBONE

Fr., trombone; It., trombone; Ger., Posaune

THE principle of the slide trombone, described in Chapter Eleven (see Fig. 63), dates from antiquity. No really essential change in the instrument has been made in at least five centuries, if we except certain alterations of mouthpiece and bell proportions indicative of changes in ideals of tone quality. Also, the tenor trombone, pitched in 9-foot B♭, seems ever to have remained the standard, typical slide trombone.

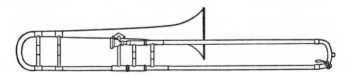

Fig. 81. B♭ Tenor Trombone

The tube is cylindrical for about two-thirds of its length, becoming conical toward the bell, which measures about 7 inches across. The mouthpiece is a shallow bowl cup, more like a large trumpet mouthpiece than one for the horn, cornet, or tuba. The slide is made with fine precision, its outer walls being about a hundredth of an inch thick. A water key is provided for drainage. The instrument is balanced in playing position by a weight situated in the U-bend of the tuning slide. In some makes of trombone the weight is contained within the transverse braces. Materials going into the trombone's construction are brass, chromium, and nickel.

267

SLIDE TECHNIQUE

The left hand holds the instrument by the mouthpipe brace and steadies the mouthpiece against the lips. The right hand operates the slide, holding the slide hand brace lightly.

In Fig. 81. the slide is seen completely closed, the ends pressing upon cork, contained in what are called the cork barrels. In improved models these cork barrels are replaced by spring barrels that permit pitch adjustments in the closed position.

When closed, the slide is in the first position, with a tube length identical with that of the natural horn in B♭ alto. The bore and mouthpiece of the trombone, however, are not designed to produce harmonics as high as those of the horn.

As the slide is extended, the positions are identified by number as each half tone alteration in pitch is reached. The distances between adjacent positions increases as the slide is further extended. From first to second position is 3¾₆ inches; from sixth to seventh position is 4¾ inches. At its greatest extent the entire instrument has a tube length of 12 feet, 7½ inches, just about the length of the classical horn in E.

The following shows the notes available in the seven slide positions. Music for the trombone is written in bass and tenor clefs, the tenor clef to save leger lines in the high register. The trombone has always been a nontransposing instrument, the notes sounding as written.

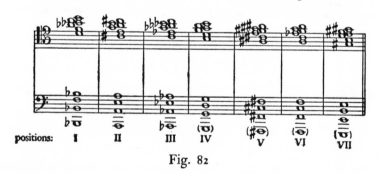

Fig. 82

The ninth and tenth partials are used chiefly in the first two positions. They are less difficult to produce in the five lower-pitched series, but the notes are better taken as lower-numbered partials in higher positions. Trombonists today play as high as the twelfth harmonic on the tenor trombone, but these extreme notes are not thus far a part of the trombone range for symphonic purposes, probably because the need for them is not felt, considering the presence of horns and trumpets. The fundamentals (pedal tones) of the first three positions are of good quality, if approached with time for adjustment of the embouchure. The low E, second harmonic in the seventh position, is the poorest note in resonance.

It is to be noted that optional alternative positions are available for many tones, but that quite a number can be obtained in only one position, especially in the lower octave. Care should be taken that wide changes of slide position do not have to be made rapidly. The following passage is very awkward if played on the tenor trombone, since it necessitates alternating seventh and first positions.

EX. 292. Bartók—*Dance Suite*   p. 66, ed. Universal

Intonation problems inherent in valve combinations are not present in the slide system. Pitch can be adjusted to perfection by slight movements of the slide.

THE ALTO TROMBONE

Until the late nineteenth century, the three trombones making up the customary trombone section of the orchestra were alto, tenor, and bass. With the ascendancy of the valve trumpet, the alto trombone gradually came to be replaced by a second tenor trombone, and the grouping—two tenor and one bass—became standard practice. French composers have shown a preference for a group of three tenor trombones, and they have been reluctant to use the bass. In general, however, when simply three trombones are indicated, it is understood that the third is a bass trombone.

The alto trombone is pitched a perfect fourth above the tenor, so its fundamental in closed position is E♭. Its playing technique is the same as that of the other trombones. Parts for it were written ordinarily in the alto clef, and this is probably one reason for the use of the alto clef for first and second trombones, seen in some scores even when no alto trombone is intended. This practice is common among Russian composers. Occasional notes for the alto trombone that are too high to be played on the tenor are most often given to the trumpet (see Ex. 295).

THE BASS TROMBONE

The bass trombone is pitched in F, a perfect fourth lower than the tenor. In England the preferred pitch is G, while in Germany in the nineteenth century bass trombones in E♭ were widely used. In the twentieth century these have all been gradually superseded by an instrument called the tenor-bass trombone, which in its present form is now called simply (and not always accurately) the bass trombone.

The tenor-bass trombone is a B♭ tenor trombone with a so-called "F attachment," a device consisting of a loop of extra tubing, accommodated within the upper U-bend, of sufficient length to give the instrument a fundamental F when added to the main tubing. A rotary valve, operated by the left thumb, controls the addition of this extra tubing in the manner of a valve on the horn.

When the tenor-bass trombone is designed principally for service as a bass trombone, the bore is enlarged, the size of the bell increased to about 9½ inches, and the F tubing equipped with a slide which, when pulled out, lowers the F to E. This last was needed to complete the filling of the gap between low E of the tenor trombone and its first pedal tone, B♭. With about 3 feet of extra tubing added, the distances between slide positions are greater, so that the slide is long enough for only six positions when the instrument is in F. The low B♮ is obtained by pulling out the E slide (Fig. 83).

Fig. 83

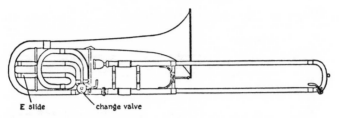

E slide   change valve

Fig. 84. Bass Trombone with F Attachment and E Slide

The advantages of the F attachment are not limited to the acquisition of notes not playable on the B♭ tube. It makes of the trombone really two instruments in one, or even three in one if the E slide is counted, a development comparable in significance to the invention of the double horn. It provides virtually unlimited possibilities of interchange through the entire range of both tenor and bass divisions.

TONGUING

All tonguings are used on the trombone, conditioned by the fact that the mouthpiece is a large one, and fast tongue strokes are fatiguing if continued long. Articulations in the low register tend to be a little sluggish. A certain heaviness is expected in the following passage. In the score, the trombones are doubled by strings, and in part by horns.

EX. 293. Wagner—*Die Götterdämmerung*   p. 309, ed. Schott

Flutter-tonguing can be employed, and there are a few examples in modern scores.

EX. 294. Schoenberg—*Five Orchestral Pieces*   p. 11, ed. Peters

Reprinted with the permission of the copyright owners C. F. Peters Corporation, New York.

LEGATO

A perfect legato is obtained only between two adjacent harmonics in the same position. Slurring two tones that require a change of slide position demands skillful coördination of tongue and slide movements. When this type of slurring is well executed, the break in continuity necessary to avoid portamento is barely discernible.

EX. 295. Schumann—*Symphony no. 3*   p. 97, ed. Philharmonia

On the other hand, it is more characteristic of trombone style to employ a soft tonguing on each note of a cantabile melody. The intervals are not slurred, but the tones are as closely connected as in a nice change of bow by the strings, except at places where breath is taken.

EX. 296. Hindemith—*Symphony: Mathis der Maler*   p. 1, ed. Schott

The trombone requires more wind than either trumpet or horn. Phrasing should be arranged to allow frequent breathing places.

TRILLS

Trills can be made with the lips on adjacent harmonics. They are therefore limited to trills of a major second. The following excerpt contains two lip trills playable in the fourth position.

EX. 297. Stravinsky—*L'Oiseau de Feu*   p. 162, ed. Broude Bros.

GLISSANDO

There is naturally a tendency to allow the intervening sounds to be heard while shifting positions, and this has been exploited as a special effect, the trombone glissando, shown in Ex. 297. The glissando on the trombone is comparable to the string glissando, and its use can easily be abused. It cannot be made over an interval larger than an augmented fourth, the total displacement of the seven positions, and a glissando is not possible if it involves a change of harmonic number, as demonstrated in the following figure.

TROMBONE IN Bb (IMPOSSIBLE)   TROMBONE IN F (GOOD)

harmonics: 2   2   2   2   3   3   2   2   2   2   2   2
positions: IV III II   I ×VII VI   VI   V IV III II   I

Fig. 85

The glissando over the overtone series of a single position, like the horn glissando, can also be played on the trombone.

EX. 298. Bartók—*Violin Concerto*   p. 133, ed. Boosey & Hawkes

TONE

The tone quality of the trombone is homogeneous throughout the range, with a natural increase in brilliance and penetrating power as the high register is approached. In the low register, an extremely soft, subdued pianissimo can be produced, especially effective in chords for three trombones.

EX. 299. Debussy—*La Mer*   p. 105, ed. Durand

The fortissimo of trombones in the low register has a dramatic, crashing sound, with tremendous power of crescendo. When uncontrolled, it causes the metal of the instrument to vibrate, giving a pronounced *cuivré* effect. In general the exaggerated brassy sonority is unpleasant, but on occasion it may not be inappropriate.

EX. 300. Sibelius—*Symphony no. 1*   p. 37, ed. Breitkopf

In medium register the trombone is closest to the horn in timbre, but with a little more solidity, even hardness, comparatively speaking. The pianissimo unison of three trombones, in the next example, makes a full, round tone, without being loud.

EX. 301. Schubert—*Symphony no. 7*   p. 30, ed. Eulenburg

The same unison in fortissimo is overpowering, especially if pitched somewhat higher. It can easily dominate the mass of sound of the whole orchestra.

EX. 302. Rimsky-Korsakoff—*Scheherazade*   p. 236, ed. Kalmus

The high register is difficult to subdue to anything less than **mezzo forte**, with average orchestral players. The extreme notes suggest tension and excitement.

EX. 303. Schmitt—*Antoine et Cléopatre*   p. 106, ed. Durand

MUTES

Muted trombones are extensively employed to reduce the volume of tone, as well as to obtain the new tone color. They are not as piercing in forte as muted trumpets. In the low register they have a sinister quality. In the following example, a novel effect is created by doubling the muted trombone in unison with low strings *col legno*.

EX. 304. Berg—*Violin Concerto*   p. 8, ed. Universal

ORCHESTRAL USES

The trombones are by tradition group instruments rather than soloists and they are used very frequently in three-part harmony, performing a harmonic background function similar to that performed by horns. In large tutti passages, the comparatively light tone of the horns is insufficient, and the trombones may be combined with them. Or, the trombones may take over the harmonic burden, leaving the horns free for melodic activities. The trombones are regularly associated with the tuba, making either a four-part texture, or a three-part harmony with the bass doubled in octaves or unison. All three trombones may join the tuba on the bass line. The trombone harmony sounds well in either open or close position. In Ex. 305 there are, in the score, full doublings by woodwind, horns, and trumpets, but the phrase is dominated by the trombone tone.

EX. 305. Brahms—*Symphony no. 4*   p. 125, ed. Kalmus

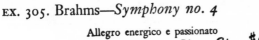

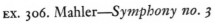

The most suitable melodies for the trombones are those having a kind of deliberate dignity and solemnity, or those of a choral type that would be sung by more than one voice (Ex. 296). Such melodies are given normally to two or three trombones in unison, or in octaves with two on the upper part. The more intimate and personal type of melody (Ex. 306), for one solo trombone, is much less common in symphonic music.

EX. 306. Mahler—*Symphony no. 3*   p. 82, ed. Boosey & Hawkes

Following are other examples of orchestral trombone writing.

Rhythmic, contrapuntal style:

EX. 307. Hindemith—*Symphonic Metamorphosis*

p. 28, ed. Associated Music Publishers

(HORNS, TRP., TUBA omitted)

Light staccato:

EX. 308. Strauss—*Till Eulenspiegel*   p. 9, ed. Philharmonia

Duet between trombone and trumpet, both muted:

EX. 309. Copland—*Concerto for Piano and Orchestra*

p. 30, ed. Cos Cob

Colorful phrase in parallel chords (doubled an octave above by oboes, English horn, and clarinets):

EX. 310. Debussy—*Ibéria*   p. 37, ed. Durand

Unison fortissimo with wide skips, covering the entire range (the tuba plays an octave below):

EX. 311. Prokofieff—*Chout*   p. 78, ed. Gutheil

THE CONTRABASS TROMBONE

Pitched in B♭, an octave below the tenor trombone, the contrabass trombone was included by Wagner in the brass section of the *Ring des Nibelungen*, the object being to extend the trombone family downward, so that it would not depend on the tuba for its low bass. This instrument has been seldom used by other composers (Strauss—*Elektra;* Schoenberg—*Gurrelieder*), and it is generally considered unsatisfactory because of the physical demands it makes upon the player.

The Italian contrabass trombone that Verdi called for (Ex. 312) was a valved instrument. Its part is usually played on the tuba.

EX. 312. Verdi—*Falstaff*   p. 316, ed. Broude Bros.

By courtesy of G. Ricordi & Co., copyright owners.

THE VALVE TROMBONE

The three-valve system has been applied to trombones. The valve trombone has had success in bands, but it is not used in the orchestra. Although the valves give greater facility in the performance of fast figures, they possess the defects in intonation of all valve systems, and the valve trombone lacks the characteristic feature of trombones—the slide—that has distinguished the trombone family for centuries.

※》 《《

THE TUBA

Fr., tuba; It., tuba; Ger., Tuba

THE tuba is the brass instrument least understood by composers. When the score calls for *tuba*, the tuba player and the conductor must decide which of several instruments is intended, and also which of several instruments will best answer to the musical needs as shown by the part written for the tuba. Even when the instrument is specified—*i.e., bass tuba* or *contrabass tuba*—it is often found that the part is better suited to a tuba of different size. Since a real bass tuba has been in use only from about 1875, it is called upon to play parts not planned for it, such as parts for the earlier small tuba or for the obsolete ophicleide.

The modern tuba player may choose from four or five different tubas. He adopts for everyday use the one that seems to him best for the general run of tuba parts, most of which are simple bass parts, lying neither too high nor too low and having no outstanding technical or musical features. On the other hand, he occasionally finds reason to select another tuba for a particular work or a special solo passage. It may happen that as many as three tubas are used by the same player in a single concert.

The tubas employed in the orchestra are pitched in 9-foot B♭, 12-foot F, 14-foot E♭, 16-foot C, and 18-foot B♭. They are constructed with a widely conical bore, except for the necessarily cylindrical valve system, and a very wide bell, details which, together with the large, deep cup mouthpiece, facilitate the sounding of the lowest notes, including pedal tones.

Both types of valve are used, rotary or piston, according to personal preference. The valve system is the regular three-valve system, plus usually a fourth valve, occasionally a fifth, and in some cases even a sixth valve.

THE FOURTH VALVE

Normally the fourth valve lowers the pitch two and one-half tones, a perfect fourth. The pitch difficulties encountered when using the third valve in combination with first and second are more pronounced in the larger instruments than, for example, in the trumpet. Since the fourth valve can be made the right length to lower the pitch a perfect fourth, it is most valuable as a substitute for the combination of first and third valves, correcting the pitch of the sixth- and seventh-valve positions. Also it is a convenience for simplifying some fingerings.

While it is true that the fourth valve offers an extension of the range downward, the notes produced by combining the fourth with other valves are hopelessly sharp, unless the instrument possesses automatic mechanism for lengthening the valve tubing.

The four-valve fingering as applied to the second harmonic of the small B♭ tuba (euphonium) is shown below. Tuba parts are regularly written at their actual sounding pitch.

Fig. 86

By the time the B♮ is reached, the accumulated discrepancy in the valve tube lengths amounts to at least a half tone, so that the note will sound C unless compensated in some way.

A fifth valve is sometimes added, most often lowering the pitch a perfect fifth and functioning in a manner similar to the fourth valve. A sixth valve may give aid to fingering by transposing down a half tone. Individual tuba players have devised various systems involving fractional tube lengths and even combining high and low instruments into a double tuba, in their efforts to solve the problems of intonation and range.

The first three valves are operated by the right-hand fingers; the fourth may be arranged for the right as well, or it may be located for the left hand, along with other extra valves.

THE TUBA IN 9-FOOT B♭

Except for some French tubas in 8-foot C, the smallest tuba in common use is that pitched in 9-foot B♭, generally called the euphonium, or tenor tuba. Other names are: Fr., *tuba basse, tuba ordinaire;* It., *tuba bassa, flicorno basso;* Ger., *Basstuba, Tenortuba.* It has usually four valves, sometimes five. Range:

Fig. 87. Tenor Tuba in B♭

The eighth partial may be exceeded by individual players. Likewise the downward limit of the pedal tones produced in the valve positions varies with player and instrument. The French tuba in 8-foot C, constructed with wide bore and equipped with six valves, can produce tones as low as those customarily written for the larger tubas.

The 9-foot tube length is identical with that of the tenor trombone and the horn in B♭ alto. The bore of the tuba is much wider than in these two instruments, placing its natural range rather lower in the harmonic series. The euphonium is also a wider-bored instrument than the baritone, a three-valved band instrument of the same length but more suited for higher parts.

THE TUBA IN 12-FOOT F

This is the most generally used all-around tuba, often called the orchestral tuba in F. It is also referred to as the bombardon, or simply the bass tuba. It may have four or five valves. Range:

Fig. 88. Bass Tuba in F

The pedal tones are of good quality but difficult. With five valves, the low F, E, and E♭ shown can be produced as second harmonics, without recourse to pedal tones. The writer has witnessed the playing on such a tuba of a complete chromatic series of pedal tones down to and including the 18-foot B♭. It is risky, however, to write lower than D. Notes higher than the eighth partial are inadvisable.

THE TUBA IN 14-FOOT E♭

This tuba is known as the E♭ bass, or bass tuba in E♭. It has four or five valves, and it is preferred by some to the F tuba because of its heavier tone and a slight advantage on the low notes. Range:

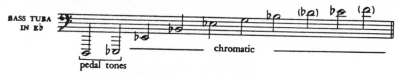

Fig. 89. Bass Tuba in E♭

THE TUBA IN 16-FOOT C

This is the instrument designated by Wagner as the *Kontrabasstuba*, and used by him as the bass of the group of Wagner tubas, to be described later. It is also called the double C tuba (CC), or contrabass tuba in C. Many players prefer this large instrument for general use, although its ponderous tone makes it more suitable for music in Wagnerian style than, for instance, the music of Debussy and Ravel. Range:

Fig. 90. Contrabass Tuba in C

The pedal tone is possible but very difficult to produce, and the valve tones just above it are unreliable. Notes above the eighth harmonic had better not be written for this tuba.

THE TUBA IN 18-FOOT Bb

More properly an instrument for military band, this huge tuba is sometimes employed in the orchestra. It is known as the double Bb bass (BBb), or contrabass tuba in Bb. Range:

Fig. 91. Contrabass Tuba in Bb

The pedal tone is barely possible. The extremely heavy sound of this tuba makes it somewhat unwieldy for orchestral combination. It is capable of a fine pianissimo, and if properly understood and skillfully handled its good qualities could be used to musical advantage.

EMBOUCHURE

In playing the tuba, the lips are compressed or tense only in the high register. Normally, they are rather loose and cushionlike, and are given added relaxation for lower notes by dropping the jaw. The lowest tones require the utmost looseness of the lips, while at the same time the capacity of the lips to vibrate must be maintained.

An enormous amount of breath is called for, especially on the large-sized tubas. It is not uncommon to breathe for single notes, in slow-moving nonlegato basses in the low register. A device for helping the holding of long bass tones was once tried, whereby air was conveyed to the mouth by a tube connected to a sort of bellows worked by the foot, but this invention appears to have remained a curiosity. Long slurs and long held notes should be used sparingly.

TONE QUALITY

The deeper mouthpiece cup, and the greater conicity and width of the bore, give the tuba a smoother, rounder, and less trenchant tone than that of trumpets and trombones. There is, in fact, more affinity with the horns in tone quality, but by reason of tone-weight the tuba is rightly associated with the "heavy brass," a group whose homogeneity is by no means perfect.

The tuba's resources in beauty of tone are best shown in soft, quiet, legato phrases in the middle register.

EX. 313. Wagner—*Eine Faust Ouverture*   p. 1, ed. Peters

Low tones can be soft and unobtrusive, but the high register tends to have a shouting quality not easily subdued. When loud, the tone is hearty and robust, capable of sounding over the orchestral tutti.

EX. 314. Strauss—*Also Sprach Zarathustra*   p. 105, ed. Aibl

THE MUTE

The tuba mute is usually a large cone made of cardboard or other light material, and over 2 feet high. It is used chiefly as a means of reducing the volume of sound. The effect is muffled, becoming strained in the high register.

EX. 315. Stravinsky—*L'Oiseau de Feu*   p. 102, ed. Broude Bros.

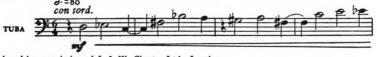

AGILITY

Were it not for the constant necessity for replenishing the wind supply, the tuba could be said to be an agile instrument. The two examples following show its remarkable capacity for active movement in the low register.

EX. 316. Hindemith—*Symphonic Metamorphosis*

p. 23, ed. Associated Music Publishers

EX. 317. Shostakovich—*Symphony no. 7*   p. 95, ed. Leeds

Wide skips are negotiated with comparative ease, and are a means of gaining interest and variety in the bass line. They may be slurred, as in Ex. 314 or detached (Ex. 318).

EX. 318. Ravel—*La Valse*   p. 87, ed. Durand

Trills are surprisingly good on the tuba, but little use for them has been found in symphonic music.

EX. 319. Wagner—*Prelude to Die Meistersinger*

p. 43, ed. Philharmonia

It is to be expected that the tenor tuba can play lively figures with more lightness and flexibility than can be had with the bass tuba. The following is an excerpt from the well-known characterization of Sancho Panza by Richard Strauss. The tenor tuba is written as a transposing instrument, sounding a major second lower. This is a departure from the usual custom, which is to write the part at actual pitch.

EX. 320. Strauss—*Don Quixote*   p. 39, ed. Philharmonia

Single-, double-, and triple-tonguing may be employed on the tuba. The following example of flutter-tonguing is quite unusual.

EX. 321. Schoenberg—*Erwartung*   p. 64, ed. Universal

The pianissimo staccato of the tuba can be compared to the double-bass pizzicato. Sharp rhythmic tonguing may become heavy and tend to drag if continued long, especially in forte.

EX. 322. Mahler—*Symphony no. 8*   p. 34, ed. Universal

ORCHESTRAL USES

The most ordinary function of the tuba is to contribute massive solidity to the bass of the orchestral tutti, doubling other bass instruments at the unison or octave below. It often acts as bass of a quartet with three trombones, and as bass of the entire brass ensemble, doubling the bass trombone, or perhaps the fourth horn. Occasionally, the tuba alone supplies the bass to a wind grouping, as in the following example.

EX. 323. Stravinsky—*Jeu de Cartes*   p. 1, ed, Schott

The tuba participates in melodic basses of a broad, expressive character (Ex. 324), and is an indispensable adjunct in ponderous, melo-
dramatic musical situations like that in Ex. 325.

EX. 324. Prokofieff—*Symphony no. 5*   p. 32, ed. Leeds

EX. 325. Respighi—*Fontane di Roma*   p. 35, ed. Ricordi

When the tuba is used as a solo instrument, the particular tuba wanted should be specified. In Ravel's score of the *Pictures at an Exhibition*, the tuba solo is preferably played on the euphonium, the small Bb tuba, yet the tuba part in the remainder of the score suggests that a larger tuba should be used. The solo (Ex. 326) is very difficult for the F tuba, and players regularly use two tubas in the performance of this work.

EX. 326. Moussorgsky-Ravel—*Tableaux d'une Exposition*
                                   p. 45, ed. Boosey & Hawkes

One may conclude that the F tuba is probably the best all-around orchestral tuba. The smaller tuba should be regarded as an accessory instrument, to be specified in the score. The Eb five spaces below the staff (14-foot Eb) is a safe bottom limit for all bass tubas. Their upper limits vary, as has been seen, being in general the eighth harmonic of the individual tube length.

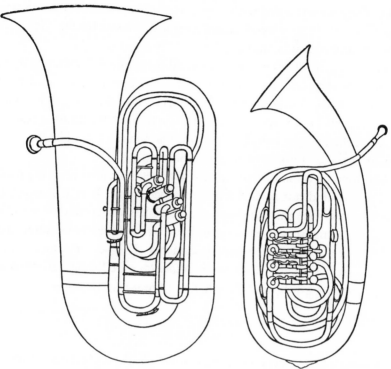

Fig. 92. (left) Orchestral Tuba in F; (right) Wagner Tuba in F

THE WAGNER TUBAS

Wagner planned to organize the brass section into four complete families, each having its distinctive tone color. The horn group was completed by raising the number to eight, the trumpets by the addition of the bass trumpet, the trombones by the addition of the contrabass trombone; and finally an independent family of tubas was conceived as consisting of two tenor and two bass tubas of a special type, added to the contrabass tuba pitched in 16-foot C.

The tenor and bass tubas designed by Wagner, sometimes referred to as the Bayreuth tubas, also called, in German, *Waldhorntuben,* and in Italian, *corno tube,* are rather more like horns than tubas. They are pitched in 9-foot B♭ and 12-foot F, hence their tube lengths are identical with horns in B♭ alto and F, and with the euphonium and F tuba. The bore is wider than that of the horn, but not as wide as that of the tuba. They are equipped with horn mouthpieces, and the intention was that they should be played as alternate instruments by the fifth, sixth, seventh, and eighth hornists.

The Wagner tuba is made in elliptical form, the bell pointing up and to one side (Fig. 92). Four valves are provided and are situated so that they may be operated with the left hand, as on the horn. The fourth valve is needed to correct pitch in the lower valve positions, a function accomplished on the horn by the right hand in the bell. The ranges are similar to those of horns of the same pitches.

The tone of these instruments is strange and individual, impossible to describe, and not to be forgotten, once heard. It is a broader, less concentrated tone than the horn tone, and less susceptible to modification. Few composers after Wagner have written for the Wagner tubas, and few orchestras possess the instruments. The outstanding examples of their use besides the *Ring of the Nibelungs* are Strauss' *Elektra*, and the Seventh, Eighth, and Ninth Symphonies of Bruckner.

NOTATION

Wagner's first notation for these tubas was the logical one of writing exactly as for horns in B♭ alto and F, sounding a major second below for the tenor and a perfect fifth below for the bass. The bass clef was used as in the "old notation" for horns. Later he changed his notation to E♭ for the tenor tubas (sounding a major sixth below), and B♭ basso for the bass tubas (sounding a major ninth below). The instruments were the same, however.

In Bruckner's Seventh Symphony and in Strauss' *Elektra*, the tenor tubas are written in B♭, sounding a major ninth below, the bass tubas in F, sounding an octave plus a perfect fifth below (Ex. 327).

In his Ninth Symphony, Bruckner wrote for the tenor tubas in B♭ sounding a major second lower, and for the bass tubas in the bass clef throughout, sounding a perfect fourth above the written notes.

The following is a familiar example of the Wagner tubas. The unison doublings by violas, 'cellos, and double-basses have been omitted.

EX. 327. Bruckner—*Symphony no. 7*   p. 57, ed. Philharmonia

THE OPHICLEIDE

In the middle of the nineteenth century the bass ophicleide was commonly used to play bass parts. It is called for in scores by Mendelssohn, Schumann, Meyerbeer, Verdi, and others, including Wagner in *Rienzi*. These parts are now played on the tuba, and the ophicleide has become obsolete.

The ophicleide, in shape, resembles a metal bassoon, except that it is much more widely conical, the bell measuring about 8 inches across. The tube is pierced with large note holes, covered by padded discs operated by keys. Opening the holes shortens the tube as in woodwinds. The mouthpiece is slightly more cupped than the horn mouthpiece, and from each of the fundamentals obtained by opening holes a few harmonics can be produced. It is said that the ophicleide, when well played, sounded not unlike the euphonium.

The bass ophicleide is pitched in either 8-foot C or 9-foot B♭, and its range is similar to that of the bassoon.

CHAPTER SIXTEEN

PERCUSSION INSTRUMENTS

INSTRUMENTS of percussion may be simply defined as those instruments in which sound is produced by striking one object with another. The result, as concerns the art of music, varies with the different instruments, from a pure musical tone to what all will agree is a mere noise. We shall deal only with instruments that have had a fair amount of use by serious composers of orchestral music. Furthermore, we shall include in the category of percussion some instruments whose playing technique is not of a percussive nature, for the reason that in practice they are assigned to percussionists to play. Finally, although the piano is clearly a percussion instrument, the keyboard instruments, except those played with mallets, will not be considered as within the percussion section.

The commonest classification of percussion instruments divides them into instruments of definite pitch (kettledrums, glockenspiel, etc.) and those of indefinite pitch (bass drum, cymbals, etc.).

A more scientific classification distinguishes those with a vibrating membrane (membranophones), such as the various drums, and those of metal, wood, or other substances capable of sounding when struck (idiophones), such as cymbals and triangle.

The student of orchestration will find a more useful guide to orchestral practice in a third classification based on the regularity with which the instruments are employed in the orchestra. In this classification there are four groups:

(*a*) The standard percussion section—the instruments most often seen in the largest number of scores, and most likely to be heard in an average concert—kettledrums, snare drum, bass drum, cymbals, triangle, tambourine, glockenspiel, wood block, tam-tam.

(*b*) Auxiliary percussion instruments—instruments only occasionally employed, to supplement or substitute for those in the standard group—castanets, xylophone, tenor drum, *tambour de Provence*, bells, antique cymbals, vibraphone.

(*c*) Sound effects—mostly imitations, realistic or suggestive, of extra-musical sounds. As there is no limit to this group, a complete list is impossible—sleigh bells, sandpaper blocks, wind machine, rattle, whip, cowbells, anvil, siren.

(*d*) Exotic instruments—for the most part, at present, instruments of Latin-American origin—maracas, claves, güiro, bongós, timbales, tom-tom, temple blocks.

KETTLEDRUMS

Fr., *timbales*; It., *timpani*; Ger., *Pauken*

The kettledrums, universally known by their Italian name, the timpani, are nearly always spoken of in the plural, since never fewer than two are called for. In the classical period, the regular practice was to specify a pair of timpani tuned to tonic and dominant. Today three and four drums are often demanded, with numerous alterations in tuning in the course of a movement.

The kettledrum is of copper and its hemispherical shape resembles a kettle resting on a tripod or stand, of which there are several types. Stretched across the top is the calfskin head, held in place by a metal hoop, and adjustable in tension by a set of tuning screws evenly spaced around the circumference.

Tuning requires great skill and an unerring sense of pitch. The timpanist is constantly retuning his drums, while the orchestra may be playing music completely dissonant with the new tuning. In recent years the introduction of mechanical kettledrums, or pedal timpani, has made this problem somewhat less difficult. By this invention the tension of the drumhead can be regulated with a foot pedal, so that the pitch may be changed even while playing. In France and Italy, some kettledrums are made to be tuned by rotating them on a vertical axis, a system that lacks some of the advantages of the pedal timpani.

Most orchestra timpanists use at least two mechanical kettledrums, and some have all their drums thus equipped.

These developments have rendered unnecessary the practice of indicating at the beginning of the score the number of timpani needed and their initial tuning, unless something out of the ordinary is required, such as five drums or more than one player. The drummer will, on looking over the part, plan out which drums to use, and the sequence of tunings. At the same time, the orchestrator needs to know on which drum a given note is to be played, and what the tuning problems are, if the timpani are to be used effectively.

Allowing for slight departures due to personal preferences, the following are the head diameters and pitch ranges of the usual orchestral timpani:

Fig. 93

There is a 32-inch drum, giving 8-foot C. The 23-inch drum (sometimes 22-inch) can reach the upper B♭. Stravinsky, in the *Sacre du Printemps*, has specified a *timpano piccolo*, giving high B♮, and Ravel stipulates in *L'Enfant et les Sortilèges* a *petite timbale en ré*, sounding the D above the staff; but these small drums, if available, certainly lack the characteristic resonance and sonority of timpani.

Overlapping of the ranges affords a choice of two drums within the octave F–F. It should be appreciated, however, that the best tone will be obtained in the middle of the range of each drum, where the head is neither too loose nor too taut. For example, the low F and F♯ will be of much better quality on the 30-inch drum than on the 28-inch.

The timpanist supplies himself with several kinds of drumsticks. The handles are wooden, and the heads of various materials—felt, flannel, cotton thread, wood, cork, sponge. The heads are small, medium, and large, and they vary in hardness, the hardest being wood, the softest, sponge. Much variety in tone quality and volume can be obtained with the different sticks. Hard sticks not only are louder but give greater clarity and definition to soft rhythmic figures. Soft sticks produce a warmer and more resonant tone. The player selects the sticks most suitable for the style of the work and for the special musical needs of each passage. Composers occasionally specify *soft sticks* (Fr., *baguettes d'éponge;* It., *bacchette di spugna;* Ger., *Schwammschlägel*), or *hard sticks* (Fr., *baguettes en bois;* It., *bacchette di legno;* Ger., *Holzschlägel*).

DRUM STROKES

The stick rebounds after each stroke. Normally the hands alternate in striking, but each rhythmic pattern, whether on one drum or more than one, will have its own set of conditions affecting the order of striking (Fig. 94). The drums are arranged with the lower-pitched drums at the player's left. All notes sound at the written pitch.

Fig. 94

The resonance of the timpani is such that the player has constantly to stop prolonged vibration by touching the head of each drum with the fingertips. It is important that all notes to be staccato should be clearly marked as such. As an added precaution, the Italian *secco* (dry) may be used with a single staccato note.

The kettledrum roll is the drum's version of a sustained tone. It is made by the rapid alternation of single strokes, and it is of powerful effect in the orchestra. The roll is written as a trill, and its exact length must be carefully shown in the notation.

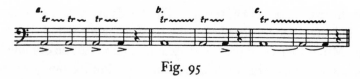

Fig. 95

In (*a*), each note is sharply accented, with a definite break in the roll. The quarter note is of course a single stroke. In (*b*), the break in the roll, between the measures, is unaccented, and is like a change from down- to up-bow by the double-basses. In (*c*), the roll is continuous, terminating without accent on the quarter note in the second measure.

All percussion instruments have the faculty of throwing into relief all dynamic changes. These should therefore be well calculated, and indicated with all possible accuracy.

ORCHESTRAL USES

The timpani are the only percussion instruments nearly always present in a score. Their utility has been appreciated by all composers in the history of orchestration. Their most important function is the dynamic reinforcement of the orchestral tutti, specifically of the bass, to which they add color and buoyancy as well. Rhythmic outlines are underscored by the addition of timpani.

Soft tones are effective in countless ways. In the following example the kettledrums alone furnish the ostinato bass.

EX. 328. Tchaikovsky—*Symphony no. 4*   p. 64, ed. Kalmus

Following is a solo passage for four drums, played by one player.

EX. 329. Holst—*The Planets*   p. 160, ed. Boosey & Hawkes

Used by permission of J. Curwen & Sons, Ltd.

Two types of glissando on the mechanical drums are shown in Ex. 330. At (*a*), (*b*), and (*c*), single strokes are given, each followed by a pedal movement changing the pitch of the drum, as indicated, while it is still in vibration from the single stroke. At (*d*), a roll is started on the G♯, continuing while the pitch is changed to C♯ by the pedal action.

EX. 330. Bartók—*Music for Strings, Percussion, and Celesta*

p. 68, ed. Universal

The following chromatic passage is likewise for the pedal drum, but it is not a glissando. It calls for a clear-cut pedal change on each half step progression.

EX. 331. D'Indy—*Jour d'Été à la Montagne*

p. 60, ed. Durand

Sometimes the kettledrums are muted by a cloth or handkerchief placed on the head opposite the striking point (It. *coperti*, covered).

A tremolo may be performed on two drums.

EX. 332. Debussy—*Nuages*

p. 17, ed. Jobert

For more forceful accents, two drums may be tuned to the same note and struck simultaneously, or both sticks may be used simultaneously on the same drum. The latter is meant in Ex. 333.

EX. 333. Mahler—*Symphony no. 4*

p. 146, ed. Philharmonia

Other special effects include using snare drum sticks on the timpani; striking near the edge of the head; and using two different sticks at once.

Many scores have called for large numbers of kettledrums, needing more than one player. The *Scene in the Fields*, in the Fantastic Symphony, by Berlioz, requires four players for four drums. The extreme is doubtless reached in the score of the Berlioz *Requiem*, in which are listed ten timpanists playing sixteen drums.

In the following rhythmic passage, two players play five timpani, including the *timpano piccolo*.

EX. 334. Stravinsky—*Le Sacre du Printemps*   p. 125, ed. Russe

THE SNARE DRUM

Identification of the various kinds of snare drum indicated in scores is often problematical. The names have different meanings in different countries, so that translations in printed scores are sometimes misleading, and this is further complicated by divergent usage by both composers and performers.

The term *snare drum* refers to the characteristic apparatus of gut strings, the snares, stretched across the under side of the lower drumhead and vibrating against it. *Side drum* is another generic term, derived from the practice of attaching the drum to a belt, and to the right side of the player, for playing while marching. Drum, in French, is *caisse* or *tambour;* in Italian, *cassa* or *tamburo;* in German, *Trommel.*

The French *caisse claire* is the smallest snare drum, being made to sound as light and clear as possible. Stravinsky specifies large and small sizes of this drum in *L'Histoire du Soldat*. The name *snare drum* usually means a drum slightly larger than the ordinary *caisse claire*, and it corresponds to the Italian *tamburo piccolo* (Ger., *kleine Trommel*). In French scores, *tambour* and *tambour militaire* (Italian, *tamburo militare*) are used for snare drum, whereas in English, military drum (also parade drum, field drum) usually means a drum larger than the common snare drum.

The distinctly larger and deeper side drum is called the tenor drum, or long drum (Fr., *caisse roulante*, It., *cassa rullante*, Ger., *Rührtrommel*). It is the only side drum without snares, and so cannot properly be called a snare drum.

The *tambour de Provence* is a special regional drum, suggestive of revolutionary times, and best remembered for its ostinato pulsation in the *Farandole* of Bizet's *L'Arlésienne*. It is the longest of the side drums, and it is also sometimes called long drum, or tabor. Its effect is usually simulated by some other instrument or imitation.

In summary, it can be said that the standard small drum is the snare drum, 14 or 15 inches in diameter and about 6 inches deep, and that the principal auxiliary is the tenor drum (*caisse roulante*), a drum of varying size, but about twice as big as the snare drum, longer in proportion to its diameter, and without snares. If other types are used, it is well to explain them clearly in a note in the score.

The upper of the two parchment heads of the snare drum is called the batter head, the lower is the snare head. They are held in place by hoops, and their tension is regulated by metal screw rods. Although the snare drum does not give a tone of definite pitch, it is an instrument of fairly high indefinite pitch, due to the action of the snares, which seem to double the frequency of the vibrations. By means of a lever the snares can be loosened, whereupon the pitch of the drum drops roughly an octave, and the tone becomes something like a tom-tom, or Indian drum. This effect is called for by marking the part *without snares* (It., *scordato* or *senza corde*). The second movement of Bartók's *Concerto for Orchestra* begins and ends with a phrase for snare drum alone, the snares loosened.

EX. 335. Bartók—*Concerto for Orchestra*   p. 29, ed. Boosey & Hawkes

Normally the drum is played with snares, maintaining its characteristic rattling sound and bright, dry tone.

The cylindrical shell of the snare drum, formerly of wood, is now made of brass. Other side drums are of wood, as a rule. The two drumsticks are of hard wood, usually hickory, with oval-shaped tips. Sticks with felt tips are sometimes used on the tenor drum, and regularly on the *tambour de Provence*.

DRUM STROKES

Music for snare drum, and for other percussion instruments of indefinite pitch, is written preferably on a single line, without clef, the stems pointing either up or down. The regular five-line staff is also used, since the manuscript paper on which composers work is already printed that way.

Drum strokes are combinations of single and double strokes. In the double stroke, the stick rebounds and repeats the note. The most important drum strokes are the roll, the flam, and the drag.

The roll is made up of rapidly alternating double strokes.

Fig. 96

In Fig. 96 are shown two ways of writing the roll. At (*a*), it is written as a tremolo (in drum notation the three crossbars mean a roll, not necessarily thirty-second notes). The notation (*b*) as a trill, has the advantage of showing the exact duration of the roll more vividly. In (*c*) the method of playing the roll is shown, right and left sticks alternating, with double strokes. The roll could just as well begin with the left stick.

Rolls are known by the number of strokes made, counting the terminating single stroke. The roll in Fig. 96 is a seventeen-stroke roll. Short rolls are shown in Fig. 97 at (*a*), the three-stroke roll, and (*b*), the five-stroke roll.

Fig. 97

The *flam* is the common stroke for a single accented note. Written as a note preceded by a single grace note (Fig. 98*a*), it is played with the hand that is to strike the principal note held higher than the other. Although both sticks hit practically at once, the principal note receives the accent. This is called a closed flam. When the grace note falls on the beat, it is an open flam. The open flam is not often used.

Fig. 98

The *drag* (or *ruff*) gives a heavier effect than the flam. It may have two grace notes before the beat, played with a double stroke (*c*), or more, as in (*d*), and using single strokes.

The *paradiddle* is not a kind of stroke, but an arrangement of single strokes to cause accents to fall alternately to right and left sticks (Fig. 99).

Fig. 99

By means of the flam, drag, and single stroke, various rhythmic nuances are conveyed. Drummers are in the habit of using these strokes even when they are not written, because of the negligence of composers in the matter of proper notation of drum music. It is most important that the composer's intentions be made as clear as possible to the performer. Rhythmic differences are especially pronounced where percussion instruments are concerned.

EX. 336. Prokofieff—*Symphony no. 5*   p. 62, ed. Leeds

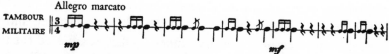

The *rim shot*, sounding like the report of a pistol, is made by placing the left stick with its tip on the head of the drum, the middle of the stick resting on the rim, and striking it sharply with the right stick. The direction to play *on the rim* produces an effect on the wooden drum, but the rim of the metal snare drum has little sonority.

The snare drum may be muffled by covering the batter head with a cloth (It., *coperto*). Another special effect is obtained by using wire brushes in place of drumsticks, making a rustling or shuffling sound.

The snare drum gives sharpness and clearness of outline to rhythmic figures and accents in the orchestral tutti. The roll is a valuable support to a crescendo, although its effect becomes dulled quite soon if prolonged. It is a common mistake to regard drums as suitable only for loud passages. The snare drum is outstandingly adapted for the concise execution of rhythmic patterns in soft dynamic nuances.

EX. 337. Ravel—*Rapsodie Espagnole*   p. 47, ed. Durand

The drum strokes used on the snare drum are employed on all other side drums, as well as on other percussion instruments played with snare drum sticks.

THE BASS DRUM

Fr., grosse caisse; It., cassa, gran cassa; Ger., grosse Trommel

The bass drum is made in sizes varying, in diameter of the head, from about 24 inches to 36 inches, and even 40 inches for big band drums. In the symphony orchestra the usual bass drum has a diameter of 30 inches, the shell being 16 inches wide, more or less. It has no snares, and the two parchment heads are carefully "tuned"—that is, adjusted for their best resonance, by screw handles spaced around the rim. The drum is supported on a special stand, or it may be equipped with spurs to prevent rolling, since it is in an upright position, the heads in a vertical plane. Most drummers play with the right hand, although the bass drum may be struck on either head.

The carrying power of the bass drum is greater than that of any other orchestral instrument. It is often remarked that its soft tones are felt rather than heard, like some of the deepest organ pipes. While it is an instrument of indefinite pitch, it frequently gives the illusion of sounding the fundamental note of harmonic groupings played by higher instruments.

The bass drumstick (Fr., *mailloche*; It., *mazza*; Ger., *Klöppel*) has a wooden handle, with a fairly soft, large knob, mostly of felt. The head is struck an upward or downward glancing blow, and the drum's resonance is such that its vibration may need to be stopped by damping with the left hand. Notes of different lengths may therefore be written. For a short, *secco* note, the damping is effected by both the left hand and the stick, which is kept against the head on striking.

Because of a slight lag in the bass drum's response, the player has to anticipate the conductor's beat in order to sound in time. This slowness in speaking is also detrimental to quickly repeated notes, and rhythmic figures of any complexity are distinctly unsuitable for the bass drum. The roll, written either as a trill or as a tremolo, is performed by holding the stick in the middle and striking alternately with butt and knob, or with a double-headed stick, or with two sticks, striking the two drumheads alternately. The roll is also played on the bass drum with two timpani sticks, the effect being like a roll on a kettledrum of extraordinary depth in pitch.

The bass drum may be written on a staff, with bass clef, or on a single line, like the snare drum.

Special effects are obtained by using snare drum sticks, wire brushes, or beating the drum with a bundle of birch rods (Ger., *Ruthe*). Muffling is accomplished by slackening the tension on the heads. A kind of damper attachment, regulated by a thumbscrew, has been invented for the bass drum.

The uses of the bass drum are dynamic, rhythmic, and coloristic. Its effectiveness is inversely proportionate to the frequency of its appearance in the score. Bass drum parts contain few notes.

THE CYMBALS

Fr., *cymbales;* It., *piatti, cinelli;* Ger., *Becken*

Cymbals, usually Turkish by tradition, are made of a brass alloy, in matched pairs, in various sizes, and in grades of thickness from paper-thin to heavy. The cymbal player of a symphony orchestra generally uses two pairs, one 15 or 16 inches in diameter, the other 18 inches.

The cymbals are not entirely flat, but slightly convex, so that just the outer edges touch. The central portion of the disc is raised in a dome shape, and at the very center a hole is drilled to allow for the attachment of a leather strap by which the cymbal is held.

The tone of the cymbals is ringing and brilliantly metallic. Small and thin Chinese cymbals used in dance bands (13 and 14 inches) give a sound described by their trade names *swish cymbal* and *sizzle cymbal*, but these are not available in the symphony orchestra except by special specification.

The normal single note stroke is the two-plate stroke, the clashing of the two cymbals together with a swinging, brushing movement, not a direct face-to-face blow. A loud two-plate stroke will cause the cymbals to sound for an astonishing length of time if they are held in the air. This effect is indicated by a tie from the note with no note following, or by the words *let ring* (Fr., *laisser vibrer*, It., *lasciare vibrare;* Ger., *klingen lassen*). Sometimes a dotted line is used to show the duration of sound wanted. In pianissimo the two cymbals are barely touched or brushed together, or the sound may be created by merely pulling them apart.

The staccato two-plate stroke is made by striking the cymbals smartly together and immediately damping by touching them to the chest. Repeated clashing makes the two-plate roll, indicated as a trill or tremolo, and marked *2 cym.*, to distinguish this rather crude effect from the roll on a single cymbal.

The single cymbal, suspended on a specially constructed bracket, gives a variety of tone colors and rhythmic effects. It may be struck with a snare drum stick, a timpani stick (hard or soft), with a metal triangle beater, or even with the fingers. A special effect is the dance band *choke*, in which the left hand grasps the cymbal, stopping its vibration with each stroke of the stick. Wire brushes and the blade of a penknife have been used on the suspended cymbal.

When two sticks are employed with the suspended cymbal, it is usually for the roll. This is best done with soft timpani sticks. The sticks play on opposite sides of the circumference of the cymbal, to keep it in balance. Having a dynamic range from the softest whisper to a triple forte of incandescent power, the cymbal roll is a brilliant means of adding excitement to the orchestral crescendo. Needless to say, it is easily overused.

The cymbal part may be written on a single line or on a staff with bass clef.

THE TAM-TAM

This instrument, called by the same name in French, Italian, and German, is also called the gong. The gong is of Far Eastern origin, and those of Chinese make are preferred to Turkish ones. It is a bronze disc, larger than a cymbal, with the rim turned down all around, preventing the outer edge from vibrating. When the instrument is struck gently, with a stick having a soft, chamois-covered head, the vibrations start in the center and seem to grow, giving off unpredictable overtones. It is extremely violent when struck with force.

The large tam-tam is 28 inches in diameter. Some orchestras have also a smaller one measuring about 20 inches, and composers occasionally stipulate large and small, or low and high, tam-tams. Each is freely suspended in a square or circular frame.

The sound has been described as dramatic. evocative, quivering, and ominous. Soft strokes are the most effective. Special tone colors are obtained with various sticks, such as the triangle beater. The tam-tam should be used very sparingly, and the intended duration of sound should be carefully marked. The part is written on a single line or on a staff.

THE TAMBOURINE

Fr., *tambour de Basque;* It., *tamburo basco, tamburino;*
Ger., *Schellentrommel, Tamburin*

The tambourine is a small drum, commonly 10 inches in diameter, with a single calfskin head. In the narrow wooden shell are openings, in which are set on wires pairs of thin brass discs, called jingles.

The playing technique of the tambourine includes the following resources:

(*a*) The left hand holds up the instrument by the rim; the head is struck with the right-hand knuckles, fist, fingertips, or the back of the hand, or it may be struck on the player's knee. Single strokes and rhythms are played in this way, the jingles sounding a kind of echo to each stroke.

(*b*) The tambourine is shaken in the air, causing only the jingles to sound. This is called the jingle roll. It is notated as a tremolo, sometimes as a trill.

(*c*) The tip of the right thumb, moistened, describes an arc on the head in such a way that it rebounds several times, causing both head and jingles to sound. This is called the thumb trill. It is recommended that the tremolo notation be reserved for the jingle roll, and the trill mark for the thumb trill, adding the words *shaken* or *with the thumb*, to avoid confusion. Some players put rosin and other substances on the head to help in achieving the thumb trill.

(*d*) The tambourine is laid, head up, on the player's lap or on a chair, and figures are played near the rim with the fingers or with drumsticks.

The first three manners are combined in all kinds of rhythmic patterns, (*a*) and (*b*) being most used. The part is written on a single line or on a staff with treble clef.

The tambourine is well established as a symphonic percussion instrument, and its use is by no means limited to musical ideas with Spanish or Italian flavor. Its color is bright, lively, and festive, the jingles contributing a sparkle to the percussion ensemble. Also, it is an instrument worthy of study for the many delicate effects it can provide. The tambourine without jingles is rarely used.

THE WOOD BLOCK

The wood block, also called Chinese block, is of Chinese origin and has been used orchestrally chiefly by American composers in the twentieth century. It is a rectangular block of resonant wood, with a resonating cavity made by cutting a slot through the block. Three sizes are usually made, 6½ inches, 7½ inches, and 8 inches in the longest dimension. A hook is provided for attaching the block to some convenient object.

Snare drum sticks or xylophone mallets are used to give single taps, or to play rhythms on the surface of the block, over the slot. The tone of the wood block is high in pitch, hard, and hollow. Its indefinite pitch varies with the size of the block. The part is on a single line or staff.

THE CASTANETS

Fr., *castagnettes;* It., *castagnette;* Ger., *Kastagnetten*

The true Spanish castanets (*castañuelas*) are hollowed-out shells of hard wood, as ebony or rosewood. Two pairs are used in playing, one smaller than the other, a pair in each hand. A string, passing through holes in the castanets, is wound around thumb and finger in such a way that the two shells can be clicked together. Great skill and art are exhibited by native players and dancers, involving the exploitation of tone color as well as rhythmic virtuosity.

The orchestral castanets cannot be said to accomplish more than a suggestion of the effect of the native instruments. A pair of castanets is hinged on the end of a handle, by means of which they are shaken like a rattle. As is to be expected, castanets are used most often to play Spanish dance rhythms, but their clicking sound has occasionally been employed for purely rhythmic purposes in absolute music. The part is on a single line or a staff.

THE TRIANGLE

Fr., *triangle;* It., *triangolo;* Ger., *Triangel*

The triangle is a bar of round steel bent into the shape of an equilateral triangle, with one corner open. A number of different sizes are made, the average orchestral triangle measuring about 6½ inches on the side. The left hand holds the triangle by a string passed through one of the closed corners, while the right hand strikes it with a short metal rod, called the triangle beater. Two beaters can be used if the triangle is hung on a support, such as the music stand. To obtain soft effects, a wooden stick may be used for a beater.

Single strokes usually are made on the base of the triangle, but some differences in loud and soft nuances are obtained by striking other points. The triangle trill, written as a trill or tremolo, is performed by rapid strokes back and forth within the upper angle. Effects similar to the flam and the drag may be used, as well as other rhythmic figures, although these will be more or less blurred by the continuous vibration of the triangle.

The tone of the triangle is high, clear, and luminous, adding brilliance, sparkle, and gaiety to the orchestral color. It is most penetrating, and can be heard in the loudest tutti. The triangle is an instrument of indefinite pitch (although some triangles wrongly give a definite note), but it will sound like upper partials of whatever fundamental harmony it accompanies.

The triangle is of such outstanding effect that it must be used with extreme economy. The trill is especially liable to abuse, and in modern times the triangle trill possesses an unfortunate resemblance to certain electric bells, the telephone bell in particular. The part is written on a single line or staff.

THE GLOCKENSPIEL

Fr., jeu de timbres, carillon; It., campanelli; Ger., Glockenspiel

The modern glockenspiel, commonly known as "the bells," consists of thirty oblong steel slabs mounted in a portable case. When the case is unfolded flat on a table, the arrangement of the slabs presents the appearance of a piano keyboard. Each piece of steel is tuned by size so that a chromatic scale is available, sounding two octaves above the following written range:

Fig. 100

Some instruments are made with a few more semitones above or below, but it is advisable to observe these limits. If the part is written only one octave below the sounds, a note to that effect should be given.

The sticks, called mallets, are light, with small round heads. The heads are of several kinds, hard rubber, soft rubber, yarn, wood, and even metal. Normally the glockenspiel is called upon to play only single melodic lines, using one stick in each hand, but it is possible for each hand to hold two or three mallets to play chords.

The tones of the glockenspiel are bright and silvery, like small bells. It is often difficult to say with certainty in which octave its pitch is located, especially with the high notes. Active figures are blurred by overlapping of the sounds, but this is a characteristic, not a defect. Following are two examples of parts for the glockenspiel.

EX. 338. Debussy—*La Mer*   p. 113, ed. Durand

EX. 339. Mahler—*Symphony no. 4*   p. 45, ed. Philharmonia

In its earlier form, the glockenspiel was an instrument played with both hands on a keyboard (used by Mozart in *The Magic Flute*). The keyed glockenspiel still exists, and must be used to play parts that cannot be executed with mallets. The mallet instrument is, however, much superior in dynamic range and tone quality.

THE VIBRAPHONE

An American development of the glockenspiel, used mostly in dance bands, is the vibraphone, played with mallets on steel bars, but deriving its individual sound from resonating tubes and a vibrating apparatus. Under each bar is a resonating tube, closed below like a stopped pipe and tuned to the note above. A disc is fitted to the open top end of each resonator, and these discs are made to revolve by an electric motor. The vibrato induced by the revolving discs prolongs the sound and, together with the resonating tubes, creates a slowly pulsating tone, which has been likened by its admirers to the sound of an impassioned human voice. It is rather like a *vox humana* stop on the organ, and it may be because of its exaggerated sweetness that so few composers have sought to introduce it into the symphony orchestra.

The range of the large vibraphone is four octaves upwards from 4-foot C, usually written at actual pitch. The instrument is equipped with a foot-operated damping device, in action much like the pianoforte damper pedal.

BELLS

Fr., cloches; It., *campane;* Ger., *Glocken*

Repeated attempts to comply with composers' specifications for the use of real, deep-toned church-tower bells in the orchestra have been unsuccessful chiefly because of the enormous size required in a bell to sound low tones. It would be out of the question to move into a concert hall a bell big enough to sound lower than middle C. Bells have what is called a hum tone, sounding an octave below the fundamental, or striking tone, but it is not relatively strong enough to pitch the bell in the lower octave. In most cases some kind of imitation has been devised, and where actual bells are used the notes are far higher in pitch than the composer's directions would indicate.

In general use as a substitute for real bells are the tubular bells, or chimes. These are hollow tubes of steel, from 1 to 2 inches in diameter, varying in length according to pitch, and hung upon a wooden frame. A set of tubular bells usually has a chromatic range as follows:

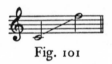

Fig. 101

A few semitones above and below this range can be provided by having extra tubes made. The part is written as in Fig. 101, and sounds at the written pitch.

The tubes are set in vibration by striking with a special hammer at a point near the top.

The uses of the bells are for the most part dramatic and realistic. Composers have always shown great interest in bell sounds, and the student of orchestration would find it profitable to make a special study of the many ways these effects have been suggested with combinations of orchestral colors.

THE ANTIQUE CYMBALS

Fr., *crotales, cymbales antiques;* It., *crotali;* Ger., *antiken Zimbeln*

These modern replicas of ancient Greek instruments are small discs of brass, some not more than a hand's breadth in diameter, thicker than ordinary cymbals, with a raised centerpiece by which to hold them. They are made in pairs, exactly shaped for specified pitches. In playing, one is held in each hand, the rims are struck together gently, and the pair are allowed to vibrate. It can be seen that two different notes in quick succession would require two players, each with a pair of cymbals. The sound is a very clear and delicate bell-like tone.

Fig. 102

Figure 102 gives four examples of the pitches written for antique cymbals by four composers.

(*a*) Berlioz—*Roméo et Juliette,* two pairs, sounding as written.

(*b*) Debussy—*L'Après-midi d'un Faune,* sounding an octave above.

(*c*) Ravel—*Daphnis et Chloé,* six pairs, sounding an octave above.

(*d*) Stravinsky—*Les Noces,* "actual pitch" noted in the score.

THE XYLOPHONE

Fr., *xylophone;* It., *xilofono, silofono;* Ger., *Xylophon*

The xylophone is like a glockenspiel except that the bars are made of rosewood instead of steel, and modern instruments are furnished with perpendicular resonators underneath the bars. The bars may be flat or rounded. The ranges of small, medium, and large xylophones are as follows:

Fig. 103

The sounds are an octave above the written notes. The exact octave, especially of upper tones, is hard to determine, and octave transpositions are freely used by players not possessing the largest instrument.

The playing technique is similar to that of the glockenspiel, with round-headed mallets made in varying degrees of hardness and resilience. Some players become specialists on the xylophone, and as such develop a dazzling virtuosity. The tone cannot be called expressive, but rather it is dry and brittle, without lasting resonance. Rapid scales, arpeggios, and figuration come out clearly without blurring.

The xylophone can be used for short solo passages, and it has many orchestral uses of a rhythmic, dynamic, and coloristic nature. Two examples of xylophone parts follow.

EX. 340. Debussy—*Gigues*   p. 29, ed. Durand

Permission granted by Durand et Cie., Paris, copyright owners; Elkan-Vogel, Philadelphia, Pa., agents.

EX. 341. Copland—*Appalachian Spring*   p. 60, ed. Boosey & Hawkes

Copyright 1945 by Hawkes & Son (London) Ltd. Used by permission.

The *marimba* may be described as a more mellow xylophone. Its resonating tubes are pitched an octave lower than those of the xylophone, and the larger instruments have a four-octave range, starting with 4-foot C. The tone of the marimba is warm and expressive, suitable for solo melodies. It has been used but rarely in the symphony orchestra, although solos with orchestral accompaniment have been written for it (Paul Creston, Darius Milhaud).

SOUND EFFECTS

Sleigh Bells (Fr., *grelots;* It., *sonagli;* Ger., *Schellen*): real sleigh bells, also known as jingles, shaken or jogged by hand (Mahler—Symphony no. 4).

Rattle (Fr., *crécelle;* It., *raganella;* Ger. *Ratsche*): ratchet, whirled around by a handle, causing a wooden slat to flap against a wooden cogwheel (Strauss—*Till Eulenspiegel*).

Wind Machine (Fr., *éoliphone;* It., *eolifono;* Ger., *Windmaschine*): large cylinder, contrived to make a whirring sound when turned by a crank. Turning faster makes a crescendo and a rise in pitch (Ravel—*Daphnis et Chloé*).

Whip (Fr., *fouet;* It., *frusta*): imitation of the crack of a whip, by clapping smartly together two hinged flat pieces of wood, also called slapstick (Milhaud—Second Symphonic Suite).

Among other sound effects found in scores are: *sandpaper blocks*, rubbed together to make a shuffling sound; *anvils*, struck with a hammer; *chains*, shaken or dropped to the floor; *cowbells* of various sizes; *sirens*, *automobile horns*, and assorted *whistles*; imitations of *birdcalls*, *lion's roar*, *thunder*; the *ticking of clocks*; and the *breaking of glass*.

EXOTIC INSTRUMENTS

LATIN-AMERICAN:

Maracas: a pair of medium-sized gourds, held one in each hand. The dried seeds inside rattle when the gourds are shaken.

Claves: a pair of short round sticks of hard wood, held so that the hollow of one hand acts as a resonating cavity when the sticks are struck together.

Güiro: a large gourd, sounded by scraping a stick over a series of notches cut in the upper surface (Fr., *râpe guero*).

Bongós: a pair of single-headed drums played by thumping with the fingers.

Timbales: a pair of single-headed drums larger than bongós, attached to a special stand and played with drumsticks, also called tom-toms.

CHINESE:

Chinese Tom-Tom: a small drum with two pigskin heads tacked on a lacquered shell, played with hard or soft drumsticks.

Temple Blocks: a set of five, tuned approximately to a pentatonic scale, and mounted on a rail to be attached to the bass drum or a special stand. The blocks are wood, generally round in shape, with slots or indentations, and usually lacquered a bright red. The mallets have flexible rattan handles and round heads of felt; or snare drum sticks may be used. The sound is hollow, between that of a gourd and that of a wood block.

INDIAN:

Indian Drum, or *Tom-Tom:* similar to the Chinese tom-tom, but with a single head fastened over a wooden bowl.

THE PERCUSSION ENSEMBLE

Percussion instruments make their effect not only as individuals but also as a unit, in which the effect of the whole may be described as the total of the effects of the parts. For example, when several percussion instruments participate in a tutti passage, the fundamental pattern of the rhythm is not played in unison by all, but each contributes a portion according to its individual nature. It is to be noted in the following example that no two instruments are given the same rhythmic pattern, but that all combine to create the over-all rhythmic design. This skillful treatment results in a maximum transparency and vitality, with changing tone colors, pitch levels, and, even more important, tone weights, on each successive eighth-note beat.

EX. 342. Ravel—*Daphnis et Chloé*   p. 307, ed. Durand

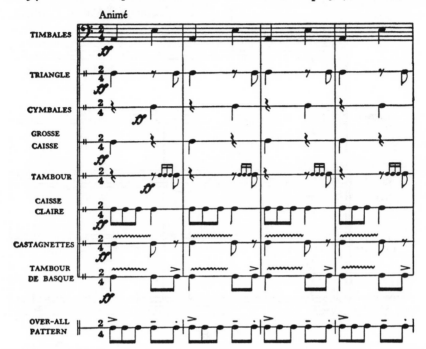

Permission granted by Durand et Cie., Paris, copyright owners; Elkan-Vogel, Philadelphia, Pa., agents.

The following is an example of unusual and imaginative scoring for percussion ensemble.

EX. 343. Hindemith—*Symphonic Metamorphosis*

p. 37, ed. Associated Music Publishers

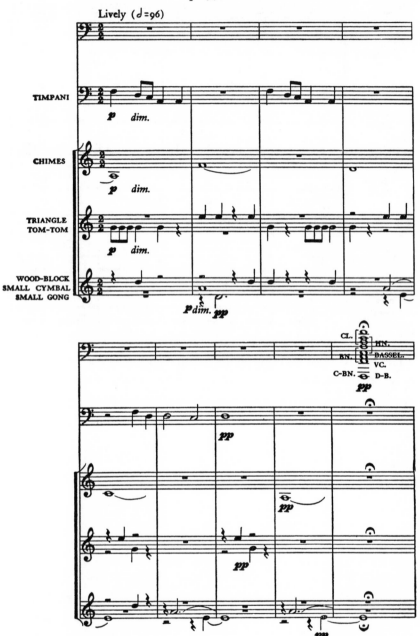

━➤➤➤ ◄◄◄━

CHAPTER SEVENTEEN

THE HARP

Fr., *harpe;* It., *arpa;* Ger., *Harfe*

THE nineteenth-century chromatic harp, having separate strings for each half tone, and also the diatonic single-action harp, are now entirely superseded by the far more versatile diatonic double-action harp. This harp has forty-seven strings tuned to the diatonic scale of C♭ major, with the following range:

Fig. 104. Harp

The strings are tuned with a key, fitting pins situated on the right-hand side of the neck of the harp. Tuning is often necessary in the course of a piece, and it can even be accomplished while notes are being played by the left hand.

From middle C up, the strings are now made of nylon. The others are of gut, the eleven lowest being wound with wire. As a help to the player in locating the right strings, the unwound C-strings are colored red, the F-strings blue.

The harp has seven pedals for altering the pitch of the strings. The traditional form of the harp and the arrangement of the pedals is shown in the following figure.

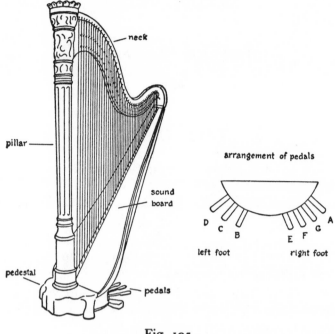

arrangement of pedals

D C B   E F G A

left foot   right foot

Fig. 105

PEDAL MECHANISM

The pedals project through openings provided with notches for three pedal positions, and they are connected with the mechanism in the neck of the harp by wires running up inside the pillar. The strings are attached below to the soundboard, and above to the pins on the left-hand side of the neck. Each string passes over two discs having pins that act to stop the string as shown in Fig. 106.

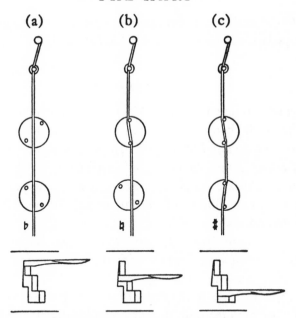

Fig. 106. Pedal Action of the Harp

In position (*a*) the pedal is in the upper notch, the pins on the discs do not touch the string, so the string vibrates in its greatest length—the "flat" position (the strings being tuned to C♭ major).

In position (*b*) the pedal is in the intermediate notch, and the upper disc has turned so that the pins stop the string, raising its pitch a half tone—the "natural position."

In position (*c*) the pedal is in the lower notch; the lower disc has turned, stopping the string and raising the pitch a whole tone—the "sharp" position.

Springs return the pedals to the upper position (flats) when they are released by the feet from the two lower notches. Each pedal acts simultaneously on all the strings of the same letter name. It is therefore not possible to have C♯ and C♮ at the same time, except enharmonically.

The lowest C♭ string lacks this mechanism. It may be tuned to another pitch before playing.

Pedal changes are made swiftly and noiselessly. A pedal may be moved during playing, when its particular string is not in use. Exceptionally, a pedal on the right-hand side may be operated by the left foot, and vice versa, and it is even possible to move two pedals at once with the same foot. A continuous chromaticism, necessitating an exaggerated use of the pedals, is, however, unsuitable for the harp.

PEDAL NOTATION

The harpist is obliged to study a new piece and plan the pedaling, marking the pedal changes where they are to be made. For this reason, it is difficult to read any but simple harp parts at sight, unless they are written by a harpist and the pedaling is marked. It is not necessary for a composer to indicate pedal changes but it is a wise practice, for by this means the practicability of chromatic movements for the harp is better understood.

At the beginning of a piece the setting of the pedals may be indicated by writing all seven scale degrees with their accidentals (Fig. 107*a*); or by arranging these in a more quickly grasped sequence, right-foot pedals above, left below, in the order of their radiation from the center (Fig. 107*b*); or by a diagram showing graphically the pedal positions (Fig. 107*c*). In the diagram, the marks above the horizontal line represent pedals in the flat position, those on the line are in the natural position, and those below, in the sharp position.

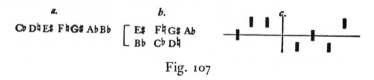

Fig. 107

The initial pedal setting having been given, each subsequent pedal change is shown by announcing the new note in advance of the time for playing it, *e.g.*, F♯, A♮. Examples of this procedure can be seen in the scores of French composers.

ENHARMONICS

Enharmonic equivalents, called by harpists homophones, are in constant use in harp playing, whether or not they appear in the notation. For instance, an F♯ might be played as G♭ in order to avoid an inconvenient pedal change. Repeated notes are preferably played by alternating two strings tuned alike.

EX. 344. Debussy—*Le Martyre de Saint Sébastien*   p. 25, ed. Durand

The enharmonic unison is a means of obtaining a richer sonority, especially useful for low-pitched tones, where the single string may lack body and carrying power.

EX. 345. Casella—*A Notte Alta*   p. 1, ed. Ricordi

Passages containing many sharps are often improved in tone quality by playing them enharmonically in flats. The strings are at their best in the flat position, at their greatest length.

It is unnecessary to attempt to anticipate in the notation all of these enharmonic practices. What is more important is to make as clear as possible the harmonic and melodic meaning of chromatic tones. This may involve writing double flats and double sharps, notes that exist on the harp solely in enharmonic form (see Ex. 346, next page).

Enharmonic tuning is frequently used in the harp glissando.

EX. 346. Dukas—*Ariane et Barbe-Bleue*   p. 442, ed. Durand

THE GLISSANDO

This characteristic feature of harp technique is no less effective for having been abused. The overworked up-beat harp glissando in the orchestral tutti has become one of the worst platitudes of music, but this fact should serve to direct attention to other more tasteful and varied possibilities in the use of glissando on the harp.

In performing the ordinary glissando, the hand sweeps across the strings more or less rapidly, keeping to the middle of the strings, the thumb catching each string when descending, the second finger when ascending (the thumb is numbered first finger as in piano playing). As this causes all the strings to sound, the setting of all seven pedals must be accounted for in the notation of the glissando.

In the following example, the preparation of three enharmonic tones is noted, since these tunings are necessary to bring all the strings in tune with the diminished seventh chord. The repeated notes resulting are not noticeable as such when the glissando is played. The setting for the second glissando lists only those strings that need to be changed. As long as there is no ambiguity as to the timing of the start and finish of the scale or arpeggio, the note values chosen do not matter. Thirty-second notes are used most often, accompanied by the indication *glissando*.

EX. 347. Debussy—*Printemps*   p. 77, ed. Durand

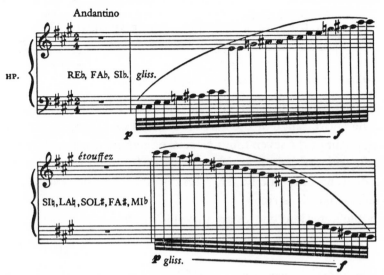

It is not necessary to write all the notes of a glissando. One octave is sufficient to show the tuning (Ex. 348), or the tuning may be shown by the pedal setting only, with just the first and last notes of the glissando written (Ex. 349).

EX. 348. Roussel—*Bacchus et Ariane, Second Suite*   p. 97, ed. Durand

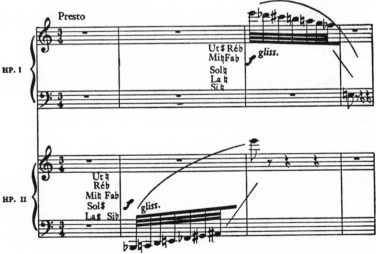

EX. 349. Bartók—*Violin Concerto*   p. 47, ed. Boosey & Hawkes

The harp glissando is played with one or both hands, and may extend over the entire range of the harp. It is based on scales, chords, or any arrangement of the seven tones. Special effects are produced by playing near the soundboard (*près de la table*), or by using the hands flat, instead of using only one finger. Also the hand may be reversed so that the nails strike the strings.

Double notes and chords are playable in glissando.

EX. 350. Debussy—*La Mer*   p. 39, ed. Durand

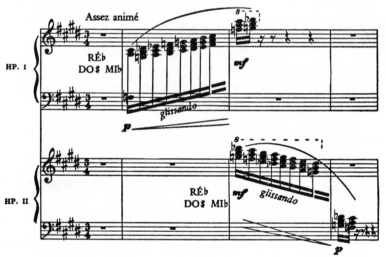

FINGERING

The strings are plucked near their middle point, with the fingertips and the outer edge of the thumb. The fifth finger is not used. On the harp there are no fingering patterns such as those occasioned by the arrangement of black and white keys on the piano keyboard. All scales are fingered alike—ascending, 4 3 2 1 4 3 2 1, descending, 1 2 3 4 1 2 3 4, etc.

EX. 351. Berlioz—*Fantastic Symphony*   p. 60, ed. Eulenburg

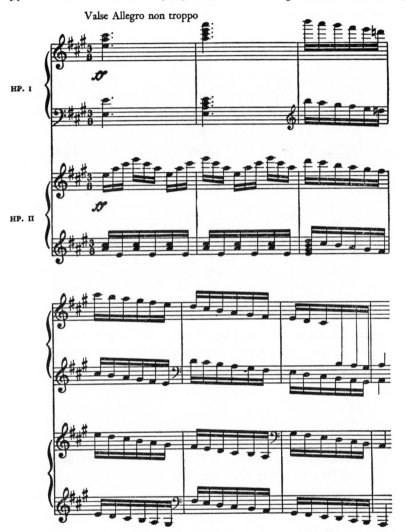

The spacing of the strings in comparison with the natural spacing of the thumb and fingers is shown in these fingerings for intervals: 1-2, seconds, thirds, and fourths; 1-3, fifths and sixths; 1-4, sevenths to tenths.

Arpeggios may be played with one hand, but are more often performed by alternating the two hands.

EX. 352. Ravel—*Le Tombeau de Couperin*   p. 14, ed. Durand

Permission granted by Durand et Cie., Paris, copyright owners; Elkan-Vogel, Philadelphia, Pa., agents.

Although both hands can play through the whole range of the instrument, the left hand more easily reaches the lowest strings, since the harp rests upon the right shoulder (and between the knees) of the player.

CHORDS

Chords for the harp should have at the most four notes to each hand, as the little finger is not used. The reach of a tenth from thumb to fourth finger is like the reach of an octave in chords for the piano.

Harp chords are normally arpeggiated slightly, from the bottom up. If a more pronounced roll is wanted, the vertical wavy line is added. When the notes are to be plucked simultaneously, a straight bracket is placed before the chord, or the direction *non arpeggiato* is written. More often the player is left to decide these matters, according to his musical judgment. Arrows are used if the chord is to be arpeggiated downwards.

EX. 353. Bartók—*Violin Concerto* p. 55, ed. Boosey & Hawkes

HARMONICS

Harmonics are typical harp sounds, and they are widely used. The only one practical is the octave harmonic, produced by stopping the node at one-half the string length and plucking the upper half of the string, all done with one hand. The node's location changes with the pedal position, the halfway point being found lower down when the string is sharp than when it is in the flat position.

The method of playing harmonics is different in the two hands, as the hands are not in the same position relative to the strings. For the right hand, the fingers are closed over the palm, the node is stopped by the second joint of the second finger, and the thumb plucks the string. The left hand is held open, the node stopped with the lower, outer side of the palm, and the strings are plucked by the thumb or fingers. Two and even three harmonics, if not over a fifth apart, can be played at once by the left hand, whereas the position of the right hand permits the production of but one harmonic at a time.

EX. 354. Ravel—*Valses Nobles et Sentimentales*   p. 18, ed. Durand

Permission granted by Durand et Cie., Paris, copyright owners; Elkan-Vogel, Philadelphia, Pa., agents.

Harmonics are best on the strings of the middle part of the range. Above A (treble clef, first leger line) the strings become too short, and in the lower register the wound strings (the bottom octave and a fourth) do not produce harmonics of characteristic tone quality.

In the notation of harp harmonics, the written note shows the string played. A small circle is added, as in harmonics of stringed instruments, and the sound is an octave above. Some harpists prefer a notation at actual pitch, but if this method is followed it should be so stated in the score.

The sound of harp harmonics is soft and delicate, suggestive of distance. It is a coloristic resource, and one that is easily covered by other sounds. Another color is made by the unison of the normal harp tone with the harmonic played on the string an octave below. Harp harmonics combine well as decorative melodic doubling of other instruments, such as muted violas, and especially the flute.

EX. 355. Debussy—*Nuages*   p. 14, ed. Jobert

(unison with flute)

SONS ÉTOUFFÉS

It is in the nature of the harp that tones should be allowed to vibrate. Dry, staccato effects are rather the exception in its idiom. In the middle and low registers the vibrations will last for some time, although in diminuendo, and it may be necessary to stop the sound. This is done by damping the strings with the flat of the hands, usually indicated by the French word *étouffez* (Ger., *abdämpfen;* Eng., *damp*). Short staccato chords may be marked *secco*, as added precaution.

The effect signified by the French *sons étouffés* calls for a special harp technique, by which each tone is damped by the finger that has just played it, as that finger is placed in position for the next note. If the notes are not closely spaced the damping has to be done by the other hand. The sound is that of a dry staccato.

EX. 356. Stravinsky—*Perséphone*   p. 44, ed. Boosey & Hawkes

PRÈS DE LA TABLE

Plucking the strings near the soundboard (*près de la table*) gives a metallic tone, somewhat like the sound of a guitar.

EX. 357. Britten—*Four Sea Interludes from Peter Grimes*

p. 74, ed. Boosey & Hawkes

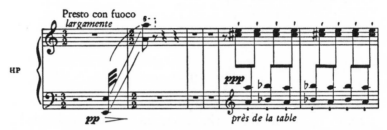

TRILLS AND TREMOLOS

Repeated plucking of one string is necessarily limited in rapidity, and harp trills and tremolos are in consequence comparatively slow. The trill can be performed by one hand (Fig. 108*a*), but more rhythmically by alternating hands (*b*). A further aid is available in the enharmonic tuning of one of the notes (*c*).

Fig. 108

The harp tremolo most often employed in orchestral scores is that called *bisbigliando* (whispering). The fingers of both hands keep the strings in a kind of delicate rustling motion, without any particular sequence of plucking. As the term implies, the effect is appropriate in soft nuances. Three or four notes within the reach of one hand are written as a tremolo.

EX. 358. Strauss—*Also Sprach Zarathustra*   p. 38, ed. Aibl

MELODIC USES

The harp's tone is resonant and strong, but it cannot be said to possess powers of melodic sostenuto. Melodic passages should be moderately active in texture, and at the same time they should not contain too many notes. The following phrase suits the harp admirably.

EX. 359. Stravinsky—*Orpheus*   p. 35, ed. Boosey & Hawkes

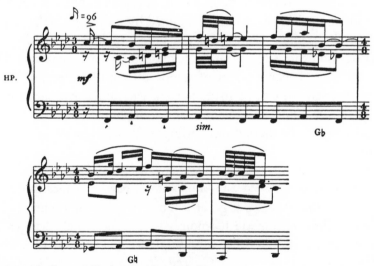

The upper octave and a half, because of the short strings, is less capable of melodic expression. The lower middle register is excellent. In the following example, the harp plays the chorale melody in canon a fifth above the muted 'cellos. There is a very soft background of muted horns and muted violins. The passage is remarkable for the impressive effect achieved with a few notes for the harp.

EX. 360. Berg—*Violin Concerto*   p. 83, ed. Universal

Accompaniment figures are an everyday function of the harp. They are usually harmonic, breaking up chords into an endless variety of arpeggios and decorative figuration for one or two harps.

Special effects, such as the use of a plectrum, or the pedal portamento made by moving the pedal after the string is plucked, have not been exploited by orchestral composers. A muted effect, not unlike the sound of a harpsichord, has been obtained by weaving a strip of paper between the strings. Composers are urged to investigate the novel coloristic and expressive resources developed by Carlos Salzedo. These have not as yet become a part of standard harp technique, so that no more than mention can be made here of the falling hail and thunder effects, the xyloflux, xylharmonic and xylophonic sounds, sounds of the tam-tam and the snare drum without snares, fluidic sounds, esoteric sounds, etc.

Most symphony orchestras possess two harps, and two are called for in scores more often than one. The second harp provides more richness and volume, and also it greatly facilitates the employment of the harp in modern chromatic harmony, where the pedal changes pose continual problems in writing for a single harp. The score of *L'Oiseau de Feu* requires three harps, *Gurrelieder* four, and in *Die Götter-dämmerung* the stipulated number of harps is six.

THE CIMBALOM

The cimbalom (It. *cimbalo ongarese*), the modern form of the ancient dulcimer, is found chiefly in Hungarian gypsy orchestras, where it is played in improvisatory style with great virtuosity. It is generally of trapezoidal shape, laid flat, and the metal strings are struck in various ways with mallets, which may be of wood or leather. Some instruments are equipped with a damper pedal device.

Outside its native environment, the cimbalom is a rare instrument, mentioned here because of a few instances of its use by important composers, who have sought to introduce its highly individual timbre and idiom into orchestral music.

The following are some modern works employing the cimbalom:

Bartók—*First Rhapsody for Violin and Orchestra*
Kodály—*Háry János Suite*
Stravinsky—*Renard*
Stravinsky—*Rag-Time*

CHAPTER EIGHTEEN

KEYBOARD INSTRUMENTS

THE PIANO

Fr., piano; It., pianoforte; Ger., Klavier

I**T IS** assumed that the reader is familiar with the pianoforte and its
technique. We are concerned here not so much with the capacities
of the piano as a solo instrument, as with its use as an orchestral instrument, occupying a status comparable, for instance, to that of the
harp or the flute.

There are five aspects to be distinguished in the association of the
piano with the orchestra:

(*a*) The early practice of employing a pianist to play along with
the orchestra to give support in weak places, and to help the group
keep time and rhythm. This is substantially the same role that was
played throughout the eighteenth century by the "maestro at the
harpsichord," who executed the realization of the figured bass on his
instrument and kept the ensemble together, but no special part was
written for the player, who read from the score. As the art of con-
ducting developed, this usage died out in the early nineteenth century.

(*b*) The piano concerto, in which the orchestra plays the accompaniment, and is subordinate throughout to the solo piano part. Characteristic examples are the piano concertos of Mozart and Beethoven. Today
a work of this type is the occasion for engaging an outstanding virtuoso
pianist, not a member of the orchestra, to play the solo part. The piano
is placed at the front of the stage.

(*c*) The composition for "Piano and Orchestra," in which the solo
piano retains its position of prominence while at the same time the

orchestra is raised to a position of equality. This is a flexible category, some features of which can be noted in the solo concertos of the preceding paragraph (the slow movement of Beethoven's Fourth Concerto). The solo part still is played by a visiting artist, but part of the time the piano is used as an orchestral instrument (D'Indy—*Symphony on a French Mountain Air*). For this reason, conductors sometimes prefer to place the piano within the orchestra rather than in front of it (Falla—*Nights in the Gardens of Spain*).

(*d*) The piano as an orchestral instrument. This situation did not come to pass until the twentieth century. The pianist is here comparatively anonymous and is a regular member of the orchestra (Copland—*Appalachian Spring*).

(*e*) The piano in the small orchestra. This is a further development of orchestral composition in the twentieth century (Stravinsky—*Suite for Small Orchestra*).

ORCHESTRAL USES

The chief use of the piano as an orchestral instrument is one of doubling. By this means an incisiveness, due to the percussive quality of the piano, is imparted to any instrument or group—strings, woodwind, brass, or percussion, in all registers. The high register of the piano is especially effective in contributing brilliance to the upper woodwind. In the following example, two piccolos go along with the piano up to its very highest note. The left-hand part doubles three oboes and the second violins, while the octave in between is played by the first violins and the xylophone.

EX. 361. Copland—*Symphony no. 3*   p. 45, ed. Boosey & Hawkes

In the next example, the right-hand notes act as strong upper partials to the left-hand part, which doubles two oboes and a trumpet. A bassoon plays in the octave below. There are other parts in the score.

EX. 362. Martinu—*Symphony no. 4*   p. 97, ed. Boosey & Hawkes

The piano is at a disadvantage associating with other instruments in parts of a sostenuto and legato character. Better results are obtained if the piano part is kept in motion, in notes of not too long duration. Doubling of pizzicato is of course very much in its style. Here it must be remarked that low-pitched staccato on the piano, when loud, often sounds upper partials with undue prominence, creating a metallic tone and disguising the pitch. This depends upon the instrument, and it is more likely to occur if a small piano is used.

EX. 363. Shostakovich—*Symphony no. 5*   p. 12, ed. Musicus

Among the numerous possibilities for the combination of the piano with other instruments, the following is particularly felicitous, with violins playing *col legno*.

EX. 364. Copland—*Symphony no. 1*   p. 8, ed. Cos Cob

SOLO PASSAGES

The piano delivers imitative thematic figures alone, just as any other instrument. It is also given important solo parts, sometimes demanding a high degree of virtuosity, although no more than that expected of other players in the modern symphony orchestra.

EX. 365. Stravinsky—*Pétrouchka*   p. 64, ed. Russe

In the following, the piano carries the thematic material, over a background of repeated sixteenth notes by three horns. Strings mark certain of the melodic notes lightly.

EX. 366. Stravinsky—*Symphony in Three Movements*

p. 27, ed. Associated Music Publishers

Copyright 1946 by Associated Music Publishers, Inc., New York. Used by permission.

PERCUSSION

Dissonant chords in the low register of the piano are used in percussive rhythmic effects.

EX. 367. Bartók—*Dance Suite*

p. 3, ed. Philharmonia

Copyright 1924 by Universal Edition. Copyright assigned 1939 to Boosey & Hawkes Ltd. Used by permission.

The piano tremolo is combined with rolls on bass drum and timpani.

EX. 368. Prokofieff—*Symphony no. 5*   p. 39, ed. Leeds

PIANO AND HARP

Some twentieth-century composers have shown a preference for the piano to be used in place of the harp, feeling perhaps that the latter instrument conveyed a certain romantic association they wished to avoid. Others have combined piano and harp, and some have used a larger grouping of piano, harps, and celesta, playing harplike arpeggios, broken chords, and figuration (D'Indy—*Summer Day on the Mountain*; Stravinsky—*L'Oiseau de Feu*). In the next example, a deep bell sound is created by the unison of two harps and the piano, with double-bass pizzicato and timpani. The latter are omitted from the example, as well as the held octave D for two bassoons, contrabassoon, bass trombone, tuba, and a bass drum roll.

EX. 369. Britten—*Sinfonia da Requiem*   p. 1, ed. Boosey & Hawkes

Unusual uses of the piano are the part for piano four hands in Debussy's *Printemps;* the employment of two pianos in Stravinsky's *Sym-*

phony of Psalms; the extraordinary orchestra of Stravinsky's *Les Noces,* composed of four pianos and percussion; and the use of an upright piano, not necessarily in tune, for local color in Copland's *Billy the Kid.*

In the small orchestra, or chamber orchestra, for which many works have been written in the twentieth century, the piano performs a variety of services. It compensates for the absence of instruments like the harp and percussion, and fills in middle parts in place of horns. Sonorous writing like the following example gives, within the perspective of the small orchestra, an impression of orchestral tutti.

EX. 370. Copland—*Music for the Theater*   p. 37, ed. Cos Cob

Scoring for the piano creates some practical difficulties that should be at least recognized by the composer. The piano tone ought to be that of a 9-foot concert grand piano, if it is to sound well in a full symphony orchestra. On a stage of insufficient size a smaller instrument may have to be used. Furthermore, to avoid much rearrangement during a concert the piano may be placed far to the side of the stage, especially if its part seems to the conductor a subordinate one. This will prove most unsatisfactory when the piano is combined with woodwinds, because of the distance. The correct position of the piano is in the center of the stage.

THE CELESTA

The celesta may be considered a kind of keyed glockenspiel, in that its tone is produced by hammers striking steel slabs. The instrument has a piano keyboard, and it resembles in appearance some modern types of miniature upright piano. Each steel bar rests upon a tuned resonating wooden box, this feature giving the celesta a softness and delicacy that distinguish it from the glockenspiel. There is also a damper pedal.

The written range of the celesta is as follows, sounding an octave higher:

Fig. 109

The gentle tones of the celesta have a bell-like ring but do not last long, nor can they be played staccato. Easily covered by other sounds in the orchestra, they are used primarily for decorative coloristic touches in soft nuances. In the following familiar motive, the celesta chords are doubled by harp, two flutes and piccolo, and three solo violins, muted.

EX. 371. Strauss—*Der Rosenkavalier*   p. 190, ed. Boosey & Hawkes

The next example shows a simple but striking use of the celesta to mark the final cadence of a symphonic movement.

EX. 372. Shostakovich—*Symphony no. 5*   p. 51, ed. Musicus

The celesta often participates in harplike tracery of the kind illustrated by this Bartók example. Here it combines with harp and piano.

EX. 373. Bartók—*Music for Strings, Percussion, and Celesta*

p. 72, ed. Universal

strings, timp., omitted

THE HARPSICHORD

Fr., *clavecin;* It., *cembalo, clavicembalo;* Ger., *Cembalo*

In the harpsichord the strings are not struck by hammers, but plucked by the action of crow quills or leather tabs. Five to eight pedals to operate register stops, and a coupler to combine the effects of the two keyboards, afford considerable dynamic variation and octave duplication above and below the note played. The written range of the harpsichord is as follows:

Fig. 110

Modern composers have shown interest in this baroque instrument, perhaps because of its increased use in the performance of early music, and have written for it in combination with the small orchestra. There is a tendency in the manufacture of contemporary harpsichords to produce instruments of greater brilliance and power, capable of sounding with the large orchestra in a large hall. This involves a sacrifice, however, of at least some of the intimacy and charm characteristic of the harpsichord.

The following are some modern works employing the harpsichord:

Falla—*El Retablo de Maese Pedro*
Falla—*Concerto for Harpsichord and Five Instruments*
Martin—*Petite Symphonie Concertante*
Poulenc—*Concert Champêtre for Harpsichord and Orchestra*
Strauss—*Dance Suite after Couperin*

THE ORGAN

In the time of Bach and Handel, the organ was an indispensable part of the instrumental forces employed in the performance of oratorios and cantatas, where it was depended upon to fill out the realization of the figured bass. As the texture of music became more homophonic and harmonic than linear, the organ was no longer needed for this function. It was not until the late nineteenth century that organ parts appeared in symphonic scores (Saint-Saëns—*Symphony no. 3*).

The organ never became an orchestral instrument in the sense that the pianoforte did, but rather it may be said to have been associated with the orchestra for certain special purposes. Works for chorus and orchestra, especially those of a religious character, frequently include the organ (Honegger—*Le Roi David*). Church and cathedral scenes in operas seldom fail to call for the obvious realism of organ music (Gounod—*Faust*). In the opening storm scene of Verdi's *Otello*, the organ supplies another realistic effect by holding the low pedal notes C, C♯, and D through fifty-three pages of score. The organ has been employed in symphonic works of the grandiose, colossal type, in which an overpowering mass of sound is striven for in the climaxes (Mahler—*Symphony no. 8*).

Not all concert halls contain organs, and organs differ widely in tone color and resources of registration. Many organ stops are imitations of orchestral instruments, and the dynamic and coloristic potentialities utilized in the combination of stops evoke a comparison with procedures in orchestration. The organ is too self-sufficient an instrument to become a part of the symphony orchestra.

THE HARMONIUM

The harmonium is a small reed organ that can be moved. It has usually two manuals (keyboards), stops and pedals. Although its tone will not be mistaken for that of a large organ, it is used as a substitute for the latter when none is available. The harmonium has been employed in the small orchestra to compensate for the deficiency in volume of wind tone (Strauss—*Ariadne auf Naxos*).

THE ONDES MARTENOT

The Ondes Martenot is an electrical instrument invented in 1928 by Maurice Martenot, and subsequently written for by many French composers. The tone originates in the pulsations made by combining two currents whose frequencies differ slightly. The resultant air waves are amplified and sounded through a loud-speaker system. A keyboard enables the player to obtain different notes by altering the frequencies by the exact amount necessary. A ribbon attached by a ring to the finger is also used for the same purpose, but with the added possibility of sounding all gradations of pitch between the notes. The range as now constructed is practically that of the piano keyboard.

By the interposition of electrical circuits overtones can be absorbed, so that the formant of the tone can be changed in infinite variety. The Ondes Martenot is still in an early experimental stage, especially as regards its use as an orchestral instrument.

The following are some works employing the Ondes Martenot:

> Canteloube—*Vercingétorix*
> Honegger—*Jeanne d'Arc au Bûcher*
> Jolivet—*Concerto for Ondes Martenot and Orchestra*
> Messiaen—*Turangalila*

TWO

ANALYSIS OF ORCHESTRATION

CHAPTER NINETEEN

TYPES OF TEXTURE—TYPE I,
ORCHESTRAL UNISON

WITH knowledge of the instruments gained from the foregoing chapters, the student is advised to read through entire parts for individual instruments in any score he intends to study. For example, let him follow the first bassoon throughout the score of the *Eroica* Symphony, noting the kind of part given the instrument, technical features such as range and difficulty, amount of playing time in comparison to the whole, and especially the relation of the part to the rest of the score at any given moment. It would afford a view of the orchestration as seen from the standpoint of a single instrument, and it would serve to summarize the participation of the particular instrument in the orchestral web. Familiar works should be chosen at first, and the student should make constant efforts to hear mentally what he sees on the printed page, correcting his pitch, if necessary, with a pitch pipe or the piano.

The objective in analysis of orchestration is to discover how the orchestra is used as a medium to present musical thought. Its immediate purpose is the simplification of the score so that order is seen in what to the layman is a "sea of notes." It is a means of studying how instruments are combined to achieve balance of sonority, unity and variety of tone color, clarity, brilliance, expressiveness, and other musical values. Ultimately, the analytical process shows the differences in orchestral style between various composers and periods.

The first step in analysis is the examination of the musical texture, apart from orchestration, to see what component elements make up the fabric of the music. As will be shown, these elements are usually few in number. They are such features as melody, harmonic background or accompaniment, contrapuntal lines, chords, etc., and in most music they are readily distinguishable.

As the second step, after the number and character of the textural elements is determined, the distribution of the instruments and sections of the orchestra among the elements is to be noted. Here a difficulty will be encountered, owing to the fact that good orchestral music is continually changing in the arrangement of the instruments, and often in the type of texture as well. It is therefore necessary to apply the analytical process to short sections of music at a time, sometimes to only a few measures. Passages should be selected that are most easily comprehended in their texture and distribution, leaving the more problematical places until skill is acquired through practice.

In the third step, a comparison of the elements should be made, evaluating the result of the distribution as to balance and contrast, and remarking any other qualities that may become evident.

The fourth step is the close examination of each element taken separately. This will take note of the choice and combination of tone colors, doubling and spacing, reinforcing of accents, etc. It often happens that an element is further divisible into what may be called subelements.

The importance of judging the movement as a whole should not be lost sight of. Proportions of tutti, unity and variety of textures and orchestral procedures, etc., are larger considerations to be weighed in relation to the form and content of the movement, and are not to be underestimated. But the inexperienced student is counseled to be patient with the analysis of short sections as a means of gaining technical facility.

A word of warning is sounded against a too pedantic and literal approach to the analysis. One seeks an answer to the question why certain procedures are followed, but, orchestration being an art and not a science, one must ever be prepared to find no good reason. Some questions are never answered. Imperfections may exist even in the works of the masters, and these are worth discovering, but it must not be forgotten that the unaccountable stroke of genius is also a reality.

TEXTURE OF ONE ELEMENT

EX. 374. D'Indy—*Istar*

p. 40, ed. Durand

When the texture is composed of but one element, this is most frequently in the nature of a melodic phrase delivered by anywhere from one to all the instruments of the orchestra. Example 374 is an actual unison—that is, without octaves—participated in by all the legato instruments within whose range the melody lies comfortably. The instruments not playing are piccolo, two flutes, two oboes, three trumpets, tuba, timpani, cymbals, triangle, two harps, and double-basses (an initial chord for harps and basses, with timpani roll, is omitted from the example).

The trumpets could have played the melody, but the low notes lie in the poorer part of their range, and the trumpet tone would tend to emerge from the blend of tone color. The trombones are asked to join very softly in what is a strong and full general sonority.

This unison provides a rich mixed timbre, somewhat dominated by the powerful string tone, with violins on the G-string, and 'cellos on the A. A kind of incandescence is contributed by the tremolo of the violas. Even the four horns, playing legato, are absorbed in the over-all sound.

EX. 375. Beethoven—*Symphony no. 9* p. 3, ed. Kalmus

Example 375 is an orchestral tutti, all the instruments taking part in a forceful statement of the melodic line as it appears in the first violins. It is not, like the preceding example, an actual unison, with all instruments on the same pitch; instead, the orchestra is distributed over four octaves, so that each instrument may participate in its best range. Taking the A of measure 1, the distribution is as follows:

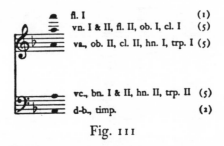

fl. I (1)
vn. I & II, fl. II, ob. I, cl. I (5)
va., ob. II, cl. II, hn. I, trp. I (5)

vc., bn. I & II, hn. II, trp. II (5)
d-b., timp. (2)

Fig. 111

It is evident that the balance is carefully arranged. The single flute on top is not more than a reinforcement of the upper partial from the lower A's. Horns III and IV could not sound the A except as a stopped tone of inferior quality.

Each part should be studied, departures from the melodic pattern noted, and reasons sought for these departures.

The brass instruments of the classical orchestra presented problems for the composer because of their limitations in available notes. If the student will write out the parts for horns in D and Bb basso, and trumpets in D, as they should be if they are to follow the melodic line, he will see that Beethoven had the choice of leaving out many notes, especially in the Bb horns and the trumpets, or substituting other notes in preference to sacrificing the tone-weight of the brass. His solution will repay careful study.

Changes in the woodwind parts are made for reasons of range (oboe II could not continue downward in measure 2), registers (flute II would be in a weak register if continued down in the same measure), and balance (note the doubling arrangement of oboes and clarinets in measure 4).

EX. 376. Stravinsky—*Symphony in Three Movements*

p. 3, ed. Associated Music Publishers

The opening unison shown in Ex. 376 is not a tutti, although loud and forceful. The trumpets and high woodwinds are reserved for the consequent part of the phrase, which follows. It is doubtful that they could have added to the incisiveness attained by this placing of strings, horns, and pianoforte. To be remarked are the accent reinforcement by the trombones, the bass clarinet and bassoons helping the upward rush of the strings, with piano glissando, and the disposition of the second violins so that they join the violas and the 'cellos on the high A♭.

EX. 377. Debussy—*Le Martyre de Saint Sébastien*   p. 1, ed. Durand

As these examples illustrate, octave reduplication is not to be considered as adding a new textural element. It is a widening of the vertical plane of sound, and the two voices are in such agreement of upper partials that the ear often accepts the interval of an octave as a unison. The habitual octave doubling of 'cellos and basses is a good illustration of this principle.

Other intervals may operate in a similar way. The common practice of doubling a melody consistently in thirds or sixths does not add a new melodic voice so much as a harmonic thickening or underlining of the single voice.

In Ex. 377, the principle is carried further, the melody proceeding in parallel minor triads. Also the parallelism is emphasized by the fact that the soprano (flute II and clarinet I) and bass (bass clarinet) are in octaves. The only unison doubling is in the upper voice, and this tends to give the phrase a pitch location in the soprano register. (This work by Debussy is orchestrated by André Caplet.)

While the example cannot be truly described as an orchestral unison, it is to be taken as an example of a texture composed of a single element.

EX. 378. Falla—*El Amor Brujo*   p. 41, ed. Chester

The texture of one element may present details of interest in the combination of tone colors. Example 378 is extremely simple in its musical material but most instructive as orchestration. It furnishes an excellent exercise in mental hearing. Let the student concentrate on hearing the separate instruments in his mind, and then attempt to imagine the combined sounds.

The double-bass harmonic sounds in unison with the viola E. An initial accent is given by the soft staccato horn and the 'cello pizzicato (note the variety of dynamic markings). At the peak of the crescendo the chalumeau clarinet trill is added, the 'cello pizzicato is marked *sforzando*, and the horn's loud, accented stopped tone gives a *cuivré* effect. In the last four measures the clarinet's role is both coloristic and dynamic.

CHAPTER TWENTY

⫸ ⫷

TYPES OF TEXTURE—TYPE II, MELODY AND ACCOMPANIMENT

IN ITS simplest and most common form, the texture of two elements is what we call homophonic texture, consisting of melody and accompaniment.

EX. 379. Mahler—*Symphony no. 4*   p. 150, ed. Philharmonia

Here the melody is given to a single instrument, the clarinet, in its middle register. The accompaniment is simple, but interesting in the choice of tone colors to combine with the clarinet in pianissimo. The harp figure is doubled by muted violas and 'cellos, divided so that the initial D is played by the violas on their C-string, accented. The portamento for the 'cellos must be delicately made. The horn D is a subtle aid to continuity and cohesion, not only horizontally but also vertically, being placed between the harp and the solo clarinet.

Refer to Ex. 380, page 366.

We shall find it convenient, in analysis, to designate the melody and the accompaniment as element A and element B, respectively. In Ex. 380, the distribution of the orchestra between the two elements may be summarized as follows:

Element A (melody): fl. I, ob. I, Eng. hn., cl. I and II
Element B (accompaniment): vn. I and II, va., vc., d-b., bn. I and II, hn. III and IV

The elements are clearly differentiated in tone color, and as a precaution the parts of element B are marked *pianissimo*, in contrast to the expressive indications for the melody. The accompaniment could, nevertheless, overwhelm the melody unless performed with understanding. It is not possible to supply by dynamic markings those prerequisites of musical intelligence and sensitivity without which no orchestration will sound well in performance.

The octaves in element A are unevenly balanced, giving the melody a pitch location in the upper octave. The two clarinets doubled by oboe and English horn make a perfect balance, except for differences in registers, and the addition of the flute makes the upper line stronger. The flute has also the effect of tempering a slight hardness present in the oboe and clarinet unison in that register.

Element B is composed of the gently pulsating divided violins and violas (without mutes), the soft low chords for horns and bassoons in measures 2 and 4, and the bass. The interlocking arrangement of the upper strings, and also that of the wind chords, are important details, as is, too, the partial doubling of the basses by the 'cellos.

EX. 380. Debussy—*L'Après-midi d'un Faune*   p. 15, ed. Kalmus

EX. 381. Beethoven—*Symphony no. 1*   p. 20, ed. Kalmus

Here element A is passed between flute and oboe in the upper octave, and from clarinet to bassoon in the octave below (the strings in measure 1 are completing the preceding phrase). In measure 4, the clarinet is omitted, a possible reason being that its entry on D might sound like a voice leading from the oboe's C to D, carefully avoided by having oboe and bassoon lead to B. When the passage is repeated a few measures later, this lower octave is played by violins, their tone and position in the orchestra offering more contrast to the oboe. Also to be noted is the subtle change from unison violins in measure 2 to thirds in measure 4. The light staccato accompaniment is throughout in contrast to the legato woodwinds.

EX. 382. Mozart—*The Marriage of Figaro: Overture*   p. 3, ed. Kalmus

It was noted in the previous chapter that doubling a melodic line in parallel intervals constituted a harmonic thickening of the melody rather than the creation of an independent element (see Ex. 377). The intervals similarly used in Ex. 382 are not literally parallel, but the texture is clearly one of only two elements, distributed as follows:

Element A (melody):   fl. I and II, ob. I and II, cl. I and II, vn. I and II

Element B (accompaniment): bn. I and II, hn. I and II, trp. I and II, timp., va., vc., d-b.

The two voices of element A are almost evenly matched, the first players having an advantage of registers and position as top voice. The first violins are the strongest, and attention is called to them by their variation from the woodwinds in measures 3 and 4. The preponderance of tone-weight lies in the upper octave of element A, the clarinets alone being placed below. This use of the clarinets in the middle register is characteristic of classical scores, where they seem often to have been given parts later assigned to trumpets when these acquired valves.

Element B, consisting of the one note D, can be subdivided into three rhythmic patterns. With element A, these patterns compose the following four-part rhythmic texture:

Fig. 112

The first violins join element B in measures 5 and 6, making a texture of part writing in the cadential chords.

EX. 383. Brahms—*Symphony no. 2*   p. 1, ed. Kalmus

The texture of Ex. 383 may be analyzed thus:

Element A (melody), meas. 2 to 5: hn. I and II, bn. I and II

                            meas. 6 to 9: fl. I and II, cl. I and II, bn. I and II

Element B (bass):   vc., d-b.

The bass is thematically important, so that there is in this texture a suggestion of the type to be described later as contrapuntal, combining two melodies. Element A, in measures 2 to 5, shows a harmonization of the melody (horn I) in parts. These parts seem inseparable from the melody even though they do not follow it in parallelism. The variety in the number of voices, and the doublings of horns and bassoons should be noticed. In measures 6 to 9, the woodwinds are evenly balanced in a wide vertical plane. Since it is on top, the first flute will naturally be heard as the most prominent voice.

EX. 384. Schumann—*Symphony no. 1*   p. 76, ed. Philharmonia

Distribution in Ex. 384:

Element A (melody):   ob. I, hn. I, vn. I and II
Element B (accompaniment): cl. I and II, bn. I and II, va., vc., d-b.

The violins play a decorative variation of the melody simultaneously with its exposition by oboe and horn in octaves. This is a not uncommon orchestral procedure. The violins are marked *pianissimo*, and the figuration is carefully provided with rests to permit the solo instruments to come through. Subsequent measures in the score contain many interesting dissonances like the E♮ in the third beat of measure 3.

The accompaniment is composed of three subelements: the sustained tones of clarinets and bassoons; the animated harmony of the violas; and the bass, the last being given a slight pulsation by the 'cellos.

The texture of this example may also be seen as an elaboration of basic four-voiced part writing.

EX. 385. Debussy—*La Mer* p. 65, ed. Durand

The composition of the accompaniment with several subelements is illustrated in Ex. 385.

Distribution:

Element A (melody):   fl. I and II
Element B (accompaniment): (a) Eng. hn., cl. I and II, bn. I and II
                            (b) hn. II and IV
                            (c) vn. I, (celesta, hp. I and II)
                            (d) vn. II, va., vc., (d-b.)

The flutes are in a rather gentle register and, although doubled, it seems on first sight unlikely that they can be heard against the array of accompanying instruments. As a matter of fact, performances prove that the flutes sound with extraordinary clarity.

All the instruments of element B are placed in registers that enable them to play as softly as necessary. The strings play with very little bow, and except for the single C♯, the basses are omitted. The low E in second and fourth horns can be produced in extreme pianissimo, the doubling being for the purpose of steadying the low tone. The three components of subelement (a) overlap one another by an eighth-note's value, with diminuendo. It is an example of a very light and transparent accompaniment.

A touch of color is added to the termination of the phrase by the celesta and harps. The score is marked *glockenspiel* (or *celesta*), but the celesta is practically always used in this piece. On the repetition of the phrase, the flutes are replaced by the first oboe.

→»» «««←

TYPES OF TEXTURE—TYPE III, SECONDARY MELODY

A TEXTURE of three elements usually consists of a primary melody, a secondary melody, and accompaniment. The secondary melody may be a completely subordinate obbligato (sometimes called countermelody), or it may have thematic significance giving it an importance equal to that of the primary melody. The decision as to which is primary and which secondary is sometimes difficult and may depend on personal interpretation and taste. The conductor who delights in "bringing out" voices intended by the composer to remain in the background is an all too-familiar figure.

EX. 386. Mozart—*Symphony in E♭*, K. 543   p. 36, ed. Kalmus

The woodwind obbligato in Ex. 386 emerges after seven measures of harmonic background of held wind chords.

The distribution of the elements is as follows:

Element A (melody):   vn. I
Element B (secondary melody): fl., cl. I and II, bn. I and II
Element C (accompaniment):   vn. II, va., vc., d-b.

The two melodic elements are contrasted in timbre as well as in melodic outline and rhythm. The first violins easily dominate the overall sonority, because of their register and energetic bowing, and also for the reason that their melody has been previously established to the ear as the primary element. They stand out despite the ideal placing of the five woodwinds in their best registers, with octave doublings.

Element C contains three harmonic voices. In the first three measures, two of these are played by the second violins as the only middle voices to balance the bass. The latter is represented in the very resonant octave reduplication of violas, 'cellos, and basses. Note that four-string basses must play the E♭ an octave higher.

EX. 387. Beethoven—*Symphony no. 7*   p. 71, ed. Kalmus

Distribution in Ex. 387:

Element A (melody):   fl. I and II, ob. I and II, cl. I and II, bn. I
                                and II, hn. I and II
Element B (secondary melody): vn. I
Element C (accompaniment):   (*a*) vn. II
                                (*b*) va., vc., d-b.
                                (*c*) trp. I and II, timp.

The rhythmic differentiation of the three elements is worthy of note. This helps the secondary melody, sustained and legato, to detach itself even though element A sounds both above and below it. The power of the first violins should not be underestimated, however.

Doublings of the wind (element A) are as follows:

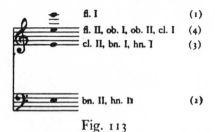

Fig. 113

Notwithstanding the larger number of instruments on the next-to-top part, the balance is in favor of the lowest octave, because of the much greater tone-weight of the horns in fortissimo. The clarinets act as a link between upper and lower tone colors. In measure 5, the horns are placed both in the upper octave, uniting on the stopped note E♭ (sounding G), and avoiding a bad stopped D in the lower octave for the second horn.

In subelement (*b*) of the accompaniment, the 'cellos are divided so that they support both the bass and the viola part. Trumpets and timpani (subelement *c*) give tonic and dominant punctuation, in classic style.

EX. 388. Berlioz—*Overture: The Roman Carnival*

p. 7, ed. Philharmonia

Distribution of the elements in Ex. 388:

Element A (melody):   va., vc., bn. I and II
Element B (secondary melody): vn. I, vn. II, fl. I, ob. I, Eng. hn.
Element C (accompaniment):   fl. II, cl. I and II, hn. I, III and IV, trp. I
                              and II, cornets I and II, timp., triangle,
                              tambourine, d-b.

Here the melody and secondary melody form a canon at the octave, with a time interval of one beat. Since the melodies are identical they are of equal importance to the ear, a slight precedence being conceded perhaps to the one that starts first, which we have called element A. Also, it may have a little more tone-weight since all the instruments playing it are in actual unison, whereas those of element B are divided in octaves (violins I and flute I on top, violins II, oboe and English horn on the bottom). The 'cellos are in a powerful position on the A-string, well supported by bassoons and violas. The latter are not in a comparable register, which would have placed them an octave higher, on their A-string. They serve here to add warmth and body rather than brilliance to the unison.

Element C could be called an accompaniment of the percussive type, a kind of harmonic coloring of the figure made by the tambourine and triangle (the triangle sounds higher in pitch than the tambourine). Brass and percussion are marked *piano*, as against *mezzo forte* for the rest of the orchestra. The arrangement of the instruments on the alternating sixteenth note beats and afterbeats of element C is as follows:

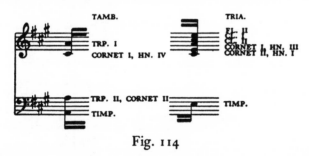

Fig. 114

The tenuto for the basses binds all together and prevents dryness in the accompaniment.

EX. 389. Milhaud—*Second Symphonic Suite*   p. 24, ed. Durand

Distribution of the elements in Ex. 389:

Element A (melody):   picc., Eng. hn.
Element B (secondary melody): vn. I and II, va., vc.
Element C (accompaniment):   (*a*) fl. I and II, ob. I and II, cl. I and II
                               (*b*) timp.
                               (*c*) hn. I, II, and III, d-b.

In this example, the secondary melody appears in the form of parallel six-four chords instead of a single line. The English horn carries the primary element, doubled two octaves above by the piccolo, marked at a considerably lower dynamic level. The various dynamic markings indicate different planes of orchestral sound, and the effect is enhanced by the presence also of different planes of harmony. Combined rhythmic patterns in element C contribute to the interest of the texture, both of the accompaniment and of the over-all rhythmic structure.

CHAPTER TWENTY-TWO

TYPES OF TEXTURE—TYPE IV,
PART WRITING

EX. 390. Franck—*Symphony*   p. 100, ed. Eulenburg

The phrase shown is based on a pattern of four-voiced part writing. The four parts are given below, and identified by letter (Fig. 115). These fundamental parts are known as "real" parts, as differentiated from parts which originate as doublings or octave reduplications.

Fig. 115

The four real parts, with their octave and unison doublings, are allotted to the thirteen wind instruments in the following manner:

A ⎡fl. I   B ⎡fl. II
8 ⎢   8 ⎢
⎣ob. I, cl. I   ⎣Eng. hn., cl. II, (ob. II)
8 ⎡
⎣bn. I, hn. I

C   bn. II, hn. II, (hn. III)   D   bass cl.

In measure 3, there are irregularities to be noted. The English horn leaves B to follow C, and oboe II enters to play the remainder of B. Bassoon I and horn I leave A and create a new voice, ending on C♯ (this makes five real parts in the cadence). Bassoon II and horn II change from C to B, while horn III plays the termination of C. These changes enable some instruments to make a better diminuendo, and at the same time the cadential harmony is enriched.

The violas add a decorative figure to the cadence, finally joining part B.

It will have been noticed that the numerical distribution of the instruments is far from equable. The octave doublings do not add materially to the tone-weight of a part, but the unison doublings do. Part A, the melody, is obviously planned as the strongest voice. Part D, the bass, appears alarmingly weak. In performance, however, the passage is very successful in its organlike sonority, if played with an ear to balance.

The part writing texture is not to be confused with that of type **II**, in which melody and accompaniment are two quite distinct elements. Here, the melody is just one of several otherwise equal voices.

EX. 391. Mozart—*Symphony in C major*, K. 200

p. 16, ed. Philharmonia

The number of real parts is most often three or four. In Ex. 391 there are only two, as follows:

Fig. 116

Distribution:

A $\Big[$ vn. I, ob. I and II   B $\Big[$ va., vc.
8 $\Big[$ vn. II   8 $\Big[$ d-b.

The horns and trumpets give an illusion of playing no other parts than these, despite their not being able to play the notes C♯, B, A, or F♯ (without recourse to stopped notes on the horn, apparently not considered good enough to use). On the second beat of measure 2, they sound the only added note, G, the open fifth being a classical formula in dominant harmony for horns and trumpets.

EX. 392. Beethoven—*Symphony no. 5*   p. 50, ed. Kalmus

Here the texture changes from three parts in the first measure to four parts in the third.

Fig. 117

Distribution in Ex. 392:

meas. 1 and 2		meas. 3		meas. 4 and 5
A ⎡vn. I	8	⎡fl. I	8	vn. I
⎣½ va., bn. I (meas. 2)		⎱vn. I, cl. I	8	
		⎣bn. I		
B ⎡vn. II	8	⎡ob. I	8	vn. II
⎣½ va., bn. II (meas. 2)		⎱vn. II, cl. II	8	
		⎣bn. II		
C		⎡ob. II	8	**va.**
		⎱½ va.	8	
		⎣½ va.		
D ⎡vc.	8	⎡vc.	8	⎡vc. 8
⎣d-b.		⎣d-b.		⎣d-b.

The expressive power of the phrase is much heightened by the variety and subtlety of this distribution. In measure 2, the sounding of the double appoggiatura in the violas, against the notes of resolution in the bassoons, is an effect characteristically orchestral. The choice of the oboe instead of flute II, to play the second part with flute I, is a favorite procedure of Beethoven.

EX. 393. Holst—*The Planets* p. 66, ed. Boosey & Hawkes

Used by permission of J. Curwen & Sons, Ltd.

On first sight, Ex. 393 looks to be a texture of seven parts. The effect is, however, of but two basic melodic lines, top and bottom, moving in contrary motion. Each voice is given harmonic "thickening," the upper moving in parallel root position triads, the lower in parallel six-four chords.

The part-writing texture, composed of real parts with or without doubling, is often found in the accompaniment element of the texture type II. Even the primary element may be constructed in part writing (see Chapter Twenty, Ex. 383). It is also present in the structure of chord connections, such as cadences, where the voice leading of the parts is felt to be important. As mentioned previously, the phrase from Schumann's First Symphony, quoted in Ex. 384, may be interpreted as an elaboration of a basic pattern of four-part writing.

≫≫ ≪≪

CHAPTER TWENTY-THREE

TYPES OF TEXTURE—TYPE V, CONTRAPUNTAL TEXTURE

THE contrapuntal texture consists entirely of melodic elements. The melodic lines may be designed in imitative counterpoint, or they may be quite independent as melodies. The texture may be fugal, or it may present a combination of melodies thematically significant, perhaps previously heard singly, and so not new to the ear.

EX. 394. Haydn—*Symphony in D (Glocken)*   p. 42, ed. Eulenburg

The simple texture of this example is very common in orchestral music. There are but two lines, starting as if in canon but continuing in predominantly consonant intervals, without close imitation. It is not very different from two-voiced part writing.

Distribution in Ex. 394:

A   8 [vn. I, fl. I and II, ob. I (ob. II, cl. I, at meas. 4) / vn. II, ob. II (cl. II, at meas. 4)

B   8 [va., vc., bn. I and II / d-b.

The cadence, measures 7 and 8, is in four-voiced part writing.

EX. 395. Mozart—*Symphony in G minor*, K. 550

p. 41, ed. Philharmonia

The contrasting patterns of the melodic rhythms, and the harmonic dissonances, make this an example of much stronger contrapuntal effect.

Distribution in Ex. 395:

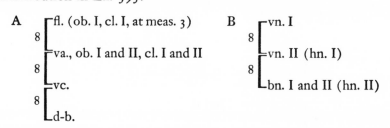

In measure 3, for the second half of the phrase, the oboes and clarinets change to octaves, strengthening the top part and giving a brighter sound than the continued unison would have made. Also the entry of the horns at that point strengthens line B where the bassoons are weaker. The horns do not attempt to finish the melody, but repeat the dominant D as extra notes. The bassoons do not play with the 'cellos and basses, as might be expected.

The vertical ranges of the two lines are significant as orchestration. Line A is the bass, but with the doubling by the flute, and the strength of the violas plus oboes and clarinets, it tends to sound in a pitch location very near to that of line B. This impression is helped by the placing of the double-basses in a fairly high register.

EX. 396. Wagner—*Prelude to Tristan und Isolde*   p. 4, ed. Kalmus

This passage is composed of three principal lines, with three less-important entering voices, the chief function of which is to add to the sonority in crescendo. These added parts are melodic, and the texture is completely contrapuntal.

Distribution in Ex. 396:

A   ⌈ob. I, cl. I   D   bn. I and II (meas. 2)
    8⌊
      cl. II, hn. I

B   ⌈vn. II   E   ⌈hn. III (meas. 4)
    8⌊   8⌊
      va.   hn. IV (meas. 4)

C   ⌈bass cl. (meas. 2), hn. II (meas. 4)   F   Eng. hn. (meas. 4)
    8⌊
      d-b., bn. III

The extra lines D, E, and F become much more significant from the middle of measure 4, the climax of the phrase. At this point the strings cease playing, and measure 5 is all wind tone in diminuendo. D, E, and F may then be considered as furnishing a continuation of lines B and C.

Attention is called to the rich tone color, and the predominance, of line A, and the low pitch of lines B and C. The few notes in measure 1, for English horn, first violins, and 'cellos, belong to the preceding phrase.

EX. 397. Milhaud—*Symphony no. 2*   p. 98, ed. Heugel

The example given is a four-part texture, a fugal stretto having two parts in augmentation (the answering of the interval of a fourth by a fifth is brought about through observance of tonal conventions of the fugue).

Distribution in Ex. 397:

A $\begin{bmatrix} \frac{1}{2} \text{ vn. I, fl. I and II} \\ 8 \\ \frac{1}{2} \text{ vn. I, ob. I and II, trp. I} \end{bmatrix}$ C $\begin{bmatrix} \frac{1}{2} \text{ vc., trb. I} \\ 8 \\ \frac{1}{2} \text{ vc., bass cl., bn. I and II, trb. II} \end{bmatrix}$

B $\begin{bmatrix} \text{vn. II, cl. I} \\ 8 \\ \text{va., cl. II, hn. I and II} \end{bmatrix}$ D $\begin{bmatrix} \text{tuba} \\ 8 \\ \text{d-b., contrabn.} \end{bmatrix}$

In the last two measures, the piccolo is added to the upper part in time to play the F♯, too high for the violins. Otherwise, the only departures from the established arrangement are the forced octave change in the basses, and the omission of three notes, one unplayable, for the contrabassoon.

The orchestra is well balanced, with the brass to the fore. The bass is deep and ponderous, no doubt an intended effect. This is an excellent example of a nearly full tutti distributed among four melodic lines.

EX. 398. Bartók—*Concerto for Orchestra*   p. 56, ed. Boosey & Hawkes

Distribution in Ex. 398:

A	vn. I, vn. II	D	va., Eng. hn.
B	vc., bass cl.	E	d-b., bn. I and II
C	hn. I and II		

In this five-part counterpoint, it could well be advanced that the violin melody is prominent enough to set it apart from the other lines. One would then describe the texture as melody and accompaniment, the accompaniment being a four-voiced contrapuntal texture. The distinction is subtle, but accented by the imitative relationships existing in the thematic content of the four subsidiary melodies.

The doublings are unison doublings, with two minor exceptions. The four notes taken an octave lower by the English horn in measure 5 are doubtless a sign that the composer did not like the sound of the high B♭ on that instrument. In the same measure the first bassoon is moved up an octave, perhaps to give clarity to the basses as they descend below the G-string. The omission of the first note, in this bassoon doubling of part E, avoids an overemphasis on the D♭, which also sounds at that moment in part B.

CHAPTER TWENTY-FOUR

TYPES OF TEXTURE—TYPE VI, CHORDS

ISOLATED chords—that is, chords affected little or none by voice leading—are to be studied for the choice of tone color, the vertical sequence of the instruments, spacing, balance, and equality of registers. All of these attributes should be considered in relation to the dynamic level and musical intent of the chord. Each chord ought to be seen in its setting in the score.

The tone color is determined primarily by the instruments selected, but it is also in a large measure affected by the manner in which the instruments are combined. The chord may be scored exclusively for woodwinds, for brass, or for strings, or it may be scored for mixtures of these. Chords for the full orchestra (tutti chords) are common. Pure colors, without unison doublings, may be used, or the chord may be made up of mixed timbres. The particular sonority of low registers, or high, may be chosen. Emphasis may be placed on double-reed tone, or on muted sounds. It should not be overlooked that the harmonic structure of the chord, its intervals, has an essential influence on its tone color, apart from the instrumental sound.

Vertical relationships between instrumental tones are important in securing an even vertical plane of sound, without noticeable breaks where one tone color adjoins another. It is customary to distinguish, in addition to octave and unison doubling, four relationships that may exist vertically between pairs of instruments. These are overlapping, superposition, interlocking, and enclosing.

Overlapping occurs when the lower of one pair of instruments is in unison with the upper of a second pair.

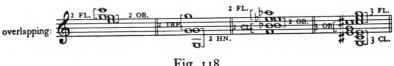

overlapping:

Fig. 118

In superposition, the two pairs are situated one above the other with no contact between them.

superposition:

Fig. 119

Interlocking is achieved by placing the lower note of the upper pair beneath the upper note of the lower pair.

interlocking:

Fig. 120

In enclosing, both notes of one pair lie between the two notes of the other pair.

enclosing:

Fig. 121

The spacing of the chord should be observed; that is, whether open or close spacing is used, and whether or not there have been left any spaces in which it would have been possible to place notes of the harmony.

The balance of a chord is judged by the relative tone-weight, or carrying power, of each note, assuming that the intent is to create a vertical plane of sound in which no tone emerges or protrudes perceptibly toward the hearer. An absolute judgment is rarely possible, because of the many questions involved, but one should form an opinion for reference when the opportunity comes to hear the chord in an orchestral performance. The largest contributing factors in balance are the number of instruments playing each note, and the relative dynamic power of the individual instruments in their particular registers.

The use of weak and strong registers is always to be taken into account where wind instruments are concerned, bearing in mind that discrepancies are often corrected by the performers in music with which they are familiar.

A chord may be deliberately overweighted in a part of its range in order to emphasize the pitch location as low, medium, or high.

Examples of isolated chords are given below, in condensed score to save space. The student is urged to examine the chords in the full scores. In the examples, all notes sound at the pitch written.

EX. 399. Weber—*Overture to Der Freischütz*   p. 24, ed. Philharmonia

(strings tremolo)

Example 399: A clear and brilliant tutti chord, occurring in the middle of the overture. The major triad in root position is naturally a most resonant chord since its factors are identified with the overtones from its lowest note. The structure of the harmonic series is also suggested by the observation that chords sound clearer when the lower intervals are the more widely spaced ones. From this standpoint, the E in the second trombone seems less ideally placed than the other notes.

Vertical relationships: superposition—flutes, oboes; trumpets, horns; interlocking—oboes, clarinets; overlapping—oboes, trumpets; trombones, bassoons. The woodwinds are placed high, above the brass, except for the overlapping with the trumpets and the placing of the bassoons in the lowest octave. The brass being so much more powerful than the woodwinds, the latter serve principally as reinforcement of upper partials.

The tremolo strings are very brilliant as placed, so that the chord is quite evenly balanced throughout. Instruments not having unison doubling are oboe I, horn I, horn IV, trombone II, and bassoon II. Except for trombone II, these receive acoustic reinforcement from the fundamental tone. Even the bassoon benefits by the strong difference tone from the octave C's.

EX. 400. Brahms—*Symphony no. 3*   p. 65, ed. Kalmus

Example 400: A soft closing chord of a slow movement. The tone color is a blend of the luminosity of the high violins and flutes, with the dark tone of the minor third, played on the C-string by the violas and doubled by the closely spaced trombones.

The spacing of the chord allows the ear to separate these two colors, through the omission of the G just above the horns. Such open spaces are often found in soft chords, and they permit the overtones of lower instruments to sound. The result is less satisfactory in loud chords, as then the overtones are not strong enough to compete with nearby instruments. Here the unison of double-basses with the open 'cello C is particularly rich in upper partials in the neighborhood of the horns and clarinets.

EX. 401. Berlioz—*Roméo et Juliette*   p. 53, ed. Eulenburg

(str. and timp. tremolo)

Example 401: This is a chord of medium low register. Note the overlapping in flutes, oboes, and clarinets, and the interlocking of violin double-stops. The major third overtone is guarded against by the strong doubling, even tripling, of the upper C's. The only parts left without doubling are flute I, kettledrum I, and the basses. There are no open spaces except the bottom octave.

The indicated crescendo from *piano* to *fortissimo*, then returning to *piano*, introduces a serious problem of balance. The trombones and timpani can easily surpass the other winds and most string sections, in power of crescendo. Horns can do better than woodwinds in this respect, especially when the latter are, as here, in their least powerful registers. The conductor will have to decide whether to limit the

amount of crescendo to the capacity of the woodwind or to sacrifice
balance to achieve the dramatic effect wanted by the composer.

EX. 402. Strauss—*Don Juan*   p. 14, ed. Kalmus

(omitted: harp arpeggio;
glockenspiel tremolo on 8ve E)

Example 402: The dynamic level marked is unusual in a complete
tutti of a large orchestra. The effect is rich and sumptuous, and could
not be obtained with the thinner texture of a smaller group of instruments. Here the extreme softness of a triple *piano* is, of course, to be
taken in a relative sense, *as soft as possible*. The instruments are not all
in weak registers, but this is not unexpected in a chord extending over
so wide a range. The two high flutes are not doubled.

This dominant major ninth is another of those chords that follow in
their structure the interval sequence of the harmonic series. The root
appears only in the lowest octave, except for the high kettledrum's F♯,
played very softly with soft sticks. From the C♯ in trombone III and
'cellos upwards, all spaces are filled with chord tones. It is of interest
that the three upper appearances of G♯, the ninth, are not doubled
(flute I, oboe I, trumpet I).

EX. 403. Stravinsky—*Symphonies of Wind Instruments*

p. 35, ed. Boosey & Hawkes

Example 403: A soft wind chord, harmonically a combination of tonic and dominant. The stopped horns, with muted trumpets, trombones, and tuba, blend on fairly equal terms with the woodwind. The woodwind doublings are worthy of close study. With the high clarinet and oboes, the three flutes make a bright color, added to the high first trumpet. There are more open than close intervals, giving room for the partials of both C and G to sound. The only close dissonance is the minor second made by the first horn against the mixed timbre of second trumpet, clarinet, and English horn.

EX. 404. W. Schuman—*Symphony no. 3* p. 81, ed. G. Schirmer

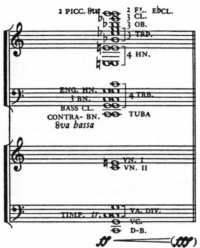

Ex. 404: Here the triads of C major and Eb major are combined into one chord, the former being situated in the lower registers and the latter in the higher pitches. The two components may be distinguished by the ear as two layers of sound, an effect further facilitated through the absence of the note G between horns and trumpets. The upper woodwinds are massed in superposition above the high trumpets, furnishing a sonority of force and brilliance for the Eb part of the chord, whereas the strings and lower winds are given positions of less intensity and carrying power. The entire chord is dominated by the brass tone, and if balance is to be achieved it will be necessary for trumpets and trombones to play somewhat under the dynamic level indicated.

EX. 405. Hindemith—*Symphony: Mathis der Maler* p. 23, ed. Schott

꘎꘎

CHAPTER TWENTY-FIVE

TYPES OF TEXTURE—TYPE VII, COMPLEX TEXTURE

W E HAVE seen how elements of a texture may be themselves divisible into smaller units or subelements. In the texture of Type I, the melodic line may be "thickened" by one or more parallel intervals, and eventually be more or less completely harmonized. The element of accompaniment (Type II) may be quite complex, and consist of a number of separate details. In Type III, more than one secondary melody may be presented, the combined melodic elements approaching a contrapuntal texture. The number of real parts or melodic voices may be increased in Types IV and V.

By combining two or more of the textures we have described as Types I to VI, a texture is created that is complex in varying degree.

Refer to Example 405 on facing page.

Example 405: The primary element in this passage is the chorale-like melody played by the first trumpet. Its thematic importance has been previously established in the piece. Here, it is presented as the top voice in a texture of part writing for the brass, with the added support of the clarinets. The secondary melody (piccolo, flutes, oboes), in contrasting rhythm, is likewise thematic, while a third melodic element consists simply of a descending scale for the strings, varied by the violins. The held pedal bass may be considered a fourth element.

The distribution of these elements may be shown in schematic form
as follows:

Element A (melody harmonized in part writing):

$$a \text{ (melody):} \quad 8 \begin{bmatrix} \text{trp. I, cl. I and II} \\ \text{hn. I, trb. I} \end{bmatrix}$$

$$b \text{ (parts):} \quad \text{hn. II, III and IV, trp. II, trb. II}$$

Element B (secondary melody):

$$8 \begin{bmatrix} \text{picc., fl.} \\ \text{ob. I and II} \end{bmatrix}$$

Element C (descending scale):

$$8 \begin{bmatrix} \text{vn. I} \\ 8 \begin{bmatrix} \text{vn. II} \\ 8 \begin{bmatrix} \text{va.} \\ \text{vc.} \end{bmatrix} \end{bmatrix} \end{bmatrix}$$

Element D (tenuto bass):

$$8 \begin{bmatrix} \text{bn. I, trb. III} \\ 8 \begin{bmatrix} \text{bn. II, tuba, } \tfrac{1}{2} \text{ d-b.} \\ \tfrac{1}{2} \text{ d-b.} \end{bmatrix} \end{bmatrix}$$

The horn and trombone do not continue their octave doubling of
the melody all the way. The part writing is in fact quite free, giving the
impression of a weaving of six parts. However, the parts are not at all
times independent voices (compare trumpet II and horn III in measures
1 and 2).

Elements A, B, and C, are marked at different dynamic levels.

EX. 406. Strauss—*Symphonia Domestica*   [facing]

p. 24, ed. Associated Music Publishers

With authorization of the original publishers Ed. Bote & G. Bock, Berlin, Wiesbaden.

Example 406: The two textures making up this page of music are both of type II, and they are closely related in thematic content. They are, however, clearly differentiated in meter and rhythm, and also in general musical character. The orchestration carries out the idea of duality by skillful use of tone colors and pitch levels.

The distribution is as follows:

Texture I:
    Element A (melody):   ob. d'am., Eng. hn., hn. I and II, vn. I, va.
    Element B (accompaniment): cl. I and II, hn. III, IV, V and VI, vn. II

Texture II:
    Element A (melody):   ob. I and II, D cl., A cl. (meas. 1), fl. I and II (from meas. 2)
    Element B (accompaniment): bn. I, II, III, and IV, timp., vc., d-b.

In texture II, a secondary melody enters in measure 4 (flute III, A clarinet). The B♭ clarinets join element A of texture I in measure 5. The sonority of texture I is large and full, while texture II is heard as though in the background. There is no octave doubling of either melody, except in measures 4 and 5 (oboe II), where the two lines are farther apart.

EX. 407. Bartók—*Concerto for Orchestra*

p. 116, ed. Boosey & Hawkes

Example 407: Two contrapuntal textures are combined here, both composed of canonic entries at a time interval of one measure. They are contrasted in rhythm and tone color. The over-all texture is spare.

In the first two measures, the oboes reinforce the first three notes of the flute entries. The clarinets are doubled in measure 5, because of their comparatively weak register, and because of their situation in the midst of so many voices.

Another kind of complex texture is not the product of a synthesis of other textures, but is an ensemble of many elements, none of which emerges as a primary element. The ear is attracted momentarily to various details, and almost at once diverted to others. Someone has aptly

called this effect of a woven musical fabric a "tapestry of sound." Example 408 is a good illustration.

EX. 408. Stravinsky—*Le Sacre du Printemps*   [facing]

p. 9, ed. Russe

Example 408: All of the motives and figures have been introduced in the preceding pages of the score, so that they are not unfamiliar to the listener. Some parts are obviously subordinate, like the chord held by the double-basses, and the figure for the bassoons might be regarded as an accompaniment figure. But the separation into melodic and accompaniment elements does not seem properly descriptive of the effect of this music.

Several groupings can be made, reducing the thirty-one instrumental parts to a considerably smaller number of elements. The following is a classification of the elements in a hypothetical order of importance. Difference of opinion is not only welcomed but encouraged.

A: D cl.
B: alternating between ob. I and D trp.
C: cl. I
D: Eng. hn.
E: picc. I and II, forming one line
F: fl. I, ob. II and III, cl. II, (later fl. in G)
G: bn. II and III, contrabn. I and II, hn. III and IV, vc. I, d-b. VI
H: fl. II, cl. III, va., having a similar function
I: bass cl.
J: fl. in G, connecting later with solo vn.
K: vc. II, d-b, I, II, III, IV, and V (chord)

The complex texture of this type is occasionally used for the evocation of a special atmosphere, or for the suggestion of extramusical ideas (Honegger—*Pacific 231*). It may be employed as a background on which to superimpose one or more melodies.

THREE

PROBLEMS IN ORCHESTRATION

CHAPTER TWENTY-SIX

-»» «-

ORCHESTRATION OF MELODY

I N THE study of harmony, counterpoint, and other technical aspects of writing music, the results of practical exercises can be tested in sound by singing, or by playing on the piano. It should be obvious that these testing methods can have little or no value to the student of orchestration. Nothing short of a well-rehearsed performance by a good orchestra can show the student the one proof he needs to have— namely, how his orchestration sounds. Even a well-intentioned "reading" will very likely give him a wrong impression of the quality of his work. Since the resources of a good orchestra are rarely, if ever, available, the student is forced to rely upon the criticism of a more experienced person, his own store of information, and the judgment of his work by analogy with similar passages in scores.

The orchestration of piano music, although providing convenient material, is an exercise too advanced and specialized for early stages in the study of orchestration. The action of the pianoforte pedal cannot, and should not, be ignored, and once the question is raised of representing its effect in terms of the orchestra there is no end to the vexing, not to say insoluble, problems for both teacher and student.

Exercises should be devised that present conditions similar to those of ordinary problems that confront a composer or orchestrator. It is also desirable that they involve contact with orchestral scores whenever that is feasible. Problems can be invented by the student or the teacher. Some suggestions as to their nature will be made in these pages.

Problem 1. Melody to be scored for strings.

Fig. 122

To derive the most benefit from exercises, one should not be satisfied to find but one or two solutions. These are nearly always immediately apparent and easy, which does not mean they may not be the best. As many solutions as possible should be found, and their relative merits and individual qualities appraised. In this way a technique of orchestration may be built up and expanded.

The possible solutions to a given problem will fall into three overlapping categories: (*a*) normal or natural; (*b*) unusual or novel; and (*c*) strange or grotesque. The first of these is of course the most important, and the most difficult. The second is perhaps more interesting, and is an essential area of inquiry for the orchestrator. The third need not be explored, since it is the easiest; in fact, arrangements of this sort are more often than not the product of ineptitude.

SOLUTION WITHOUT DOUBLING

The melody should be listened to mentally as played by each of the strings, first as it is written, then in octave transposition. Transposition by other intervals is also to be considered. For instance, placing the part a fifth lower would make quite a different effect on violas or 'cellos. Other than octave transpositions will not usually be discussed in these chapters, for reasons of space.

If the melody is assigned to double-basses, without transposition, it would sound an octave lower, and although it is not impossible of execution thus, the result would be most unusual, even strange. Written down an octave, it is in a good range for the basses, but it would sound better with octave doubling by the 'cellos. The melody as it stands is entirely suitable for violins or violas.

Other possibilities are the reduction in the number of instruments in a section and the use of solo players.

UNISON DOUBLING

Possibilities for unison doubling in the strings are: vn. I + vn. II, vn. I + va., vn. I + vc., vn. II + va., vn. II + vc., va. + vc., vn. I + vn. II + va., vn. I + vn. II + vc., vn. I + va. + vc., vn. II + va. + vc. The 'cellos seem out of place in these doublings because the intensity of the high tones on the A-string contrasts with the tone quality of the other instruments. The penetrating sound of the viola A-string can be avoided by marking the last half of the melody *sul D*.

The unison of violin I and violin II, with or without violas, gives breadth and power. It is often used to maintain predominance of a melody against a full background. The violas add much warmth and tone-weight to the combination.

OCTAVE DOUBLING

$$8\begin{bmatrix} \text{vn. I} \\ \text{vn. II} \end{bmatrix} \quad 8\begin{bmatrix} \text{vn. I} \\ \text{va.} \end{bmatrix} \quad 8\begin{bmatrix} \text{vn. I} \\ \text{vc.} \end{bmatrix} \quad 8\begin{bmatrix} \text{va.} \\ \text{vc.} \end{bmatrix} \quad 8\begin{bmatrix} \text{va.} \\ \text{d-b.} \end{bmatrix} \quad 8\begin{bmatrix} \text{vc.} \\ \text{d-b.} \end{bmatrix}$$

These are the most common arrangements in octave doubling, the first two requiring the placing of violin I an octave higher (Fig. 123a). The combination of violas and 'cellos seems ideal for the present melody (Fig. 123b). Combining violas and basses this way is not practical here because of the high pitch of the bass part. If the violas are replaced by 'cellos, the part can be put in the lower octave (Fig. 123c).

Fig. 123

Inversion of the natural order of pitch of the instruments (placing violas above violins, 'cellos above violas) is to be considered an unusual arrangement, used for special effect. This principle applies even to placing violin II above violin I.

TWO-OCTAVE DOUBLING

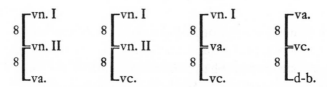

The first of the above schemes carries the first violins into the extreme high range, and it is of ethereal effect. Widening the sonority over two octaves enriches the tone, and at the same time renders it more impersonal in expression. This quality is enhanced, and an impression of aloofness imparted by omitting the middle voice (Fig. 124*a*).

Octave doublings may extend over three and four octaves, Fig. 124, (*b*) and (*c*).

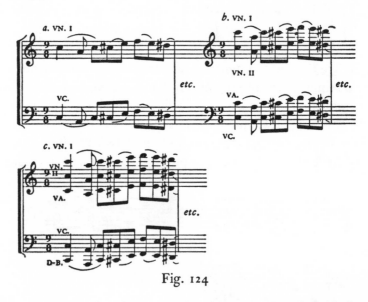

Fig. 124

These resources of variety are enlarged by the use of divided strings, and by combining unison doubling with octave doubling. Division of violin II to preserve balance is shown in Fig. 125 (*a*), unison doubling to emphasize the lower voice (*b*), and accenting the upper voice by the same means (*c*).

Fig. 125

MELODY FOR WOODWINDS

Problem 2. Melody to be scored for woodwinds.

Fig. 126

The instruments available in all problems are, unless otherwise stated, those of the standard symphony orchestra with woodwind by threes, four horns, three trumpets, three trombones, tuba, harp, percussion, and strings. In the woodwind section, the third family members are presumed to be the auxiliary instruments—piccolo, English horn, bass clarinet, and contrabassoon. Needless to say, it is not expected that all the available instruments will be used in each problem. The acquisition of an instinctive feeling for the orchestra as an instrument is furthered, however, by a continued awareness of the presence of those instruments that do not happen to be playing.

SOLUTION WITHOUT DOUBLING

To one experienced in orchestral writing a melody will at once suggest certain instruments, or perhaps one particular instrument most suited for its performance. A composer usually creates melodies with the instruments in mind, although he is conscious of the fact that a melody written for one instrument can perfectly well be assigned to another, with or without minor changes or transposition.

As for the student, he should consider each instrument in turn, observe its suitability to the melody in respect to range and other technical points, never omitting the effort to hear mentally the sound of each instrument. Following are some typical observations relevant to problem 2.

Piccolo—sounds an octave higher; the melody is good as it stands; if written an octave higher, the sound might be too shrill, unless in large combinations.

Flute—comparatively gentle in this range; probably better an octave higher.

Oboe—staccato and accents better than those of the flute; excellent range and style; also suitable an octave lower, rather rough.

English horn—part to be written a fifth higher, hence too high in the pitch given; better an octave lower; less in character than the oboe.

Clarinet—in good range and style, especially the sixteenth note figure; staccato a little heavier than on the oboe; also good an octave below, but quieter; part written a major second higher.

Bass clarinet—write out in both French and German notation (see Chapter Nine); given pitch too high, possible an octave lower but best range two octaves down; good style, staccato a little slow.

Bassoon—excellent one octave lower; sharp, dry staccato, appropriate character; two octaves lower playable but subdued in quality; three octaves lower possible but sluggish.

Contrabassoon—part to be written two octaves lower, sounds still another octave down; speaks slowly in this type of music; better omit some notes; perhaps give it only the accents and slurs occurring in measures 2, 3, and 4.

UNISON DOUBLING

Unison doubling involves the creation of mixed timbres. This was of less importance in dealing with strings, which are far more alike in tone color than are the woodwind instruments. Furthermore, the greater disparity in the different registers of each woodwind instrument renders the matter of their combination more complex.

Two instruments playing in unison reinforce each other, but at the same time each tends to cancel some of the intensity of the other's tone. The unison of two instruments of the same kind possesses somewhat less than twice the tone-weight and carrying power of one. Also, the subtle fluctuations of expressive playing are bound to be in large part destroyed when two play in unison.

Unison doublings are used for dynamic reinforcement and to obtain new tone colors. The student should store up in his memory as many of these mixed timbres as he can by hearing orchestras, with knowledge of the scores. They cannot be described in words. When two instruments of different tone colors play a melody in unison, the predominance of one or the other color will vary throughout the phrase, as the relative intensities vary.

It will be useful to the student to consider the possibilities of unison doubling in the following list:

picc. + fl.	fl. + bn.	Eng. hn. + bn.
picc. + ob.	ob. + Eng. hn.	cl. + bass cl.
picc. + cl.	ob. + cl.	cl. + bn.
fl. + ob.	ob. + bass cl.	bass cl. + bn.
fl. + Eng. hn.	ob. + bn.	bass cl. + contrabn.
fl. + cl.	Eng. hn. + cl.	bn. + contrabn.
fl. + bass cl.	Eng. hn. + bass cl.	

As far as problem 2 is concerned, oboe and clarinet cannot play high enough to double the piccolo, unless the clarinet is asked to ascend to high C; and because of the first B♭, the flute cannot play an octave lower to double the English horn, bass clarinet, or bassoon. The combinations with contrabassoon are not satisfactory for this melody.

The best rhythmic staccato will be obtained with oboe plus clarinet;

in the octave below with clarinet plus bassoon; and in the high octave with flute plus piccolo.

Further possibilities are the unison doublings of three or more instruments.

Octave doubling involves the equalizing of registers to preserve balance. Ordinarily, two instruments of the same kind, as two oboes, do not balance an octave apart because of the difference in registers. This is not a rule, but rather a caution to serve as a guide in considering individual cases. It is perhaps oftener true than not, but the peculiarities of the instrument in question, the pitch of the octave, and the dynamic level, affect the validity of this as a principle.

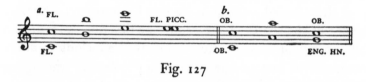

Fig. 127

In Fig. 127 (*a*), the octave C for two flutes will be in uneven balance, whereas the octave B is quite good. The high E is much more brilliant than the lower E. The usefulness of the auxiliary instruments is shown by the combination of flute and piccolo, the piccolo sounding the octave above from a fingering identical with that of the flute. In (*b*) the octave C, in contrast to that for two flutes, has the lower note the stronger of the two. The octave A is in good balance. The octave C is much better balanced if the English horn replaces the second oboe, playing a written G on the instrument.

A melody such as we are considering in problem 2, covering a range of an octave, needs careful attention to the matter of registers when assigned to woodwind in octaves. Following are some workable solutions.

Fig. 128

Another often stated rule is that instruments must be kept in the natural order of pitch; namely, flute above oboe, oboe above clarinet, clarinet above bassoon. Inspection of almost any score will reveal violations of this rule, inevitable considering the extent to which the ranges overlap. There is nevertheless the prestige of usage to support the principle, and those combinations we classify as normal or natural will usually conform in a general way. Inversions of the order, when they prove successful in balance, come under the heading of unusual or novel arrangements (Fig. 129).

Fig. 129

Doublings embracing two or more octaves may be used (Fig. 130a), and for special effect two instruments may play at a distance of two or more octaves apart (Fig. 130b).

Fig. 130

Unison doublings are combined with octave doublings for added strength, to emphasize a particular pitch location, or to correct balance that may be faulty because of disparity in registers. For example, in Fig. 130(*a*), the balance would be improved by doubling both clarinet and bassoon with other instruments, the bassoon being especially at a disadvantage.

MELODY FOR BRASS

Problem 3. Melody to be scored for brass.

Fig. 131

SOLUTION WITHOUT DOUBLING

Trumpet—good range as written; playable an octave lower, but first two measures too low for good effect.

Horn—too high as written; good an octave lower; two octaves lower possible, but too low to sound well alone.

Trombone—good an octave lower; also good two octaves lower but less appropriate.

Tuba—one octave lower suitable only for the euphonium; for the bass tuba in F, good two octaves lower; also three octaves lower if combined with heavy sonorities.

UNISON DOUBLING

The unison of two or three trumpets is excellent, and in general preferable to octave doubling in which the third trumpet is placed low. Horns may play two, three, or four on the same part. If pitched two octaves below the melody as given, the second and fourth horns would play in unison. One octave below the given pitch is a good range for the unison of three trombones. The unison of horns and trombones is effective and normal. The fourth horn might double the tuba, two octaves below the melody as given.

OCTAVE DOUBLING

Fig. 132

These combinations have each a slight unevenness due to differences in registers, but they do not show the audible differences in attack exhibited by the combinations in Fig. 133 (the entire melody should be taken into consideration).

Fig. 133

Here the difference in articulation between the action of slides and that of valves is quite noticeable; also the slowness of the horn to speak. The horn also lacks tone-weight, compared with its companions in the brass section. These discrepancies are to a large extent mitigated, or covered, by the use of unison doubling and mixed timbres (Fig. 134).

Fig. 134

THE GROUPS COMBINED

Problem 4. Melody to be scored for strings, woodwind, and brass.

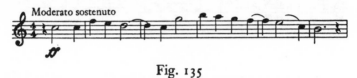

Fig. 135

STRINGS AND WOODWIND

A woodwind instrument may double a string section at the octave above or below, *e.g.*, flute above violin I, bassoon below. This usually sounds well in soft nuances, but when loud it is necessary to double the woodwind part to balance the strings. The unison doubling of strings by woodwind is common. All combinations are good, wherever the ranges coincide. Considering the extent of the string ranges, there are few doublings that do not offer at least a restricted possibility. The student may compare the ranges to see what these are. Some unisons of strings and woodwind seem especially congenial and colorful, although it should be emphasized that the kind of music being played is of paramount importance in this respect. Also the different intensities will create different tone colors in different parts of the range. As illustration, let the following combinations be considered throughout the range of the wind instrument: vn. + fl., va. + Eng. hn., vc. + bass cl., d-b. + contrabn.

In general, when a single woodwind is added to a string part it serves to strengthen the string tone, and if the dynamic level is fairly loud its own color will be more or less absorbed. If the woodwind is doubled by another woodwind, the wind tone begins noticeably to assert itself.

BRASS AND WOODWIND

Associating with brass, the woodwind finds itself again in company with sonorities more powerful than its own. The horns are more capable than the heavy brass of blending with woodwind, their tone being much less unyielding. They are therefore a helpful link between the two groups. In *piano*, octave doublings are of good effect between trumpet and flute, horn and flute, oboe, or clarinet. In *forte*, the woodwinds act as reinforcement of upper partials of the brass, and they require as much doubling as may be available, if a balance is to be approximated. The low-pitched bassoons and bass clarinet cannot perform this function, so they are usually engaged in doubling the bass, with the tuba, third trombone, and fourth horn.

Unison doubling of trumpets by woodwind (clarinets and oboes) adds a certain amount of tone-weight, but it reduces the characteristic brilliance of the trumpet tone. Horns make effective unisons with clarinets and bassoons. Woodwind unisons with trombones are not often useful. The tuba combines quite well with bass clarinet and contrabassoon.

STRINGS, WOODWIND, AND BRASS

Since problem 4 does not specify a full tutti, the melody may be scored for only part of the three instrumental groups, even thinly. Far from discouraging this type of solution to the problem, let us say that the use of pure colors, that is without much unison doubling, leads to a more interesting, clear, and transparent orchestral sonority, greatly to be desired. On the other hand, considering the orchestra as a whole as an instrument, it is necessary to acquire some early familiarity with the rather commonplace process of handling large groups of instruments in a normal way.

Among the many alternatives existing, two different approaches are suggested below. In Fig. 136(a), the sound is concentrated in a narrow range, one octave, and, since the effect intended is that of an orchestral fortissimo, nearly all the instruments are used. This makes a very thick tone, with much unison doubling. The instruments of the lowest octave, double-basses and contrabassoon, have been omitted in the interest of concentration in the single octave. The tuba is omitted, and also the second and third trumpets, to save the over-all tone from being completely that of the brass, especially in measure 4. The piccolo is not used lest the range be widened by another octave.

In Fig. 136(*b*), the range is widened to four octaves, giving a more brilliant result. All the instruments are included (all shown at actual pitch).

Fig. 136

In the suggested solutions to the foregoing problems, the arrangements given are intended to continue throughout the phrase. Actually, both unison and octave doublings may be introduced for only part of a melody, for reasons of intensity or volume, changing color, or sudden accent. Doublings will usually accumulate in the course of a gradual crescendo. A melodic line extending over a very wide range will necessitate joining one tone color to another. If possible, the joining is made where there is not a marked contrast of registers, and the parts are overlapped by at least one note (Fig. 137).

Fig. 137

The following melodies are to be scored in various ways, for different combinations of strings, woodwind, and brass.

Problem 5.

Fig. 138

Problem 6.

Fig. 139

Problem 7.

Fig. 140.

Problem 8.

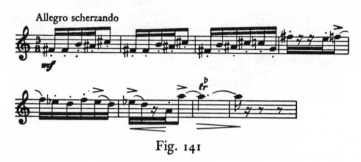

Fig. 141

CHAPTER TWENTY-SEVEN

BACKGROUND AND ACCOMPANIMENT

THE arrangement of the accompaniment to a melody is more a matter of composition than of applying orchestral procedures. The rhythmic style and the texture of the background is just as much a part of the composer's thought as the melody itself. Harmonically, the accompaniment supplies tonal orientation for the melody, harmonic color through the choice of chord structures, and the motion of harmonic rhythm through the pattern of root changes. It also supplies rhythmic designs and pulsation that establish the underlying rate of motion of the music, a function that can affect vitally the musical meaning of the melody itself. The background is important in setting an over-all mood or atmosphere.

Orchestration must confirm and enhance these musical qualities, and it should not distort them by ostentatious display of orchestral "effects" irrelevant to the musical meaning. The accompaniment may or may not be contrasted in tone color with the melody, although such contrast is one means of securing detachment of the melody from the background. A melody with accompaniment is very often played exclusively by strings, less often by woodwinds or brass. It is valuable practice to try scoring phrases for the three groups separately.

It goes without saying that a melody should not be overwhelmed in sound by its accompaniment. Skillfully managed, however, the accompaniment may be quite elaborate and still permit a melody played softly by one or two instruments to be perfectly heard. This is what is meant by transparency in orchestral texture. The sonority is heard as the total effect of a number of details. A good example may be seen in Chapter Twenty, Fig. 385, from Debussy's *La Mer*.

The alternatives in the arrangement of an accompaniment are so many that copious perusal and analysis of orchestral scores of all styles and periods becomes of prime importance in a study of the subject. An essential point to remember is that orchestral figuration and idiomatic writing originate in the techniques of the instruments, another reason for avoiding as much as possible the use of piano music in the study of orchestration. The best exercises are those which bring about closer contact with scores.

Four types of exercise are suggested:

1. Make a reduction of a passage in a score, containing a melody with accompaniment. Do not show the names of instruments. Rescore the passage and compare the result with the original. This is more profitable when a second person makes the reduction, but one person can derive much from the practice.

2. Supply an original melody and harmonic background, the latter in simple harmonic skeleton form, to be orchestrated for various instrumental groupings.

3. Similar to type 2, but with the kind of figuration and other details of the accompaniment prescribed. Certain instruments may also be stipulated.

4. Select a passage from orchestral literature, having a melody and accompaniment. Reorchestrate the passage in different ways, radically changing the distribution of the two elements, *e.g.*, melody in woodwind instead of strings, etc., but preserving as far as possible the original musical style. This is a real composer's problem, one that often presents itself in the working out of a composition. Variants in the conditions of the problem will at once come to mind, such as changing the dynamic level from *piano* to *fortissimo*, or transposing the passage up a fifth, operations requiring no little readjustment in the scoring. A most valuable by-product of this exercise will be the acquired intimate knowledge of the original orchestration.

Problem 9.

Fig. 142

This texture of two elements is to be orchestrated in the following ways:
   (a) *For strings only (it is understood that element B as given is the harmonic skeleton for an accompaniment to be devised).*
   (b) *With the melody in the woodwind, accompaniment in the strings.*
   (c) *With the melody in the strings, accompaniment in the woodwind.*
   (d) *With the groups mixed, and with the addition of horns.*

Solution (a). Strings alone.

Fig. 143

Doubtless the first solution that suggests itself will be the obvious one of assigning the given parts as they stand to the string sections in normal order, *viz.*, soprano, vn. I; alto, vn. II; tenor, va.; bass, vc., with or without double-basses. As a matter of fact, this is an excellent arrangement, and it would sound very well indeed.

The solution given in Fig. 143 is lighter in texture, and has the advantage of imparting a sense of motion at the beginning.

Solution (b). Melody in the woodwind.

Fig. 144

This accompaniment is designed for transparency and lightness. It can be divided into two subelements: (*a*) vn. I and II; (*b*) va., vc., having rests at different points. Double-basses are often omitted in a musical situation of this kind. The partial doubling by the flute is for variety.

Solution (c). Melody in strings.

Fig. 145

In the solution shown, the intention was to create somewhat more interesting tone colors. The melody is played by divided first violins in octaves, and a solo 'cello in the octave below, the tone thus obtained being thinner, and at the same time more intense and personal, than if all the first and second violins, with the full 'cello section, had been used. The bass line is given to the bass clarinet, partially doubled by the English horn and bassoon. Clarinets and flutes contribute motion and the remaining factors of the harmony. The cadential measures show a four-voiced texture of part writing.

Solution (d). The groups mixed.

Fig. 146

A warmer and more ample sonority was sought in this version. The melody, starting with the octaves, fl. I, vn. I, vc. + hn., stronger in the horn and 'cello register, is given varied treatment from measure 4. The quarter-note motive is passed over to the high flute, ob. I entering an octave below. In measure 5 the combination is fl., vn. I, vc. + Eng. hn., the latter replacing hn. I, and the oboe changing to a harmonic part. For the last three measures the melody is in one octave, vn. I. + ob. II, vc. + Eng. hn., the flutes calling momentary attention to a secondary voice.

The accompaniment consists of the syncopated motive, cl. I and II + vn. II div., based on notes of the harmony and arranged to have a melodic curve of its own. It is joined by the horns at the cadence. This is supplemented by the motive in the violas marking the second beats. The bass is possibly a little too heavy because of the low pitch of the double-basses. Their tone is clarified by the doubling in the bassoons, also needed on account of the distance of the bass from the other parts. Putting the basses in the upper octave would change the over-all sound by increasing their melodic intensity, especially at measures 5 and 6.

Problem 10.

Fig. 147. Brahms—*Symphony no. 2*   p. 19, ed. Kalmus

The passage is to be reorchestrated, changing the instrumentation assigned to the two elements, melody and accompaniment.

Typical solution.

Fig. 148

Since, in the original scoring, the horn is in a rather high register, it was decided to give the melody to 'cellos high on the A-string, modifying the intensity by the unison of violas, who would not be playing on their A-string. In the accompaniment, the held tones of the strings are replaced by a full horn quartet. It did not seem advisable to double the initial A of the melody, as in the original, because in the new situation the first horn would certainly be too prominent, as compared to the first violins. The pedal A of the double-basses is well suited to the octave of fourth horn and contrabassoon. For the arpeggio figure, a single instrument would be less appropriate in style than the more impersonal ensemble of bassoons, clarinets, and flute, considering the use of both violas and 'cellos for the melody.

Problem 11.

Fig. 149

Rescore the given passage in more than one way, then compare the results with the original score, Mendelssohn—Symphony no. 3 (Scottish), p. 112, ed. Eulenburg.

Problem 12.

Fig. 150. Mozart—*Symphony in D*, K. 504   p. 14, ed. Philharmonia

Score the phrase in three different versions for woodwind only, adding two horns in one version.

Problem 13.

Fig. 151. Tchaikovsky—*Symphony no. 4*   p. 5, ed. Kalmus

Rescore the passage above in the following ways:

(a) Element A in the strings, element B in the woodwind, mezzo forte.

(b) For woodwind only, in close position, not over two octaves in total spread, piano.

(c) For woodwind and horns, forte.

(d) Element A in strings and woodwind, element B in the brass, fortissimo.

Problem 14.

Fig. 152

This phrase is to be orchestrated in two versions, the melody to be given to the flute in the first version, to a solo violin in the second.

❯❯❯ ❮❮❮

SCORING OF CHORDS

THE composer or orchestrator who scores chords with consistent success from the standpoint of balance of tone, smooth blend of instrumental color, and appropriate dynamic effect, does so because of a reliable memory of the sound made by each instrument at any given pitch and dynamic level. He does not do so because of formulas and devices learned from books. Chords for orchestra cannot be constructed by rule except in a very elementary sense, imitating what others have done before. Imitation has some value for study purposes, but it should not be concluded that what sounds well in one musical situation will necessarily be appropriate in another.

Especially in the combination of instrumental sounds, any stated principle is immediately subject to qualification from so many angles that its usefulness is brought into question. It is the aim of the present study to make clear the nature of these qualifying aspects in the scoring of chords.

NUMERICAL BALANCE

When we say a chord is balanced we seem to imply that it forms a flat vertical plane of sound, with no individual voices protruding or sounding more prominent than the others. It is possible to doubt that such a chord can be written, given the assortment of instruments we are committed to employ, and more than that, given the chord tones and intervals predetermined by our musical language. This equilibrium of tone is not assured simply by having the same number of instruments on each note of the chord. In fact, the chord in Fig. 153(a), with one instrument to each note, is nevertheless quite badly balanced.

Fig. 153

It will be hardly necessary to point out, in chord (a), the overpowering tone of the high notes for the three brass instruments, the comparative weakness of the low-pitched flutes, and the striking contrast of the oboe C with the second flute and the soft bassoon A.

A rearrangement of the same instruments is made in chord (b), resulting in considerable improvement in the balance. The brass are now much less strident, the flutes are in better position to be heard, and the octave C of oboe and bassoon is a more even sound. However, the chord remains in unsatisfactory balance, due to the difference in strength of woodwind and brass in *forte*. It should be noted, incidentally, that the rough, strident quality of chord (a) has been sacrificed.

In (c) three more woodwinds have been added, making unison doublings to try to match the tone-weight of the brass. At this point, mention must be made of the inadequacy of the horn to equal the *forte* of trumpet and trombone. Two horns would be better than one, but this only helps the brass the more to overpower the woodwind.

The same chord is arranged for strings at (d). In counting the number of instruments assigned to a part, it is the custom to count a section of strings (violin I, violin II, etc.) as one instrument. This is a convenient principle and is strongly supported by the practice of composers, although it admits a wide margin of error. To begin with, the number of players to a section varies between orchestras. Then there is the matter of divided strings, whereby a half or a third of a section is to be regarded as a single instrument, as indeed it can be, except by comparison with another string section which happens not to be divided. Finally, when we realize that a solo violin is entirely worthy to be counted a single instrument (see Chapter Two, page 63), we see that the computation of numerical balances is far from simple.

These remarks are not meant to convey a sense of hopelessness or futility in the effort to achieve a balance in scoring. The fact that an ideal may be beyond attainment should not be a deterrent to the will to approach it as nearly as possible. Two important points are to be stressed here. First, a trained musical ear and musical memory are indispensable, so that one hears mentally, and more and more accurately, what one writes. These are acquired by unceasing efforts and a lifetime's experience. Second, the coöperation of conductor and performers plays an enormous part in the balance of sonorities. In a good orchestra each player tries, instinctively or consciously, to make his part sound in balance with the others. The better the scoring, the more successful his endeavors will be.

BALANCE OF REGISTERS

In comparison with the winds, the string section is homogeneous in tone throughout, although, as we know, each stringed instrument has portions of its range that are less brilliant than others—the D-string in all of them, for example. But in the combining of wind instruments, the equalizing of registers is an ever-present preoccupation. In general, an unevenness results from the association, in a chord, of a weak with a strong register of the same instrument (Fig. 154a). Likewise, combining tones of the weak register of one instrument with tones of the strong register of another instrument will probably result in poor balance (Fig. 154b).

Fig. 154

It cannot be too strongly emphasized that examples of chords for instrumental combinations have validity only for the pitch at which they are given. If a chord is transposed, the relationship of registers changes. In Fig. 154(c), flute and oboe will be found to be nicely balanced, while in (d) the flute has a distinct advantage over the oboe. One may say the situation is different with each half-tone transposition. Unison doubling can be used to strengthen the weaker voice.

TONALITY

There are sometimes reasons for having some tones of a chord stronger than others. One of these concerns the tonal function of the chord. In orchestration, just as in conventional harmonic theory, the tonal degrees of the key (tonic, dominant, and subdominant), being structurally more important to the tonality, may be doubled more than the modal degrees (mediant and submediant). In (a) of Fig. 155, the single F of the first trombone is sufficient to give major identification to the harmony against ten other instruments on the root and fifth, and the chord suggests the keys of A♭, G♭, and D♭. The minor triad at (b), having extra weight on G, might be construed as supertonic harmony of the key of D major. If the extra doubling were shifted to the B, as in (c), the chord would no longer suggest D, but rather a key in which B is a tonal degree, e.g., E minor or B minor. In a chord like (d), presuming the intent to be the avoidance of tonality, care is taken not to suggest tonality by a similar emphasis on certain chord members.

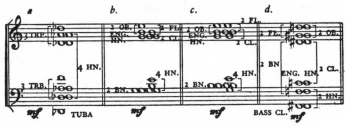

Fig. 155

SPACING

Overtones from the lower notes are sometimes disturbing in a chord, and may need to be canceled by upper tones. This may be one reason for loud chords being almost invariably in close position, with chord tones present wherever possible. If spaces were left to permit the overtones to sound, as in a major triad, the partials would hardly be strong enough for an even balance. On the other hand, soft chords in woodwinds are often attractively colored by the sound of overtones in open spaces. These effects are more often than not unpredictable, and their success the result of experiment.

The conflict of upper partials created by close spacing in low registers is usually avoided. It is easy to see what would be the product in middle register overtones of the diminished seventh chord in Fig. 156(*a*). The sound is a synthesis of C major, E♭ major, F♯ major, and A major.

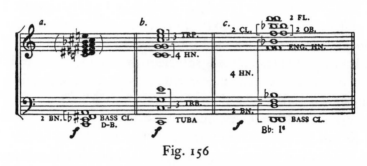

Fig. 156

Such a chord might be used in a percussive effect. If the chord is put up an octave, or better still two octaves, the overtones become very much thinner and less noticeable. Below 4-foot C, intervals smaller than a fifth or fourth are generally avoided if clarity is desired. The ideal spacing following the outline of the harmonic series (Fig. 156*b*) is possible only in root position major chords.

Harmonic principles of doubling are sometimes responsible for the appearance of spaces as large as a fifth in upper parts. Figure 156(*c*) observes the usage of omitting reduplication of the bass in upper voices.

BLEND OF TONE COLORS

Factors in the smooth blending of tone colors have been described in Chapter Twenty-four, p. 396 and following. One need but add here that every imaginable association of tone colors can be found useful in the scoring of chords. The student should experiment with the arrangement of chords, applying the devices of unison doubling, overlapping, superposition, interlocking, and enclosing, and try to judge their effect. A general statement as to the relative value of these devices in achieving an even blend of timbres cannot and should not be made.

TUTTI CHORDS

A tutti chord, employing the full orchestra, occurs most often in *forte* or *fortissimo*, at moments of climax or in a brilliant ending. It is inevitable that such a chord will be dominated by the brass. Consequently, the first step in its construction is to make certain that the brass as a unit will sound well. The brass section, within itself, is in turn dominated by trumpets and trombones. Placing of the less powerful horns is sometimes problematical in arranging a brass chord.

Two principal methods of approach to the use of horns in a tutti chord can be broadly discerned: (*a*) the four horns may be doubled two by two and employed as two voices on an equal footing with trumpets and trombones (Fig. 157*a*); (*b*) the trumpets and trombones may first be scored as a satisfactory unit, adding the tuba on the bass. A natural octave relationship is often to be found between trumpets and trombones (Fig. 157*b*). The horns may then be arranged in a four-part grouping and placed alongside the heavy brass (Fig. 157*c*).

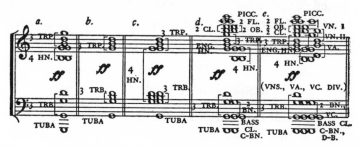

Fig. 157

The woodwinds cannot be planned to sound satisfactorily by themselves, since the presence of the brass renders them useless in the middle register. The high-pitched woodwind are better situated above the brass, where they will add brilliance by reinforcing upper partials. The low woodwind, bassoons and bass clarinet, contribute the most in their low registers, so they are placed with the bass (Fig. 157*d*). The English horn is often at a loss to find a good location, since it is not strong in the high register. It is given almost any doubling in preference to omitting it from the tutti.

The strings are free to be placed where they will best sound as a section. They may be divided to make a richer sonority (Fig. 157e).

Let it be said at once that the chief value of this recipe for a tutti chord lies in its utility as a commonplace from which to survey other and more interesting possibilities.

DYNAMIC LEVEL

The temptation to mark different dynamic levels for brass and woodwind must be resisted. If this system is used for the purpose of correcting the inherent inequalities in the orchestral groups it will be meaningless when called into play for legitimate special effect. Dynamic indications are admittedly far from logical or accurate, and the fact must be acknowledged that a *forte* or a *mezzo forte* is not a measurable quantity but a comparative over-all designation of a dynamic level to which all are bidden to adapt themselves.

Muted brass and stopped horns are more comparable to woodwind in both color and tone-weight, but the capacity of the brass to play softly, muted or not, is not to be overlooked.

Thin and thick sonorities are not to be regarded as synonymous with soft and loud, respectively.

RANGE AND PITCH LOCATION

Orchestral chords may vary in range from the total spread in pitch of the whole orchestra to a concentration within a small interval, in loud and soft nuances. The entire chord may be located in a high, medium, or low register. A chord of wide pitch range may be given emphasis in the high, medium, or low register, by manipulating the balance of tone-weight.

We have been considering chords in an abstract sense as far as time values are concerned, as though they were to be held long enough for the balance and other qualities to be plainly heard. In a staccato chord, the finely calculated blend of tone color is less important than the placing of each instrument so that it is able to give its best staccato or accent. In working out the problems that follow, a condensed plan of the chord should first be made, like those shown. Then the chord should be written out in score, with a time value assigned and correctly notated.

Except in problem 18, the pitch range is optional.

Problem 15. Score the tonic triad of A major in root position, **forte,** *for these three groups, separately:*
(a) *Full strings.*
(b) *Full woodwind by threes.*
(c) *Full brass (3 trp., 4 hn., 3 trb., tuba).*

Problem 16. Score a dominant seventh chord, built on C as a root, having its third, E, in the bass, pianissimo, *for 2 fl., 2 ob., Eng. hn., 2 cl., bass cl., and 2 bn.*

Problem 17. Score a minor triad, with root B, **forte,** *for strings, woodwind by threes, and four horns.*

Problem 18. Score the chords in Fig. 158, keeping the pitches given, according to the listed specifications:

Fig. 158

(a) *For 2 fl., 2 ob., 2 cl., 2 bn., showing interlocking.*
(b) *For woodwind by threes and four horns.*
(c) *For three different combinations selected from woodwind and horns.*
(d) *For full tutti.*

CHAPTER TWENTY-NINE

VOICE LEADING AND
COUNTERPOINT

THE interplay between the horizontal onward movement of melodic forces and the vertical static sonority made by resonance and the superposing of intervals is an ever-present basic fact of the art of music. Counterpoint, the combination of melodies, creates harmony through the coincidence of melodic tones. Harmony creates melodic movement by the effect of progression from one vertical sonority to another. The art of orchestration is concerned at all times with the interpretation of these two opposing yet complementary forces.

In the preceding chapter, those elementary considerations that affect the vertical arrangement of chords were outlined. It is not too much to say that any of these considerations may be overruled or superseded by the consequences of melodic progression. The orchestra is composed almost entirely of singing instrumental voices. The listener may not be able to follow them all, on first hearing an unfamiliar work, but the melodic conduct of each and every voice is of paramount importance in musical coherence and meaning.

The distinction was made in Chapter Twenty-two between real parts and reduplications of these parts brought about by octave doubling. Orchestration of a texture of part writing will illustrate the application of this concept.

Problem 19. Score the harmonic progression I, V, VI, in C major, piano, *for* (a) *strings;* (b) *woodwind; and* (c) *brass. Employ a basic texture of three real parts.*

Solution (a). The three real parts should first be written out in correct harmonic progression, as played by three of the instruments designated (Fig. 159a).

Fig. 159

Since there remain two more string sections, the octave doubling of the two outside parts at once suggests itself (*b*). Needless to add, these are not the "consecutive octaves" of harmonic theory, but reduplications of correct real parts. It is also to be remarked that the balance of tone is not upset by the octave doublings.

Any one or all the parts may be doubled, either at the octave or at the unison, the latter having the effect of increasing the tone-weight of the part doubled. Generally, care is taken to preserve the integrity of the bass part, avoiding doubling it above lest it become confused with the upper voices (*c*), or doubling another part so low as to sound below the bass (*d*). An arrangement like that in (*e*), having the voice just above the bass in octaves with the highest part, is not considered the best arrangement, since the upper voices are too definitely separated from the bass by being thus circumscribed. Other settings can be made, including those with divided strings and with unison doubling.

Solution (b).

Fig. 160

In Fig. 160 are shown woodwind arrangements, increasing the number of parts to as many as eight in (c), by reduplication and without departing from the original three real parts. The final chord of (c) would not be thought good in either spacing or balance if it were an isolated chord, but as the result of voice leading it is perfectly acceptable.

Solution (c).

Fig. 161

In Fig. 161(c), unison doublings are employed on the original three parts, leaving undoubled the two octave reduplications above and the octave below in the tuba.

CHORALE STYLE

Problem 20. Orchestrate the following phrase, using the full tutti of strings, woodwind, and brass.

Fig. 162 Bach—*Chorale: Ein' feste Burg*   no. 20, ed. Breitkopf & Härtel

The chorale style is common in orchestral music, employing either small groups of instruments or the massive effect of the whole orchestra. The latter seems appropriate for the excerpt given, with the mass of tone centered chiefly in the middle or vocal register.

The strings fall quite naturally into the most obvious distribution:

part A, violin I; B, violin II; C, viola; D, violoncello, and the double-basses also on part D, sounding an octave lower.

The arrangement of the brass is facilitated by doubling the melody in the tenor register:

Fig. 163

On the fifth beat the shift of trombones II and III was felt to be necessary for two reasons. The third trombone needed moving to the upper octave as the bass line was getting too low for good quality of tone. The introduction at this point of part B for the second trombone avoids the effect of division described above (see Fig. 159e).

The woodwinds will be divided between the bass and the octave and the unison doubling of violins and trumpets. The piccolo will be written in its lowest octave so that it will sound no higher than the flutes.

Fig. 164

The complete score is as follows:

Fig. 165

Problem 21. Orchestrate the following fragment of four-part counterpoint:

Fig. 166. Bach—*The Art of the Fugue: Contrapunctus* X

It would be possible to score this phrase in a manner similar to that used for the chorale, allotting all four parts to strings, woodwinds, or brass, and combining the groups or not. The sound would be satisfactory, provided the instruments were assigned parts suitable to their ranges. However, when the texture is more truly contrapuntal, the voices having been given melodic and rhythmic independence and individuality, an orchestration itself more contrapuntal in style is called for. This is accomplished by treating each voice individually, creating in this instance four different tone colors, each suited to the character of its melody, and all participating in an evenly balanced sonority.

The possibilities should be exhaustively studied, each voice being regarded as a problem in the orchestration of melody. Unison and octave doublings as well as pure instrumental colors should be tried. The final selection will demand the exercise of taste, ingenuity, and imagination.

The solution offered shows the following distribution:

A   ⌈picc.
    8⌊
      ⌈ob. I
    8⌊
      Eng. hn. (from meas. 3)

C   hn. II, va.

B   ⌈fl. I
    8⌊cl. I

D   ⌈bn. I and II
    8⌊d-b.

Typical solution:

Fig. 167

Problem 22.

Fig. 168

Score the three given harmonic progressions in the following ways:
(a) For full woodwind plus two horns.
(b) For brass and woodwind.
(c) For strings, woodwind, and four horns.

Problem 23. Orchestrate the following phrase in two versions, one piano, *for strings and woodwind, the other* forte, *using the full tutti of strings, woodwind, and brass.*

Fig. 169. Bach—*Chorale: Es ist genug*   no. 216, ed. Breitkopf & Härtel

Problem 24. Score the following fragment for brass and woodwind.

Fig. 170. Bach—*Well-Tempered Clavier, Book II, Fugue no. 5*

PROBLEMS

Problem 25. Rescore the following passage so that the element now played by woodwind will be in the strings, and that now played by strings will be in the woodwind. The complete section of woodwind by threes is to be considered available.

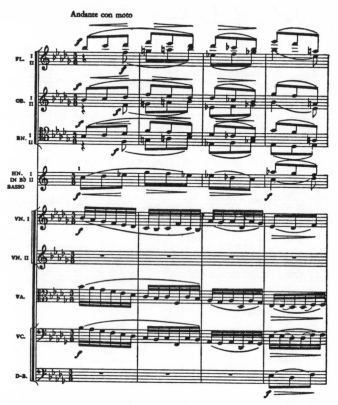

Fig. 171. Brahms—*Variations on a Theme by Haydn.* p. 24, ed. Eulenburg

‐≫‐≪‐

CONCLUSION

I
T IS perhaps useful to repeat that no part of this book pretends to
exhaustive treatment of its subject matter. The intention has been
to present the first stages of study in each chapter, in the anticipation that the student will in each instance continue investigations of his
own. Some suggestions may be offered as to the nature of further
studies.

The importance of a thorough knowledge of the instruments cannot be too strongly emphasized. Good writing for the instruments is
indisputably the largest single factor in good orchestration. One might
with considerable reason declare that if the parts are well written for
the separate instruments the ensemble is bound to sound well, and that
if the parts are poorly suited to the instruments the total effect is bound
to be unsatisfactory. Insufficient acquaintance with the instruments is
by far the most outstanding defect to be noted in the scores of inexperienced composers. The composer or specialist in orchestration must constantly and perpetually keep adding to his store of information in this
department of his technique, gathering data from every conceivable
source.

Analysis of scores is next in importance, and it should become a daily
habit. Sections taken for analysis will be progressively longer compared with the short fragments used in the first stages, thus affording
the opportunity of observing the perpetual changes in texture and distribution, and the expansion and contraction of the instrumental forces
for dynamic purposes. Eventually, a whole movement will be studied
especially for the application of principles of unity and variety through
orchestration. The student is advised to exercise patience, and to select
for his early analyses only those passages that are clear in their texture,

unless he has the help and advice of a more experienced person. Above all, he must guard against being satisfied with a hasty and superficial analysis.

For practice in orchestration, the invention of additional problems similar to those offered is again recommended, particularly the kind that involve contact with standard scores. Whole pieces will eventually be orchestrated for practice in the organization of unity and variety of texture and tone color, and in securing appropriateness and unity of style. These pieces may be piano reductions of orchestral works, either published or made by the student himself. If piano pieces are used, they should be carefully chosen to have as little as possible of purely pianistic, idiomatic writing, and pedal effects.

Those gifted for composition will wish to try their hand at original pieces for orchestra. A good plan is to compose a sketch in the form of textural elements and then orchestrate it. However, it is not suggested that one method is better than another in the personal matter of composition.

Qualities to seek in orchestration are clarity, naturalness, beauty of sound, fidelity to the original musical thought, and an imaginative scoring of renewing interest without fussiness. The orchestration should have its origin in the musical material. It should not be composed of admired sound combinations copied from the works of others. Formulas and "devices" are the death of creative orchestration.

The author's intention will have been realized if this book is found to provide a workable basis for the expansion of knowledge of the art of orchestration, leading in the direction of a mastery attainable, in the final analysis, only through self-reliant individual initiative and effort.

INDEX